TAX SMARTS
for small
business

James O. Parker
Attorney at Law

D1514911

SPHINX® PUBLISHING
AN IMPRINT OF SOURCEBOOKS, INC.®
NAPERVILLE, ILLINOIS
www.SphinxLegal.com

First Edition, 2004

Published by: **Sphinx® Publishing, An Imprint of Sourcebooks, Inc.®**

Naperville Office
P.O. Box 4410
Naperville, Illinois 60567-4410
630-961-3900
Fax: 630-961-2168
www.sourcebooks.com
www.SphinxLegal.com

This publication is designed to provide accurate and authoritative information in regard to the subject
matter covered. It is sold with the understanding that the publisher is not engaged in rendering legal,
accounting, or other professional service. If legal advice or other expert assistance is required, the services of a competent professional person should be sought.

From a Declaration of Principles Jointly Adopted by a Committee of the
American Bar Association and a Committee of Publishers and Associations

This product is not a substitute for legal advice.

Disclaimer required by Texas statutes.

Library of Congress Cataloging-in-Publication Data
Parker, James O., 1948-
   Tax smarts for small business / by James O. Parker.-- 1st ed.
      p. cm.
   ISBN 1-57248-366-0 (alk. paper)
   1. Small business--Taxation--Law and legislation--United States. 2.
Self-employed--Taxation--Law and legislation--United States. I. Title.

KF6491.Z9 P37 2004
343.7305'268--dc22
                                            2004022490

Printed and bound in the United States of America.

VP Paperback — 10 9 8 7 6 5 4 3 2 1

Contents

Introduction

During the nearly twenty-five years that I have practiced law, many of my clients have been small businesses. Many of those clients have struggled with tax issues. Often they have gotten into trouble without even realizing the potential problems that they were facing. In many cases, the U.S. tax laws have become so complex that it is difficult to offer advice that makes any sense to a client who has absolutely no tax background. As a result, I have often found myself conducting a *mini tax course* for my clients. I did this in order to enable him or her to fully understand the tax consequences that he or she was facing in making such decisions as which type of entity to select for a new company or whether to hire employees or use the services of independent contractors.

On several occasions, I have been asked to recommend a book aimed at tax issues specifically for small businesses. Although there is no shortage of books on U.S. tax law in general and on how to prepare a tax return, there is little to choose from in the way of tax books that are geared toward helping owners, operators, and advisors of small businesses make informed decisions concerning their tax matters. Having earned an advanced law degree in taxation; having taught various business courses (including tax) for twenty-seven years; and, having been involved as an owner in several small businesses, I was encouraged that I could put together a book that would be of value to small business owners and operators in coping with their tax issues.

The objective of the book that I have written, *Tax Smarts for Small Business*, is to alert small business owners and operators to provisions in the Internal Revenue Code—the basic tax law of the United States—that are most likely to have a significant affect on them. It places emphasis on fundamentals in hopes of creating awareness of tax issues so that small business owners and operators will know what they need to further consider and investigate regarding tax issues and in making business decisions. There will be times when such readers can find the specific answers that they seek in this book. There will be other times when they simply learn that they have tax issues that require the need for the services of a tax expert.

For those who desire to conduct further research into a tax issue on their own, relevant sections of the Internal Revenue Code (I.R.C.) are cited, as are relevant Treasury Regulations, which are interpretations of the I.R.C. by the Treasury and the Internal Revenue Service (IRS). There are also numerous references in the book to publications distributed by the IRS that further explain specific aspects of the I.R.C. and often give specific instructions on how to prepare some aspect of a party's tax return.

The book begins with an analysis of what constitutes income in general for purposes of U.S. federal income tax laws and devotes subsequent chapters to the determination of gross income, adjusted gross income, and taxable income. Identifying and determining income is a fundamental concept in U.S. tax law. Considerable attention is devoted to deductions that reduce taxpayers' taxable incomes. Entire chapters have been allocated to the home office expense deduction and to deductions for losses and bad debts. There is a chapter devoted to the basic types of federal taxes that small businesses and their owners face and a general explanation of how those taxes are calculated.

After taking the reader to the point of determining tax liability, subsequent chapters explore the various tax credits available to offset that tax liability; how the choice of business entity affects ones tax liability; and, what options are available to owners of small businesses in the form of retirement plans. The book concludes with an explanation of the employer's duty to withhold taxes from the earnings of his or her employees and pay the money to the U.S. Treasury.

The first step in solving any problem is to recognize that a problem exists. This book should go a long way toward helping owners and operators of small businesses recognize tax issues and deal with them *before* they become serious problems.

Great effort has been expended to ensure the accuracy of the material in this book. However, tax laws are open to interpretation and are subject to *constant change.* Therefore, it is advisable to confirm the continued accuracy of materials contained in this book before relying on them.

Chapter 1

Income

There are many types of taxes that businesses face. Some of those taxes are based on how the business is organized, others have to do with what the business does or produces. Of all the taxes imposed on a business (as well as its owners), income tax affects each and every business. Determining this tax can be daunting, but it begins with establishing what *income* is.

REALIZING INCOME

There are several different approaches to calculating income for tax purposes. This book will use a system that requires *realization* of income before it is taxed. Until some event occurs that causes income to be received, either *actually* or *constructively*, by a party, it is not considered to be *realized* and is, therefore, not subjected to taxation.

EXAMPLE: John bought 100 shares of stock in a local bank at its inception. The bank did well in its first year of operation. The stock rose in value from $10.00 on January 2nd to $18.00 by December 15th of that same year. Even though John's net worth increased by $800.00 due to the stock appreciation, he will have no tax consequences from the stock's appreciation unless he actually sells the stock, thereby *realizing* the gain.

CONSTRUCTIVE RECEIPT

Although we normally think of income as involving the *receipt of funds*, there are numerous instances when a party will be deemed to have *realized income* despite not having received anything. The concept of *constructive receipt of income* has largely been brought about due to efforts by taxpayers to escape or postpone taxation, or due to their efforts to shift the tax away from themselves and on to someone else.

Once income becomes fully *available* to a taxpayer, he or she is regarded as having *received* it for taxation purposes, whether he or she really received it or not. Taxation will be imposed on such income at the time it is constructively received, rather that when it is *actually* received. However, if there are substantial limitations or restrictions on a party's right to receive income, or if the party that owes the income is unable to pay it, the income will not be considered to be constructively received.

EXAMPLE: Jane is a roofer. Under the terms of her agreements with two local builders, she is to be paid upon completion of her work on each house. On December 31st, the last day of the tax year, she had just finished a house for Quality Construction Co., but the owner could not pay her. The bank where he had gotten his construction loan required that an inspector verify completion of the work before he could draw additional funds on his line of credit. The inspector would not be available until after the first of the year. Jane was almost through with her second project, a house for Platinum Homes, Inc., but needed about one more day to finish it.

Since Jane did not actually have access to payment in the first instance due to the contractor's inability to pay her, and in the second instance because she had not completed the work as required by her contract, she will not be deemed to have constructively received payment from either contractor. However, if Jane finished the house for Platinum Homes on

December 28th but waits until January 2nd to pick up her check, she will be considered to have constructively received the money in December.

Furthermore, taxpayers will also have income attributed to them when they divert income, such as reinvesting taxable stock dividends to buy more stock or when someone pays a debt on their behalf and the payment is not considered to be a *gift*. The fact that payments are made *in kind*, rather than in money, will have no bearing on otherwise taxable payments.

ASSIGNMENT OF INCOME

Often, in an effort to escape taxes, someone who has earned income will designate another party to actually receive the income. This is usually done to satisfy an obligation or to place the taxable income onto a person whose income (and thus tax liability) will be less.

When the IRS (Internal Revenue Service) determines that there has been an *assignment of income*, it will generally take the approach that the party who assigned his or her right to the income will be deemed to have constructively received it. Taxes will then be assessed on the assigned income to the party who assigned it. Any taxes that may be due on the income from the party to whom it was assigned will be unaffected.

EXAMPLE: Jeff trims trees on weekends to supplement his income. He was to be paid $1,000 for work he did at several rental properties owned by one person. Upon completion of the work, he had the property owner write a check for $500 to Rachel to pay her for painting Jeff's kitchen and a check for $500 to Jeff's son, Hank, a young child who had no income of his own. Jeff did not report the $1,000 payment on his own tax return, but Rachel reported the $500 that she received. Hank's income was so low that he was not required to file a return.

The IRS would consider Jeff to have constructively received $1,000, resulting in him having under reported his income by $1,000 for the year. The fact that Jeff had to recognize the

$1,000 as reportable income would not affect the fact that the $500 that Rachel received was taxable to her, since she received it in exchange for her labor. The $500 payment to Hank, however, would be recharacterized as a *gift* since he did nothing to earn it.

In addition to instances where taxpayers deliberately attempt to escape taxation by assigning income, there are cases in which they unknowingly are deemed to make *income assignments*. This is particularly common in instances where company profits are used to pay former owners or partners for their share of a company or its assets.

EXAMPLE: Joe and Bobbie, part owners of a local sales organization, entered into an agreement to buy out two other owners of the partnership. It was agreed that the former owners would be paid for their interests in the partnership by receiving half of the profits generated for the next five years.

The proper tax treatment of the profits paid to the former owners would be to report those profits as income to Joe and Bobbie, which were then paid to the former owners for the sale of their interests in the partnership. Joe and Bobbie would be required to report the payments to the former owners as regular income of their own from the partnership. The former owners would report the payments received for their partnership interests as receipts from the sale of an asset.

METHOD OF ACCOUNTING

A major factor affecting the timing of realization of income is the taxpayer's *method of accounting*. Individuals generally adopt the *cash method of accounting*. This means they must recognize and report their income as they receive it—either actually *or* constructively.

Payments-in-kind, such as building a fence in exchange for an air compressor, are to be reported as receipts under the cash method of accounting, using the *fair market value* of the goods or services received as the value to be reported. Likewise, under the cash method of accounting, *business expenses* that may be deducted in calculating net income are not to be taken until they are actually paid.

Accrual Method

Not every taxpayer is permitted to use the cash method of accounting. Under current U.S. tax law, some businesses must use the *accrual method of accounting*. Section 446-1(c)(2) of the current Internal Revenue Code (I.R.C.) states that corporations that sell goods are required to adopt the accrual method of accounting. It requires recognition of obligations that are merely owed as having been fully paid. Expenses are treated in a consistent manner as well, since businesses on the accrual method of accounting are allowed to take deductions for business expenses when they are incurred, rather than having to wait until they are actually paid.

The theory behind requiring businesses that sell goods to adopt the accrual method of accounting is that they could time the payment of their obligations in a way that would permit them to distort the incidence of taxation if they were allowed to use the cash method. By prepaying rent, the costs of services, or other obligations of the company, and taking a deduction for those payments against current income, they would be able to reduce the amount of profits that they realized for the year.

However, there are a number of exceptions that permit companies that would otherwise be required to use the accrual method of accounting to use the cash method. Those exceptions are generally based on whether the organization is primarily a *goods-based* business or a *service-based* business, and the dollar amount of sales the business generates. Businesses that fall into the exception include:

- ◆ farming;
- ◆ corporations with average annual gross receipts for each of the prior tax years ending after December 16, 1998, under $1,000,000;
- ◆ corporations that strictly provide services and whose annual sales averaged less than $5,000,000 over the last three taxable years;
- ◆ qualified personal service corporation whose shareholders are employed by the business and actively participate in the oper-

ation of it, even with gross sales in excess of the $5,000,000 three-taxable-year average; and,

◆ otherwise eligible businesses with average gross receipts of less than $10,000,000 over the last three years unless they fall within certain codes of the *North American Industry Classification System (NAICS)*. These generally consist of companies that deal in goods, and industries involved in mining, manufacturing, wholesale trade, retail trade, or certain information industries.

Companies that are considered to be *tax shelters* are not allowed to use the cash method of accounting, even if they do not sell goods. Code Section 464(e)(2) defines a tax shelter as an entity, other than a C corporation, from which more than 35% of losses for tax purposes that it generates is attributed to owners who do not actively participate in the management of the entity.

Consequence of Accounting Method

Companies that do not make a profit will not suffer significant ill consequences from having to use the accrual method of accounting. However, a problem arises when a company on the accrual method of accounting has profits that take the form of *accounts receivable*. The result is a tax liability due to the profit earned, but no cash with which to pay the taxes on that profit because the profit is merely a receivable.

EXAMPLE: Mid-America Steel Distributors, Inc. buys and resells steel components to commercial contractors. The goods are delivered to its customers who pay for the goods on an average of sixty to ninety days later. At the end of the tax year, Mid-America showed profit of $660,000, but its accounts receivable increased by $700,000. The corporation will report to the IRS that each of the three owners had a $220,000 profit from the company, on which each will be required to pay taxes. But, since the profit took the form of an increase in accounts receivable, the profit will not be available for distribution to the owners.

Chapter 2
Gross Income

Regardless of which accounting method a party uses, once it is determined that an individual possesses realized income that is subject to taxation, there are numerous factors that must be taken into consideration in order to arrive at the party's tax liability. The process begins with the determination of *gross income*. Section 61 of the Code defines *gross income* as including *all income from whatever source derived* unless there are provisions in the tax laws to the contrary. Section 61 goes on to list the major sources of gross income, but cautions that the potential sources of gross income are not limited only to those listed.

COMPENSATION FOR SERVICES

The first source of gross income listed in the Code Sec. 61 is *compensation for services, including fees, fringe benefits, and similar items*. As long as a party is paid for services rendered, the receipts are income, despite what name they may be called. *Payments*, such as *tips* or *bonuses*, even if made without any legal obligation, are included within the definition of gross income. Payments from an employer, such as *sick pay,* are also included.

BUSINESS INCOME

Gross income derived from business, calculated by reducing gross receipts by the cost of goods sold, is included in the Sec. 61 list of gross income sources. However, businesses have some latitude in determining the value of their cost of goods sold. This can be accomplished in the *method of inventory accounting* the business adopts.

FIFO Inventory Accounting

Traditionally, businesses were required to regard the goods that they had sold as being those that had been held in inventory the longest, a procedure known as the *first-in, first-out* or *FIFO method of inventory accounting*. During periods of relatively stable prices, using the FIFO method of inventory accounting creates no particular problems. However, during periods of inflation, the FIFO method causes profits to be distorted. They appear higher than they really are since the older, less costly inventory that yielded an apparently high profit from its sale, must be replaced with similar inventory items that are more costly.

EXAMPLE: Hometown Lumber Co. had 5,000 sheets of half inch 4x8 plywood in inventory. The oldest 1,000 of those sheets cost $3.50 each. The next oldest 2,000 cost $3.75 each and the last batch of 2,000 cost $4.00 each. Hometown, which is on the FIFO method of inventory accounting, filled a 1,000 sheet order at $4.50 a sheet. When it ordered 1,000 sheets to replace those it sold, it had to pay $4.40 a sheet for them. Hometown's gross profit will be determined by subtracting the cost of the oldest 1,000 sheets, $3,500, from the gross sale price of $4,500 for a total of $1,000. However, Hometown will have to use $4,400 of its gross receipts to replace the 1,000 sheets that it sold, leaving only $100. This would not even be enough to pay the taxes on the $1,000 gross profit.

LIFO Inventory Accounting

In order to avoid the profit distortions caused by the FIFO method of inventory accounting during inflationary periods, Congress enacted the Code Sec. 472 that allows taxpayers to adopt a *last-in, first-out method*, known as *LIFO*. Election of this method (made by sending in a completed *Form 970* along with the tax return for the first period that LIFO is used), permits sellers to more accurately reflect the replacement cost of their cost of goods sold.

EXAMPLE: If, in the example above, Hometown had been using the LIFO method of inventory accounting, its cost of goods sold would have been based on the most recent purchase price of $4.00 per sheet of plywood. This would result in a total cost of $4,000 for the thousand sheets. When subtracted from the $4,500 sale price, this would leave a gross profit of $500, rather than the $1,000 resulting from the FIFO method.

Although reducing income by use of the LIFO inventory accounting method may be appealing to the degree that it reduces taxes, business operators may be less enthusiastic about showing reduced profits to owners, investors, or creditors. To alleviate this, Sec. 472(c) of the Code permits business operators to make a notation in their financial statements showing what the operation's profits would have been using the traditional FIFO method.

Specific Identification Inventory Accounting

Sellers of goods that are *specifically identified* to each transaction will not face problems from income distortion due to their choice of inventory accounting method. They can readily ascertain their cost in the specific item being sold and use that figure for their cost of goods sold.

EXAMPLE: Clyde operates a used car lot where he keeps about twenty-four cars in inventory. He has a record of how much he pays for each car that he buys. As he sells a car, he can readily ascertain his cost in acquiring that car and include that figure as part of his cost of goods sold in order to calculate gross income.

GAIN FROM DEALINGS IN PROPERTY

Gross income includes *gains derived from dealings in property*. This encompasses not only the sale of real estate, but also the sale of the rights of ownership in intangible property, such as a trademark or contract rights.

It is of particular importance that Sec. 61 limits the amount included in gross income from dealings in property to *gain* rather than gross receipts. That limits taxation to what we generally think of as *profit* attributable to such dealings. Gain is the difference in the amount realized from the transaction and the taxpayer's adjusted basis in the property.

The amount realized is generally the amount received for the property (in cash and/or the fair market value of trade) minus its *basis*. *Basis* can be an incredibly difficult amount to determine, but a starting point in that determination is the purchase price of the item. Adjustments can be made to that amount to arrive at an *adjusted basis*. Section 1016 of the Code allows for additions to basis for expenditures made on the property, such as putting in a parking lot, and deductions for losses taken on property for tax purposes, such as an uninsured fire loss. It allows for certain receipts attributable to the property, such as insurance proceeds for damage to property that is not repaired. It also requires a reduction in basis for any depreciation taken on the property, but prohibits adjustments in basis for taxes or interest paid in connection with the property.

EXAMPLE: Terry bought a house for $65,000 and rented it out. Over a period of several years, he took $8,000 in depreciation on the property, paid $4,200 in taxes and $3,000 for insurance, spent a total of $2,000 on clean-up and routine maintenance, and collected $5,000 in insurance proceeds due to destruction of a detached storage shed which he never replaced. Terry's basis in the property will be reduced by the $8,000 in depreciation that he took on the property and by the $5,000 in insurance proceeds that he collected for the loss of the storage shed that was not replaced.

However, none of his expenditures for property taxes, insurance, or routine cleanup and maintenance will affect his basis in the property. His adjusted basis at this point is

$52,000. If he sold it for the same $65,000 price that he had paid, he would have a gain of $13,000 on the sale of the house.

CAPITAL GAINS AND LOSSES

Taxpayers who sell capital assets that they have held for over one year are usually entitled to have their gains (known as *long-term capital gains*) taxed at a substantially lower rate than their ordinary income. There is also special tax treatment for losses realized on the sale of *capital assets*.

DETERMINING WHETHER PROPERTY IS A CAPITAL ASSET

The determination of whether an asset is a capital asset is based on how the owner uses it or obtained it, rather than the specific type of asset involved. The same asset can be a capital asset in the hands of one taxpayer, but not in the hands of another. Guidance for determining whether or not an asset is a capital asset is provided by the Code Sec. 1221 that describes the uses and sources of acquisition of property that disqualify it from being considered a capital asset. Property used in a trade or in the ordinary course of the taxpayer's business that is excluded from consideration as a capital asset includes:

- ◆ inventory;
- ◆ real estate;
- ◆ personal property that the taxpayer is allowed to depreciate;
- ◆ accounts receivable;
- ◆ promissory notes acquired from the sale of goods or services; and,
- ◆ intellectual property under certain conditions.

EXAMPLE: When the price of gold took a significant dip, Stella, who makes jewelry, bought $50,000 worth of gold for use in her business. At the same time, Baddar, a convenience store owner, thought that gold was likely to go back up in value and bought $100,000 worth of gold as a speculation. Fourteen months later, Stella still had most of the gold that she had bought because most of her customers were buying silver jewelry, so she sold 80% of the gold that she had bought for a profit of $30,000. At that same time, Baddar sold his entire gold holdings for a profit of $75,000. Stella's profit on the sale of her gold will be ordinary income since she is in the business of selling gold and her motivation for buying it was to use it as inventory. Baddar's gain will be a capital gain, since he purchased the gold as an investment.

Determining the Amount of Capital Gain or Loss

When a capital asset is sold and the sale price exceeds the seller's adjusted basis in the property, the amount received in excess of the asset's adjusted basis is a *capital gain*. If the sale price of a capital asset is less than the seller's adjusted basis in the property, the difference is a *capital loss*. Capital gains and losses can also result from transfers other than sales, such as when a taxpayer suffers a casualty or theft loss and the insurance company's payment for the loss is either greater or less than the taxpayer's adjusted basis in the property that was stolen or destroyed.

Usually, the sale price of a capital asset is simply the amount of money that a party was paid for the asset. However, if a party receives noncash property or a combination of cash and noncash property in exchange for the property, the sale price will be equal to the fair market value of the noncash property received plus any cash paid. When a combination of cash and noncash property is exchanged for an asset, the noncash part of the payment is referred to as *boot*.

Multiple transactions in the course of one year must follow special *netting rules*. Short-term capital gains are netted against short-term capital losses and long-term capital gains are netted against long-term capital losses. If the netting of short-term gains and losses yields a net gain, it must be netted against net long-term capital losses and any remaining gain will be taxed as ordinary income. If the netting of both short-term gains and losses and long-term gains and losses each result in gains, the net short-term gain will be taxed as ordinary income. The long-term gain will be kept separate and taxed at the more favorable long-term rates.

If the netting of short-term gains and losses results in a net short-term loss, it will be netted against net long-term gains. But, if the netting of short-term gains and losses results in a loss and the netting of long-term gains and losses yields a loss as well, the net short-term loss must be used to offset ordinary income to the extent permitted by law first, and then the net long-term loss may be used if the short-term loss is exhausted without fully offsetting the amount of ordinary income permitted. The maximum amount of ordinary income that can be offset with either short-term or long-term capital losses per year is $3,000. Any unused capital losses may be carried forward until used up.

EXAMPLE: Jasmine sold stock that she had owned for six months and made a $5,000 profit. She sold a futures contract that she had held for forty-five days and lost $3,000. She sold a bond that she had owned for two years and made $6,000 on it and sold some stock that she had owned for three years at a $4,500 loss.

Jasmine must net her short-term losses and gains to arrive at a net short-term capital gain of $2,000 ($5,000 - $3,000). She must then net the $6,000 long-term capital gain on the bond against the $4,500 long-term capital loss on the stock for a net long-term capital gain of $1,500. Since both the netting of short-term gains and losses and the netting of long-term gains and losses resulted in net gains, the net short-term gain will be taxed as ordinary income and Jasmine will have a long-term capital gain of $1,500.

Tax Treatment of Long-term Capital Gains

With the passage of the 2003 *Jobs and Growth Tax Relief Reconciliation Act* (*JGTRRA*), the tax rate on most long-term capital gains for most taxpayers on transactions occurring on or after May 6, 2003, but before January 1, 2009, was reduced from 28% to 15%. For taxpayers whose net long-term capital gains would be taxed in either the 10% or 15% tax bracket had the gains been ordinary income, JGTRRA imposes a tax rate of only 5%. It is scheduled to drop to 0% in 2008. The 28% rate remains in effect for collectibles that are held for over one year, such as coins, stamps, artwork, and antiques, and also for gains on the sale of stock in small businesses that qualify to be taxed under the Code Sec. 1202.

There is a 25% long-term capital gain tax rate on the long-term gain realized from the sale of certain real estate that is subject to depreciation known as Sec. 1250 property, to the extent that the gain is attributable to recovery of *straight line depreciation* taken on the property. To the extent that gain on Sec. 1250 property is attributable to depreciation taken on the property in excess of straight line, it is taxed as ordinary income. To the degree that the gain on Sec. 1250 property is attributable to actual increase in the value of the property, it is taxed at the 15% rate.

Corporations

Corporations are not entitled to any tax relief on their long-term capital gains. Such gains are taxed no differently than ordinary corporate income. Furthermore, corporations cannot use any of their capital losses to offset ordinary income, although they are permitted to use capital losses to offset capital gains.

Losses from Sale of Small Business Stock—Sec. 1244

Taxpayers who suffer losses on *small business stock* upon its sale, exchange, or due to the stock having become worthless, are allowed to treat up to $50,000 of such losses per year as ordinary loss. Married taxpayers who file joint returns are permitted to treat up to $100,000 of such losses as ordinary losses per year. The impact of these provisions in the Code Sec. 1244, is that an investor who realizes sizable losses on a small business stock, is often referred to as *Sec. 1244 stock*. The investor is permitted to use those losses, up to the extent of the maximum limit, to offset ordinary income. (Net capital losses from assets other than Sec. 1244 stock may be used to offset only $3,000 of ordinary income per year.) If a taxpayer's loss from Sec. 1244 property exceeds the statutory limit for deduction as ordinary losses, the excess will be classified as a capital loss. Taxpayers who do not have enough ordinary income to fully utilize the allowable ordinary loss deduction provided for in Sec. 1244 may carry those losses back two years as a *net operating loss deduction*. Taxpayers may carry them forward for up to twenty years.

In order to qualify as a small business for purposes of Sec. 1244, the company must be a domestic corporation with an aggregate capital under $1,000,000. A further requirement for a company's stock to qualify as *Sec. 1244 stock* is that during the last five years, or the duration of the company's existence if it has not been in business for five years, the company must have derived more than 50% of its aggregate gross receipts from sources other than royalties, rents, dividends, interest, annuities, or the sale or exchange of securities.

Partial Exclusion of Gains from Sale of Small Business Stock

Investors who acquire original issue stock in a *qualified C corporation* and hold the stock for over five years are permitted by the Code Sec. 1202 to exclude half of their gain from the sale of the stock from taxation altogether. The maximum amount that they are permitted to exclude is the larger of $10,000,000 or ten times the taxpayer's aggregate adjusted basis in the stock.

In order to be a qualified corporation for purposes of Sec. 1202, at least 80% of the corporation's assets must be used in the active conduct of one or more trades or businesses. Most trades or businesses will qualify for Sec. 1202 treatment, including service businesses, farming, businesses providing financial services, businesses providing food and/or lodging, as well as businesses actually engaged in the production of goods. A corporation is also limited to a maximum of $50,000,000 in gross assets immediately after issuance of its stock in order to qualify as a small business for purposes of Sec. 1202. Furthermore, only stock that was issued after August 10, 1993, qualifies for the exclusion.

Prior to passage of the *JGTRRA (Jobs and Growth Tax Relief Reconciliation Act)* in 2003, the 50% exclusion from taxation offered by Sec. 1202 was a tremendous benefit. However, under the provisions of JGTRRA, the remaining gain after the excluded half is taken into consideration is taxed at the pre-JGTRRA rate of 28%. Ordinarily, most long-term capital gains are taxed at only 15% until the end of 2008 when the old rates are set to return. Therefore, the net effect of Sec. 1202, under current provisions, is a tax savings of only one percentage point of the qualified gain. (The 28% rate on half of the gain is the equivalent of 14% on the entire gain—1% less than the 15% rate.)

DEFERRING RECOGNITION OF CAPITAL GAINS

Provisions within the Internal Revenue Code that allow the recognition of capital gains to be deferred accomplish this by allowing the taxpayer to transfer his or her basis from the property that sold to qualifying property acquired. The result is a mere *postponement* of gain because, if the replacement properties are sold, the low basis transferred to them will result in recognition of the previously deferred gain, unless the gain can be further deferred. However, that does not mean that the ability to defer recognition of gain is not beneficial. By being able to defer recognition of gain on the sale or exchange of capital assets, businessmen and investors will have the full amount of funds they receive with which to acquire the replacements they need.

Rollover of Gain from Qualified Small Business Stock

Taxpayers (other than corporations) who sell qualified small business stock that they have held for more than six months are allowed, by the Code Sec. 1045, to defer recognition of any gain on the sale if they purchase replacement qualified small business stock within sixty days of having sold the shares. (In order for stock to be considered *qualified small business stock*, it must meet the definition set forth in the Code Sec. 1202, as previously discussed.) The taxpayer's basis in any qualified small business stock purchased within the sixty day period for tax-deferred replacement will be reduced to the extent that the gain was deferred on the qualified small business stock that was previously sold. If a taxpayer uses only part of the proceeds received from the sale of qualified small business stock to acquire a qualified replacement, he or she will still be allowed to defer gains on that part of the proceeds from the sale. However, the taxpayer will be required to recognize the gain on the balance of the proceeds.

Like-kind Exchanges

Section 1031 of the Internal Revenue Code provides for nonrecognition of gain or loss when property held for productive use in a trade, business, or for investment is exchanged solely for property of *like-kind* that will also be held either for productive use in a trade, business, or for investment. However, not all property qualifies. Among the more notable items that are specifically excluded from eligibility for deferment of recognition of gains under Sec. 1031 are inventory, securities, notes, and interests in partnerships. However, the provisions of Sec. 1031 do apply to holdings of real estate, both improved and unimproved, held for investment or for productive use in a trade or business. Like-kind exchanges involving such realty is quite common.

CONVERSIONS OF PROPERTY

Parties who convert their personal-use property to a business use will not be taxed on the conversion. However, if depreciation was taken on the property, its basis will be adjusted. The new basis will be either the lower of its fair market value at the time of the conversion *or* the owner's adjusted basis in that property at that time.

If a taxpayer converts business property to personal use, there will be no recognition of either gain or loss from the conversion, similar to the personal-to-business conversion. This is because there is no event that triggers realization of gain or loss when a party retains ownership of an asset, but merely alters the use.

Involuntary Conversion

Occasionally, a taxpayer surrenders his or her interest in either real estate or personal property despite not choosing to do so. Such transfers, known as *involuntary conversions*, include:

- ◆ forced sales due to a governmental entity exercising its rights of seizure, requisition, or condemnation;
- ◆ theft compensated for by insurance;
- ◆ casualty loss compensated for by insurance; and,
- ◆ livestock destroyed by or on account of disease or weather-related conditions, such as flood or drought.

When an involuntary conversion occurs, the Code Sec. 1033 permits the property owner to postpone recognition of any gain from it if replacement property (*similar or related in service or use to the involuntarily converted property*) is purchased within two years after the close of the first taxable year in which any of the gain from the conversion is realized. A taxpayer must recognize gains on any proceeds from an involuntary conversion that are not used to acquire qualified replacement property.

REPORTING CAPITAL GAINS AND LOSSES

Capital gains are reported on Schedule D. There are separate Schedule D forms for individuals and corporations. The Schedule D for partnerships provides a vehicle for identifying capital gains and losses. These forms are designed so their identities can be preserved and reported in appropriate shares to the individual partners.

There are provisions for calculating capital gains on the front of Schedule D. There are also lines for the inclusion of capital gains and losses that are calculated on other forms and transferred to Schedule D. The back of Schedule D for individuals contains the steps for calculating the tax liability for those who have long-term capital gains for the tax year.

INTEREST

Interest (money received by a party for letting someone else use his or her money) is included in Sec. 61(a)(4) as a source of gross income. (However, the Code Sec. 103 permits exclusion of interest received from tax free bonds.)

One of the more troublesome aspects concerning the inclusion of interest in gross income is the concept of *imputed interest*. Whenever tax-payers lend money that is to be paid back at some future time, or sell goods that are to be paid for at a future time, and do not specify if the borrower is to pay interest or not, the IRS will impute interest on the transaction. As a result, part of the proceeds collected by the lender or creditor will be recharacterized as interest and taxed accordingly. Interest will also be imputed on interest-free loans that are never repaid because the lender forgives the indebtedness, making it a *gift*. *Gifts* that exceed a certain annual dollar amount are subject to additional tax related rules.

When interest is imputed, the *applicable federal rate* (the rate paid by the federal government on funds that it borrows for a similar period) is used. The rates are calculated monthly and include a short-term rate for loans of three years or less, a mid-term rate for loans of over three years, but not over nine years duration, and a long-term rate for loans with a duration in excess of nine years.

EXAMPLE: Jed wanted to give some money to his daughter, Ellie Mae, so that she could buy a pet store. In order to avoid state and federal gift tax consequences, he gave her a $500,000 interest-free loan to be paid back from pet store profits. The IRS will impute interest on the loan resulting in taxable income to Jed that will be regarded as a gift to Ellie Mae since he chose not to collect it.

RENTS

Still another source of gross income, listed in Sec. 61(a)(5), is *rents.* The term *rents* refers to money received for letting someone else use the recipient's real estate or personal property. Only the net income from the rental of property is included in a taxpayer's gross income. Deductions are allowed for expenses, such as maintenance, taxes, insurance, advertising, and repairs associated with rental activities, as well as depreciation of the rental property.

It is not uncommon for leases on real estate to provide that upon expiration of the lease or breach of the lease by the tenant, all improvements to the property that were made by the tenant will be forfeited, without charge, to the owner of the property. Section 109 of the Internal Revenue Code provides that such improvements that are forfeited by a tenant to a property owner under such lease provisions will not constitute income to the owner. However, any payments made by a tenant to an owner to permit him or her to terminate the lease early shall constitute ordinary income.

Internal Revenue Code Sec. 469 disallows the use of *passive activity losses* to offset any type of income other than *passive activity income*. Rental real estate activities are specifically included in the Sec. 469 definition of passive activities that are otherwise defined as those in which the taxpayer did not *materially participate*. Despite the fact that rental real estate activity is considered a passive activity, Sec. 469(i) contains an exception that permits a person to offset up to $25,000 of non-passive activity income with losses from rental real estate if his or her adjusted gross income does not exceed $100,000. If a party's adjusted gross income exceeds $100,000, the $25,000 rental income loss that a taxpayer would be otherwise eligible to use to offset nonpassive losses will be reduced by 50% of the amount by which his or her adjusted gross income exceeds $100,000. At an adjusted gross income amount of $150,000, the offset amount becomes zero.

EXAMPLE: Devon rented space to Dennis so that he could open a restaurant. Devon required Dennis to make improvements to the space to make it more suitable for use as a restaurant. He stipulated in the lease that the improvements would become Devon's property upon termination of the lease due to either its expiration or breach by Dennis. The restaurant was unpopular and Dennis became insolvent and closed the restaurant after only six months. Devon was able to quickly rent the space to another tenant at somewhat more rent due to the improvements that Dennis had made.

Devon's adjusted gross income for the year was $120,000 before considering his $45,000 loss from his rental activity. Devon can use only $15,000 of his rental losses to offset part of his $120,000 adjusted gross income. This is because his adjusted gross income exceeded $100,000 by $20,000 and the $25,000 offset for rental losses must be reduced by half of the overage ($25,000 − ($20,000/2) = $15,000).

The value of the improvements made by Dennis that became Devon's property upon termination of the lease, will not be considered rental income or any other type of income to Devon.

ROYALTIES

Payments for the right to use property such as written materials, patents, trademarks, and formulas are referred to as *royalties*. This term also describes payments for the right to exploit natural resources such as oil, minerals, or timber. Royalties are included in gross income and are regarded as ordinary income.

DIVIDENDS

If a corporation that has not elected to be taxed under subchapter S of the Internal Revenue Code makes a *nonliquidating distribution* of cash or property from either current or accumulated earnings and profits, it constitutes a *dividend*. The dividend is includible in the recipient's gross income under the provisions of Sec. 61(a)(7).

Any payment by such a corporation will be viewed as merely a return of capital, also known as a *nimble dividend*, to the extent that the payment exceeds the company's earnings and profits. Rather than being included in the recipient's gross income, nimble dividends merely reduce the party's adjusted basis in the stock for which the dividend was paid. Once a recipient's adjusted basis in a company's stock is reduced to zero, any further nimble dividends paid by the company will be classified as capital gains.

The concept of *earnings and profits* is an accounting device used solely to determine whether or not a corporation's dividend payments are includible in the recipient's gross income or are to be regarded as a return of part or all of his or her capital investment in the corporation. The calculation of earnings and profits starts with the corporation's taxable income, to which is added the previously excluded items of death benefits received from life insurance, interest on obligations of states and their political subdivisions, certain compensation for injuries or sickness, and amounts of recovery of previously deducted bad debts and prior taxes. Next, the deduction for dividends received, the net operating loss deduction, and the capital loss carry-backs and carry-forwards are added back.

Certain items that were not allowed as deductions in calculating a corporation's taxable income, such as business expense deductions that were disallowed because they were either unsubstantiated or disallowed by statute, federal income taxes, losses from dealings with related parties, and certain life insurance premiums must then be subtracted from the total. After a further adjustment to convert accelerated depreciation to straight line, the result is the earnings and profits in the case of most corporations.

EXAMPLE: Monica invested $25,000 in a fan shop, The Big Wind, Inc. and was issued stock accordingly. She also borrowed money on behalf of the company, which did not elect to be taxed as an S corporation and was, therefore, a C corporation. Despite the fact that the company had no earnings and profits in its first year of operation, Monica paid herself a $10,000 dividend. Monica will not be required to include the $10,000 dividend in her gross income, but her adjusted basis in her stock on Big Wind, Inc. will be reduced from $25,000 to $15,000.

DISTRIBUTIVE SHARE OF PARTNERSHIP INCOME

Section 61(a)(13) provides that a partner's distributive share of partnership gross income shall be included in gross income. Partnerships and entities that are taxed as partnerships, such as eligible corporations whose owners have elected to be taxed under provisions of subchapter S of the Internal Revenue Code, must file annual tax returns, but do not incur tax liabilities. Such organizations show their income on their tax returns and then further show each partner's distributive share of the organization's income or loss. Each owner's distributive share of income from such organizations will be reported to the owner and the IRS. It must be included in gross income regardless of whether or not a distribution was actually received. (Further discussion of calculation of distributive shares of partnership income and taxation of undistributed shares may be found in Chapter 10.)

EXAMPLE: Tina is a partner in an interior decorating company. Her distributive share of partnership income for the last tax year was $28,000. However, the partners decided to leave all earnings in the partnership and use them to buy a van and some fixtures for their store. Despite the fact that Tina did not actually receive her distributive share of partnership income, she still must include it in her gross income on her tax return.

LOANS

Although funds received as proceeds of a loan are not considered to be income, there are a number of situations involving loans that can result in the realization of taxable income. There are instances in which taxpayers have attempted to escape taxation by characterizing payments that they were to receive as if they were loans, although they were not actually obligated to ever repay the money. To the degree that these sham *loans* are really payments for goods or services, they will be recharacterized appropriately as income. Penalties and interest will be assessed on top of tax liabilities when there is a resulting tax deficiency. If nothing is given in exchange for the sham loan, it will be recharacterized as a gift. It will not result in any income tax liability to the recipient, but may generate a gift tax liability for the donor.

Even when loans are originally bona fide legal obligations that the borrowers intend to repay, there can still be realization of taxable income to the debtor in the event that the debt is forgiven or canceled. Unless it can be shown that the canceled amount of a debt was a gift, Sec. 61(a)(12) provides that the canceled amount will be regarded as income to the debtor. Income due to cancellation of debt can arise whether the debt is entirely or only partially canceled unless the party whose debt was canceled is either insolvent or bankrupt. A debt that is owed to a corporation by one of its stockholders that is forgiven will be regarded as a dividend to the stockholder. Otherwise, canceled debt is generally treated as ordinary income.

EXAMPLE: Sarah owes an $8,500 deficiency on a car that she failed to pay for, was repossessed, and sold. The finance company that she owes has agreed to take $2,500 as full payment of the debt and write off the remaining $6,000. Sarah will have to report the $6,000 discount as income if she settles with the finance company for $2,500.

SPECIFICALLY EXCLUDED SOURCES OF INCOME

There are a number of sources of income that, due to legislative grace, are not regarded as gross income to the recipient. Among the most important statutory exclusions from gross income are:

- gifts and inheritances;
- most insurance proceeds;
- some disability income;
- many of the fringe benefits provided by employers to their employees;
- the part of the proceeds from a sale of assets that represents recovery of adjusted basis;
- much of the gain from the sale of primary residences; and,
- half of the gain from the sale or exchange of qualified small business stock.

Gifts and Inheritances

Money or property received by taxpayers as a gift will not be subject to income tax. However, included in gross income are gifts that are transfers from employers *to (or for) the benefit of an employee*, except for employee *achievement awards for years of service* or *safety awards* that do not total more than $400 in cost to the employer for the year. (These are provided for in the Code Sec. 74(c) and *de minimis fringe benefits* as provided for in Sec. 132(e).)

EXAMPLE: Safronia is a salesperson for a mattress company. Her salary is $5,000 a month. She had an exceptional year in 2003 and was the top producer for the entire company. At the annual awards banquet, she was given a sterling silver pen in recognition of ten years of service with the company and a $10,000 bonus in recognition of her record sales for the year. The company was under no obligation to give her anything beyond her salary. The company had never given such a bonus before, but the managers decided that they wanted to do something special for Safronia since her sales were double those of the next highest salesperson.

As long as the cost of the pen plus the cost of any other service or safety awards given to Safronia over the course of the year did not exceed $400 and she had not received a length of service award in the last four years, she can exclude its value from her gross income. However, she must include the $10,000 bonus in her gross income, even though her employer was not obligated to give it to her. (If the pen had been given to her in recognition of her sales performance, its value would be includible in her gross income, as well.)

It is possible for a gift that appears to otherwise qualify for exclusion from gross income to be deemed a part of the recipient's gross income if it can be shown that the *gift* was actually payment for goods or services. The fact that the payment is labeled as a gift will not govern its treatment when the transfer was not made as the result of donative intent.

Insurance Proceeds

Insurance proceeds are another source of revenue that often is not subject to income taxation. Among the most important determinants of whether or not insurance proceeds will be included in the recipient's gross income are whether:

- ◆ a tax deduction was taken by the business entity that paid the premiums;
- ◆ the proceeds of the policy replaced income for the recipient; and,
- ◆ a party who received proceeds for damaged or stolen property realized a gain as a result.

Life Insurance Proceeds

Proceeds from life insurance policies offer a source of sizable payments without income tax consequences. However, there is an exception that renders life insurance proceeds taxable when the premiums are paid by business entities for policies that they own and the premiums paid are taken as a deductible expense for tax purposes. Publication 525 (available from the IRS without charge) offers considerable information concerning whether or not various life insurance proceeds are taxable.

EXAMPLE: The owners of Prestige Shoe Store, Inc. decided to buy life insurance on the lives of each of the owners, since all held important jobs in the company. The policies that are generally referred to as *key man insurance*, were to be paid for and owned by the company. The company also bought a $50,000 life insurance policy for each employee and paid the premiums on them, but those policies were owned by the individual employees whose lives were insured.

If the company takes a tax deduction for the premiums it pays on the key man policies, whenever an insured party dies and Prestige Shoe Stores, Inc. collects the proceeds of the policy, those proceeds will be fully taxable as income to Prestige. If the company had not taken a tax deduction for the premiums that it had paid on the key man policies, it could have collected proceeds from those policies free of income taxation.

Even if Prestige deducts the premiums that it pays for the $50,000 life insurance policy that it provides for each employee, it will have no income tax consequences when payments are made to a deceased employee's beneficiaries since the policy was not owned by the company. The beneficiaries of the individual policies will not be required to pay income taxes on the $50,000 that they receive, since such payments qualify for exclusion from gross income.

Whether the premiums paid by employers for the life insurance they provide to employees will be includible in the gross incomes of the employees depends on the nature of the policy provided, the amount of coverage provided, and whether the company discriminates in favor of key employees in providing the coverage. Premiums paid by an employer for up to $50,000 of group term life insurance per employee are not taxable income to the employee. If an employee is provided more than $50,000 of group term life insurance, he or she must report the premiums for coverage in excess of the $50,000 as income. However, if the employer's group life insurance plan discriminates in favor of key employees, such as providing coverage equal to three times annual salary for key employees, but only two times annual salary for others, the entire premium paid by the employer for the key employee's policy will be fully taxable to that employee, but not to the other employees who had not received favorable treatment.

If the employer provides employees with life insurance that includes permanent benefits, such as paid-up permanent coverage or cash-value (rather than term insurance that does not accumulate cash value), the entirety of the premiums paid by the employer for the coverage for each employee will be considered income to each employee.

Medical Insurance Benefits

Insurance proceeds paid to an injured party to cover the costs of medical care or as compensation for pain and suffering will not be considered taxable income. However, insurance payments to replace income lost while recuperating from an injury are considered to be part of the recipient's gross income. This is true unless the payments are received under provisions of a no-fault car insurance policy, an accident, or health insurance policy for which the recipient had paid the premiums with after-tax earnings.

Benefits paid from an accident or heath insurance policy paid for by the recipient's employer, or through a plan that the employer established and/or funded, are not included in gross income if certain conditions are met. The Code Sec. 105 provides that the value of the benefits shall not be included in the recipient's gross income if the proceeds are paid directly or as a reimbursement to the taxpayer, for medical care for the recipient, his or her spouse, or a dependent.

Also excluded from gross income by Sec. 105 are payments from those sources for permanent disability or disfigurement of such parties. However, those exclusions will not apply if the company has a self-insured medical reimbursement plan that discriminates in favor of highly compensated employees.

In order to avoid being considered discriminating in favor of highly compensated employees, either 70% or more of an organization's employees must benefit from its self-insured medical reimbursement plan or at least 80% of those who qualify must benefit and at least 70% of the employees must qualify. Among the primary groups that Sec. 105

allows an employer to disqualify from participation in their self-insured medical reimbursement plan are:

- ◆ employees with less than three years of service;
- ◆ employees under the age of 25; and,
- ◆ seasonal or part time employees.

Another major advantage of employer-provided health and accident insurance or self-insured plans is that the Code Sec. 106 excludes the amount of the employer's payments from inclusion in their employees' gross incomes, despite the fact that most of the benefits received by employees from the coverage is excluded as well. However, the employers are still allowed to deduct the costs they incur for such plans and insurance coverage.

Property and Casualty Insurance Benefits

Payments received for stolen or damaged property are generally not includible in the recipient's gross income. However, if the payment received causes the recipient to realize a gain on the stolen or destroyed property, that gain is reportable income.

Disability Income

Whether income paid to a recipient to replace income lost due to inability to work, illness, or disability (referred to as *disability income*) is included in gross income depends on whether it was the recipient or the employer that bore the cost of obtaining the benefit was the recipient. Section 105 of the Code provides that if a party's employer pays the premium for a recipient's disability income policy or makes contributions into a fund from which benefits are to be paid, any benefits collected from such sources are fully includible in the recipient's gross income.

EXAMPLE: Amit works for Road Kill Shock Absorber Co. It offers a disability income policy to employees under a plan in which the company pays half of the premium that is not included in the employee's gross income and the employee pays half of the premium from after-tax earnings. Amit enrolled in the plan. In his sixth year of employment, he was stricken with

Goldfish Pox, a rare disease transmitted by squirrels, and was unable to work for six months. He drew $12,000 in disability income from his policy.

Since he had paid 50% of the premiums with after-tax earnings, 50% of the benefits will be excluded from his gross income, but the other 50% will be included since 50% of the premiums were paid with funds that were excluded from his gross income. Any funds paid to him to cover the cost of medical treatment will be excluded regardless of who paid the premiums for their coverage.

The provisions of Sec. 106 not only exclude payments for healthcare by an employer for employees from inclusion in the employees' gross incomes (see *Medical Insurance Benefits* discussed earlier in this chapter), but also exclude premiums paid by an employer for disability and health care policies for their employees from such inclusion. This provision offers employers a way to enhance their compensation packages at the expense of the U.S. Treasury. By paying premiums for health insurance and disability coverage for their employees, employers are able to provide their workers with a tax-free benefit, while still being allowed to take a deduction for the benefit themselves.

Fringe Benefits

In an effort to attract and retain employees, it is common for employers to offer benefits beyond the basic wages and salaries that they pay. Many of these incentives, known as *fringe benefits*, are excluded from an employee's gross income as long as they are not simply a form of disguised salary. If the parties eligible to receive certain fringe benefits are limited to *highly compensated employees*, it is assumed that the benefits are an attempt to pass off salary as a fringe benefit and the benefits are not excludible from the gross incomes of the recipients.

Internal Revenue Code Sec. 414(q) defines a highly compensated employee as one who owned 5% or more of the company they worked for during the year in question or the preceding year or one who earned in excess of $80,000, subject to adjustments for inflation from 1997, when the standard was set. There are a number of fringe benefits that, when not limited to highly compensated employees, will qualify for exclusion from the gross income of the recipients by virtue of the Code Sec. 132.

No Additional Cost Service

Companies that regularly market services to the public may make those services available to their employees without charge. The value of the services will not be included in the employees' gross incomes when they take advantage of the offer. For this exclusion to apply, the employer must be able to provide the service to the employee without incurring a substantial increase in cost. Also, the benefit cannot be *limited* to highly compensated employees.

EXAMPLE: James works at a golf course on weekends. He is allowed to play golf without charge during the week as a benefit of his employment, as are all of the employees of the golf course. Since the golf course will not experience any substantial increase in its costs for letting employees play without charge and the benefit is offered on a nondiscriminating basis to all employees, the value of the benefit will be excluded from the gross incomes of the golf course employees.

Qualified Employee Discount

It is common for employers to offer *discounts* to their employees on the goods or services that they regularly sell to the public. These discounts can meet the definition of the Code Sec. 132(c) for *qualified employee discounts* to the degree that these discounts do not exceed the employer's *gross profit percentage* on goods or 20% of the price at which services are offered by the employer to its customers. Discounts are excluded from the gross income of any employee receiving them.

The gross profit percentage limitation imposed on discounts on goods sold by an employer prevents employers from providing employees with a tax-free subsidy by selling them goods below their cost. In a further attempt to prevent employers from providing employee compensation disguised as discounts for goods or services, Sec. 132(c) does not permit employers to acquire goods or services that are not part of their regular line of business, sell them at a discount to an employee, and still exclude the discount from his or her gross income.

Also, discounts on real estate and investment property of any kind are not eligible for exclusion from gross income under Sec. 132(c). As with other fringe benefits, offering employee discounts only to highly compensated employees disqualifies them for exclusion from gross income.

EXAMPLE: Alan is a bond salesman at a brokerage house. Fearing a return of inflation, he decided to buy some gold. He bought it through his company receiving a 20% discount on their normal commission. Since the discount that Alan received was a discount on his employer's services, rather than on actual investment property, and it did not exceed 20%, he can exclude the discount from his gross income. Any discount on the price of the gold would have been fully includible in his gross income since the gold is investment property.

Working Condition Fringe Benefits

Any expenses paid by an employer on behalf of an employee, or reimbursed by an employer to an employee, that the employee would have been entitled to a tax deduction for had he or she paid them qualify for exclusion from the employee's gross income as a *working condition fringe benefit* under the Code Sec. 132(a)(3). Although Sec. 132(d) defines working condition fringe benefits in terms of those paid on behalf of employees, Treasury Regulation Sec. 1.132-1(b)(2) defines *employee* to include those *employed* by the employer, a *partner* who performs services for the partnership, a *director* of the employer, or even an *independent contractor* who performs services for the employer. The expenses paid by the employer must each meet the definition of an ordinary, necessary, business expense, as provided in Sec. 162, or depreciation, as provided in Sec. 167, in order to qualify for exclusion from gross income as a working condition fringe benefit.

If an employee is reimbursed for expenses that qualify as a working condition fringe benefit, he or she must keep records of the expenses. An employee must either use the funds for the qualified expenses or return any overage to the employer in order to exclude the reimbursement from gross income. Limiting working condition fringe benefits to highly compensated employees is permissible.

EXAMPLE: Ignatz is employed at a cheese processing plant. He is provided with a laptop computer so that he can maintain up-to-the-minute information concerning orders, production, and shipments. He uses the computer entirely for business. The value of Ignatz's use of the computer will be excluded from his gross income as a working condition fringe benefit.

De Minimis Fringe Benefit

If a benefit that is provided by an employer to employees is so small that accounting for it would be *unreasonable* or *administratively impracticable*, it is known as a *de minimis fringe benefit* and is excluded by the Code Sec. 131(a)(4) from inclusion in the recipient's gross income. This section of the Code specifically addresses an *eating facility* operated by an employer for the benefit of employees. It provides that as long as such a facility is on or close to the employer's business premises and employees are charged enough to cover the direct operating costs of the facility, the value of the benefit derived from the facility by the employees will be excluded from their gross incomes. Access to the facility must not be limited to highly compensated employees.

Treasury Regulation 1.132-6 offers substantial detail as to what constitutes a de minimis fringe. Of key importance in determining whether a benefit is a *de minimis fringe benefit* is the frequency with which the benefit is provided to a specific employee. The Regulation points out that if a company with a substantial number of employees were to provide a free meal on a daily basis to just one of its employees that, while its cost may well be de minimis from the company's point of view, the value of such meals would clearly not be de minimis from the recipient's point of view. Among the specific benefits cited by the Regulation as de minimis fringes are:

♦ *discount public transit passes* provided by employers to employees to help defray commuting costs as long as the discount does not exceed $21 per month;

- *occasional meal money* or *transportation fare* provided to an employee because he or she had to work beyond his or her normal work schedule;
- *occasional use of the employer's copy machine* for personal use;
- *occasional parties*, *picnics for employees and their guests*, or *group meals*;
- *noncash gifts of low market value* for holidays or special circumstances, such as due to illness;
- *occasional tickets to shows or sporting events*; and,
- *coffee*, *soft drinks*, or *doughnuts* provided by an employer for employees.

These benefits do not have to be made available to all employees, regardless of income, in order to qualify for exclusion from gross income.

Qualified Transportation Fringe

Employers may provide employees with *transportation* from their residence to their place of employment without including the value of the transportation in the gross incomes of their employees as long as:

- the transportation is provided in a vehicle that seats at least six in addition to the driver;
- at least half of the seats are occupied by commuter employees when the vehicle is in use; and,
- at least 80% of the miles put on the vehicle are for the purpose of transporting workers between their residence and place of employment.

Section 132(f) establishes that *qualified transportation fringe*, also permits employers to pay directly for or reimburse employees for transit passes up to $100 per month or fees for parking at or near the employer's place of business up to $175 per month.

The *transit pass allowance* is permitted not withstanding the limits on this item when it is considered to be a de minimis fringe. These limits are subject to adjustment for inflation in increments of $5.00. If an employee uses his or her parking allowance to obtain residential parking, the benefit is ineligible for exclusion from gross income, even if he or she had a home-based office.

Gyms and Athletic Facilities

Section 132(j)(4) permits employers to provide a *gym* or other *athletic facility* to their employees without having to include the value of that benefit in their gross incomes. To qualify under this provision, the facility must be operated by the employer, on the employer's premises, with its use restricted substantially to employees and their spouses and dependents.

Qualified Moving Expense Reimbursement

The Code Sec. 217 provides if an employee were eligible to take a deduction for *moving expenses* and paid those expenses, but the employer either paid or reimbursed him or her for those expenses, Sec. 132(g) permits exclusion of that benefit from the employee's gross income. (Details for qualifying for a deduction for moving expenses under Sec. 217 are provided in Chapter 3.)

Qualified Retirement Planning Services

Another benefit that employers can offer employees without having to include its value in their employee's gross incomes is *qualified retirement planning services*. Section 132(m) states that the benefit can include the cost of retirement planning advice or information to an employee or to the employee's spouse, as long as the benefit is not restricted to highly compensated employees.

Dependent Care Assistance Program

Employers who establish a separate written plan of *dependent care assistance* for the benefit of their employees to allow them to maintain their employment can provide up to $5,000 worth of such assistance ($2,500 if the employee is married and files separately) to each employee each year without including its value in the recipient's gross income. Among the requirements set forth in the Code Sec. 129(d) for such a program to qualify for the gross income exclusion are:

- the program cannot discriminate in favor of highly compensated employees;
- no more than 25% of the benefits paid for by the employer can go to parties who own 5% or more of the company; and,
- those eligible for the benefit must be given reasonable notice of the availability of the benefit.

Because the purpose of the benefit must be that it enables the recipient to maintain employment, an employee and the employee's spouse, if the employee is married, must have income that was earned from employment that was at least as much as the value of the dependent care received. Payments to a dependent of an employee or spouse of an employee and payments to an employee's child who is under the age of 19 do not qualify for exclusion under Sec. 129.

EXAMPLE: Phil is senior vice president of Intercity Freight Co. His wife does not work outside their home, but has agreed to do volunteer work for Save Our Ferns, a local environmentalist group. Intercity has a qualified dependent care assistance program and Phil's wife leaves their nine year old daughter at the company's day care while doing her volunteer work. The value of the day care services provided for Phil's daughter is fully includible in Phil's gross income since his wife had no earned income. Had the value of the day care services been $4,000 for the year and Phil's wife had earned $1,500 from a temporary job that she had held, then $1,500 would be excludible from Phil's gross income, but his employer must include the remaining $2,500 in his gross income.

Recovery of Adjusted Basis from a Sale

To the degree that a taxpayer sells or otherwise disposes of assets and merely recovers the amount invested in the property, there will be no tax consequences from that transaction. Section 1001 of the Internal Revenue Code provides that only the gain from the sale of goods shall be included in a taxpayer's gross income. The part of the proceeds from such sales that constitutes the seller's adjusted basis in the property is what is viewed as his or her investment in it. That portion of the proceeds is not included in gross income.

Qualified Small Business Stock

For shareholders who have owned their shares in a C corporation for over five years, the Code Sec. 1202 may allow them to altogether exclude from taxation 50% of their gain from the sale of those shares. In order to qualify for the 50% exclusion, the stock must be *qualified business stock*.

The Code provides the test for qualified business stock. The stock must be issued by a C corporation after the date of enactment of the *Revenue Reconciliation Act of 1993*, and acquired by the shareholder at its original issue in exchange for money, other property, or as compensation for services provided to the corporation. It is permissible for a stockholder to have acquired *initial issue shares* through an underwriter, as well as directly from the corporation, but shares acquired by an underwriter in exchange for his or her services as an intermediary in selling the corporation's stock do not qualify, nor do shares obtained by any shareholder in exchange for other stock.

A further requirement of the Code Sec. 1202 is that the corporation be an *active business*, except for a special rule waiving the requirement for specialized small business investment companies. In order to qualify as an active business, the Code requires that at least 80% of the corporation's assets be used by the company to actively conduct one or more *qualified trades* or *businesses*. All trades or businesses qualify under the Code Sec. 1202(e)(3), except the ones that it specifically excludes. The exclusions consist of professional service companies such as those involved in banking, leasing, or investing; farming operations including tree harvesting; mineral or oil and gas extraction; and hotel, motel, and restaurant operations. The corporation must also be an *eligible* corporation that requires it be a domestic corporation and not one of the few types of companies listed in the Code Sec. 1202(e)(4).

Although the Code specifically states that these provisions are for *small business stock*, the companies involved can actually have assets of up to $50,000,000 and still qualify. In addition, shareholders may use the 50% exclusion on at least $10,000,000 of eligible gains from the sale of qualified small business stock. These provisions have historically made the C corporation an especially attractive choice for promoters who were planning on starting a company in hopes of eventually selling it once it was well established. However, the benefit of Sec. 1202 has largely dissipated due to recent changes in the tax treatment of capital gains.

Chapter 3
Adjusted Gross Income

After determining gross income, the next step toward eventually arriving at a taxpayer's tax liability is to calculate *adjusted gross income*. Adjusted gross income is defined in Internal Revenue Code Sec. 62 as gross income, less certain specific expenses set forth in that section. Of the dozen categories of deductions set forth in Sec. 62, several have only a relatively modest economic impact in general, and little, if any, specifically impact on small businesses. Included in that category are deductions for *jury duty pay* that a recipient must pay over to his or her employer in order to be eligible to receive full pay from his or her employer for time spent on jury duty; deductions for required repayments of certain *unemployment compensation benefits*; deductions for *penalties paid for early withdrawal* of certificates of deposit or other timed accounts; and deductions for *interest on education loans*.

A deduction for alimony payments completes the transfer of the incidence of taxation from the payor to the recipient and, although the economic impact of this provision is undoubtedly significant, it does not directly impact the income of small businesses. The provisions of Sec. 62 that permit deductions for deprecation for life tenants of property and for the costs of reforestation expenses may be important to those qualified to use them, but most small businesses will be unaffected by those provisions.

The remainder of the deductions specifically allowed by Sec. 62 are of importance, in some degree, to most small businesses and/or self-employed taxpayers. For the most part, they focus on allowing small businesses and the self-employed to adjust their gross income to reflect the *cost of doing business*. Still other provisions are designed to help self-employed taxpayers offset the value of the fringe benefit packages and other economic benefits that they lose by being self-employed, rather than working for someone else.

For the great majority of small businesses, the most important provisions of Sec. 62 are those that permit deductions of the costs incurred by them in generating their gross income and deductions for losses from sale or exchange of property. Were it not for these deductions, businesses, self-employed workers, and employees who incur business-related expenses would be required to pay taxes on their gross incomes. The result would be inappropriately high taxes due to overstated income levels that could tax many small businesses out of existence.

LOSSES FROM SALE OR EXCHANGE OF PROPERTY

The provisions in the Code Sec. 62 for the deduction of losses from the sale or exchange of property permits those engaged in the trade or business of buying and selling property to offset the results of their unprofitable transactions against the results of their profitable transactions and pay taxes on only the net income from such activities. In order to be eligible to take a deduction for losses from the *sale or exchange of property*, an actual transaction must be completed so that the loss is realized. The taxpayer taking the loss must have entered into the transaction in connection with a trade or business that he or she was engaged in for a profit.

EXAMPLE: Ben regularly ran an advertisement in a local newspaper offering to buy houses from those wanting to sell in a hurry. He would buy houses at prices that he believed were somewhat below their full market value, perform any needed repairs, and then market them in a more traditional manner in an effort to make a profit on each house.

Lee and Tiffany called Ben seeking an offer on their home that had been custom built for them for $350,000. The owners had attempted to market the house, but due to a poor local economy, were confronted with a soft real estate market and were unsuccessful. However, since Lee had been forced to change jobs and take a sizable pay cut, they felt compelled to sell and took Ben's offer of $275,000 for their house.

After painting and cleaning the house, Ben put it on the market but met with limited interest in what was one of the more expensive houses in a town whose economy showed few signs of recovery. After holding the house for six months and incurring expenses of $5,000 in connection with its ownership, Ben accepted an offer for the house of $250,000.

Since Lee and Tiffany used the house as their personal residence, rather than acquiring it in connection with a trade or business, they will not be entitled to take a deduction for the $75,000 loss they sustained on it. If Ben closes the transaction for the sale of the house, he will be entitled to take a deduction for the $25,000 loss he sustained on it and the $5,000 incurred in expenses.

EXPENSES RELATED TO RENTS AND ROYALTIES

Section 62 also provides for a specific deduction for expenses *attributable to property held for the production of rents or royalties*. Such income for individuals is calculated on Schedule E of *Form 1040*. It lists about a dozen specific expenses eligible for deduction, provides a few lines entitled *other* for the deduction of allowable expenses that are not specifically enumerated, and makes provision for the deduction of depreciation or depletion of income-producing property. In addition to the list of Schedule E deductible expenses that include commissions, advertising, mortgage interest, taxes, insurance, and repairs, almost any expense reasonably related to the production of rents or royalties should meet the requirement of being *attributable* to the property used to produce the income.

EXAMPLE: Dimitry owns a condominium in Miami. He rents it out for $1,000 per month. Among the expenses that he pays are $200 per month in condominium maintenance fees, $20 per month to an exterminator to spray for bugs, and $50 a month for a security patrol service. Dimitry may take a deduction for all of those expenses.

TRADE AND BUSINESS DEDUCTIONS

The first deduction listed among those in the Code Sec. 62 that may be subtracted from gross income to arrive at adjusted gross income is the deduction for *trade and business expenses* incurred by businesses and self-employed taxpayers. A similar provision is listed for business related expenses incurred by employees in the *fulfillment of their employment duties*. In addition to the fact that those deductions permit a taxpayer to reduce gross income to more accurately reflect true business income, it is especially significant that those deductions, as with all of the deductions listed in Sec. 62, are what tax practitioners commonly refer to as *above-the-line* deductions.

The *line* that they refer to is the line on tax returns that contains the figure for adjusted gross income. Above-the-line deductions are those subtracted from gross income in order to arrive at adjusted gross income, offer the advantage that they are fully deductible, and will definitely result in a reduction in the taxpayer's income that will be subject to federal taxation. However, *below-the-line* deductions may not help reduce a taxpayer's tax liability at all since they are subject to various limitations that do not apply to above the line deductions. The specifics concerning the limitations imposed on some of the more common below-the-line deductions are discussed in the following sections on deductions.

Section 162 of the Internal Revenue Code imposes the requirement that expenses be *ordinary and necessary expenses paid or incurred during the taxable year in carrying on a trade or business* in order for a taxpayer to be allowed to deduct them from gross receipts to arrive at taxable income. Although the definition seems straight forward, its application can prove difficult.

Parties Qualified to Take the Deductions

In order for a taxpayer to take a deduction of any kind as a business expense, the party must be engaged in a trade or business. Someone operating a retail store or providing service, such as an engineer or an attorney, will generally have no problem meeting this requirement. Most of the cases in which there is a question as to whether a person or organization is actually engaged in a trade or business arise when the participant is involved only part-time or sporadically. In order to be considered to be carrying on a trade or business, a taxpayer must:

- ◆ have begun the endeavor with the intent to make a profit;
- ◆ consistently and significantly participate in the venture;
- ◆ demonstrate a commitment to the enterprise; and,
- ◆ conduct the operation in a business-like manner.

The fact that an activity actually generates a loss rather than a profit will not be fatal to it being considered a trade or business as long as it was started with the intent to make a profit.

Commitment to an enterprise may be demonstrated by such things as:

- ◆ attendance at seminars or trade shows;
- ◆ taking formal courses to gain expertise in operation of the business; or,
- ◆ engaging in any other activity aimed at improving the party's ability to operate the enterprise profitably.

If a purported business activity is determined not to be a trade or business, it will likely be classified as a *hobby*. A deduction for expenses will be allowed only to the degree necessary to offset gross income from the activity, thereby eliminating the deductibility of any losses generated by the venture.

EXAMPLE: Frank, manager of an electronics store, is especially fond of baseball cards. He has become quite knowledgeable in evaluating cards. He travels to large baseball card shows in search of cards he needs to fill out his collection. He runs an advertisement in a magazine offering to buy cards. If he buys collections that contain duplicates, he will sometimes offer them for sale online.

If Frank were to file a tax return showing his baseball card sales as a business and deduct all of his expenses, thereby generating a loss used to offset part of his regular income, the loss would be disallowed since his purpose in travelling to card shows is primarily to complete his personal collection. Sales are merely incidental and sporadic. Frank's activity is clearly a hobby.

However, if, after developing expertise in collecting baseball cards as a hobby, Frank decided to capitalize on that expertise by starting a baseball card business, then the results would be different. If he ran ads and attended shows in order to obtain inventory to supply his regular, ongoing Internet-based marketing operation, it would appear that Frank had developed a trade or business and would be eligible to deduct his expenses associated with it.

Ordinary and Necessary Requirement

The next hurdle in establishing the deductibility of business expenses is proof that they are *ordinary and necessary*. Several allowable business expenses that are deductible are enumerated in the Code Sec. 162. Included are salary expenses, travel expenses, and rent. These are just a starting point for most businesses. Any other business-related expenses may be deducted as long as they are shown to be both ordinary and necessary.

Ordinary Expense

There is no clear cut test to determine whether or not an expense is *ordinary* for the business wishing to deduct it. In general, the courts have traditionally considered the issue of whether a business expense should be considered ordinary for a given taxpayer from two distinctly different points of view. On the one hand, courts consider whether a given expense that a business had deducted was *appropriate for that business in light of the type of business* that it does. Courts have not required that expenditures of the type for which a deduction is sought be typical of businesses in their field or even that they were historically incurred by the company in question. The key determinant seems to be whether the expenditure was a *reasonable one for that taxpayer at the time it was made*. This is true even if it does not result in any improvement in the profitability of the business.

EXAMPLE: Zack owned and operated a machine shop. He decided to hire a consultant to analyze his business operation and make suggestions on how to improve efficiency and increase profitability. He had never hired a consultant before, but hoped to gain a significant advantage from doing so. No other machine shops of his size had ever hired such a consultant, as far as he knew.

Zack paid the consultant a fee of $5,000. However, his recommendations seemed so radical to Zack that he decided not to implement any of them. Zack's expenditure for the consultant would be considered ordinary, since there is a reasonable business purpose for it. This is despite the fact that he had never used a consultant before and does not intend to do so again; no other businesses of his type had been using consultants; and, he did not actually profit from the consultant's advice.

The other aspect of *ordinary* that courts analyze in considering whether or not a business expense should be deductible also focuses on the reasonableness of the expenditure. But, rather than involving the question of whether the purpose of the expenditure was reasonable, it deals with the issue of *whether the amount of the expenditure was reasonable*. Expenditures for business purposes that are clearly ordinary will likely still be considered nondeductible if they are considered to be *extravagant*. The determination as to whether a business expenditure is reasonable or lavish must be made on an individual basis depending on the circumstances of the expenditure and the nature of the taxpayer's business.

EXAMPLE: Alfred operates a company that collects samples of air, water, and soil so that they can be analyzed for pollution content. He needs a boat in order to collect water samples from various places within local lakes. Alfred decided to buy a top of the line Bass boat, fully equipped for fishing. Alfred should not be allowed to take a business deduction for the boat since it is unreasonably elaborate for his business needs and is not an ordinary expense for such businesses. However, if Alfred had been a professional Bass fisherman, his purchase of such a boat would have easily qualified as ordinary for his trade.

Necessary Expense

The concept of *necessary* has also been the topic of analysis in numerous court cases. Necessary is *not* to be construed as *essential* or *indispensable*. In practice, the requirement that an expense must be necessary in order to be deductible is not much different than the requirement that it must be ordinary. As long as it can be shown that an expenditure was reasonable, both from the perspective that it would be beneficial to the business and that it was not lavish, it should qualify as a necessary expenditure for tax purposes.

In the event of an audit by the IRS, auditors keep a watchful eye for business deductions that were actually for items for *personal use*. That is the abuse that the ordinary and necessary requirement of Sec. 162 is primarily aimed at preventing.

Specific Deductions

A basic checklist of deductible business expenses available to employers can be found on the very forms provided by the IRS for filing annual business income tax returns. Schedule C of *Form 1040*, the form that *sole proprietors* must use to report their business income, contains a list of twenty-six specific deductible business expenses in Part II of the form. The 27th line of the form, labeled *other expenses*, provides space for the total of the expenses that are unique to the particular taxpayer's business. *Form 1065* for partnerships and *Form 1120* for corporations also contain sections that enumerate deductible expenses for calculating annual income, but the lists are not nearly as extensive as the one in Schedule C.

The allowable deductions for employee compensation provided for in the Code Sec. 162 are addressed in all three of the basic annual tax return forms. However, in Schedule C of the *Form 1040* there are separate lines provided for *commissions and fees* and *wages*. Still further breakdowns for the components of employee compensation consisting of *employee benefit programs* and *pension or profit sharing plans* are also listed.

Payments to independent contractors who provide services to businesses on a nonemployee basis are deductible business expenses and are specifically enumerated as *legal and professional services* on Schedule C. A designated line for the deduction of *rents* as provided for in Sec. 162 is also contained in each of the three basic income tax return forms, as is a line for deducting *interest expenses*, as provided for in the Code Sec. 163. A specific line for deducting *advertising expenses* is provided for in Schedule C and on *Form 1120*, but it would have to be included as part of the *other deduction* total on *Form 1065*.

Expenditures for *supplies, repairs and maintenance, utilities, office expense, insurance, telephone expense*, and a host of other business expenses are fully deductible by businesses regardless of the form they must use to report their annual income and despite the possible lack of a specific line on which to list each expense. Section 164 of the Code permits businesses to take a deduction for *taxes* and *licensing fees* that they must pay, but excludes any deduction for federal income taxes, thereby limiting that deduction to state and local income taxes.

Although the Code Sec. 162 specifically provides for deductibility of *traveling expenses* associated with carrying on a trade or business, quite a number of past disputes have arisen between taxpayers and IRS auditors over allowance of specific travel-related deductions. As a result, rather than merely relying on the ordinary and necessary test for determining the deductibility, expenditures for *auto expense* and for *meals* and *entertainment* have been singled out. A more extensive guideline concerning their deductibility have been set forth. (See Chapter 4 for more information.) Extensive guidelines have also been promulgated concerning the allowance for *depreciation* that businesses may take as a deductible business expense.

Auto Expenses

Car and truck expenses are common deductions for most businesses. This deduction lends itself to abuse by taxpayers and is generally targeted for close scrutiny by IRS audits. The maximum deduction that taxpayers may take for wear and tear (known as depreciation) for passenger cars per year is set forth in annual Revenue Procedures that are promulgated by the IRS in accordance with the Internal Revenue Code.

In addition to depreciation, taxpayers may deduct the cost of *fuel*, *maintenance*, *insurance*, and *license fees* that they incur in connection with an automobile used for business purposes. However, the deduction for depreciation and expenses associated with an automobile is limited to its *use in business matters*. To the degree that an automobile is put to personal use, deductions are not allowed.

Taxpayers are also prohibited from taking a deduction for automobile expenses and depreciation for miles driven *commuting* to and from their places of employment. Therefore, if a vehicle is used for business purposes as well as personal and/or commuting use, it is essential that records be kept for each type of use in order to support taking a deduction for the business portion of the expenses and depreciation. Such a record usually takes the form of a log book in which the beginning and ending mileage on the vehicle's odometer are recorded each time the vehicle is used for business purposes. It is also necessary that receipts or other records of automobile expenses be kept in support of the deduction for business use of a car or truck.

If an automobile is used only partly for business, the deductions for depreciation of the vehicle and for the expense of operating it must be prorated based on the percentage of business use. For example, if the taxpayer's log book showed that a vehicle had been driven a total of 20,000 miles during the tax year and 15,000 of those miles were for business, he or she would be entitled to deduct 75% of the allowable depreciation and expenses from gross business income.

Establishing a system in which a separate business entity owns an automobile and then supplies it to the owner who is also an employee may appear to transfer the employee's personal use and commuting miles into deductible expenses, but it will not. It is true that the business entity will be allowed to take a deduction for depreciation and other expenses associated with the vehicle that it provides to an employee. However, Regulation Sec. 1.61-21(b)(4) then requires that the employee recognize the value of the commuting or personal use as taxable income. Regulation Sec. 1.61-21(d)(2)(iii) contains tables that show the *fair lease value* of vehicles based on their fair market values.

Therefore, despite the fact that the employer's depreciation deduction for the vehicle will be subject to severe limitations, the income that the employee must recognize due to personal use of it will likely exceed the deduction that the business entity gets to take for that portion of the use, since it is based on the full market value of the vehicle without regard to the limits on value for depreciation purposes. If the vehicle is a relatively expensive one, the difference between the employer's deduction for the vehicle for the portion attributed to the employee's personal and commuting use and the income that the employee must report due to that use can be sizable.

EXAMPLE: Speedy Construction Company supplied a new sport utility vehicle that cost $40,000 to its general manager, Rob. He was allowed to take it home and use personally, as well as for work. He kept a log book that indicated that his personal use constituted 50% of the miles driven for the taxable year. If it were determined that the appropriate depreciation allowance for the year for the vehicle should be $7,000, but the applicable Revenue Procedure stipulated that the maximum depreciation deduction allowable for business use of the vehicle would be $3,060 for the year, then Rob would be required to recognize $3,500. That would be 50% of the depreciable value of the vehicle, as income for the 50% personal use of the vehicle that he was provided for the year. Speedy Construction would be allowed only $1,530 (half of the maximum $3,060 full year's depreciation allowed by the Revenue Procedure) as a deduction for depreciation for business use of the vehicle for the year.

Leased Vehicles

More and more businesses and individuals are *leasing* their vehicles. In such cases there will be no deduction for depreciation, even for the vehicle's business use. Instead, when a leased vehicle is used for business, the taxpayer may deduct the appropriate portion of the lease payments. However, in order to prevent parties from taking deductions for luxury cars, limitations have been placed on the amount of the lease payments that are considered deductible. The limitations on the deductibility of lease payments for automobiles used in business are designed to start at the level of the lease payments on a vehicle with approximately the same fair market value as that of a vehicle on which a taxpayer may take a depreciation deduction without limitation.

Cents Per Mile

As an alternative to taking a deduction for depreciation or lease payments, and then a further deduction for the actual expense of operating an automobile, Sec. 1.61-21(e) of the Treasury Regulations allows taxpayers the option of a deduction on the basis of a specified number of *cents per mile* driven for business purposes. The actual amount of the cents allowed as a deduction for business use of an automobile is set each year and may even vary during the course of a single year. Although taxpayers who use the cents per mile option for calculating their deduction for automobile use will not be required to keep receipts and other proof of their actual expenses associated with the vehicle's operation, they will still need to keep a detailed log of miles driven for business purposes.

Using the cents per mile option is not available if:

♦ the provisions of the Code Sec. 179 were used to offset any of its cost during the year of acquisition;

♦ the vehicle has been depreciated using any method other than straight line;

♦ the vehicle is used for hire (such as when used in a limousine service);

♦ more than one vehicle is used by the taxpayer for business use at the same time; or,

◆ if the vehicle has been leased by the taxpayer, rather than purchased, and the taxpayer has taken a deduction for the lease payments made for the year.

Meals and Entertainment

Additional business expenses that have historically been closely scrutinized by the IRS are the costs of business *meals and entertainment*. A deduction for meal expenses incurred while away from home on business is permitted by the Code Sec. 162 as long as the meal is not considered lavish or extravagant. However, Sec. 274(n) limits the amount of the deduction to 50% of the amount of the expenditure.

Even though a taxpayer is not away from home, he or she may still be allowed a business expense deduction for the cost of meals while on business with customers or potential customers. Section 1.274-2 of the Treasury Regulations sets forth the criteria that must be met in order for such expenditures to be deductible as a business expense. It requires that the taxpayer be able to show that the expenditure for such meals was *directly related to the active conduct of the taxpayer's trade or business* or that the expenditure was *associated with the active conduct of the taxpayer's trade or business*.

One or both of these criteria will generally be met if *bona fide business discussions* take place before, during, or after the meal. However, even when it can be shown that the meal was *directly related to* or *associated with* the active conduct of the taxpayer's business, no deduction will be allowed for the portion of the cost of the meal deemed to be lavish or extravagant. Section 274(n) of the Code will limit the deduction for the qualified part of the meal expense to only 50% of its cost, although both the reasonable costs of the taxpayer's own meal as well as those provided for business guests will qualify for the 50% deduction.

Another requirement of the Code Sec. 274 is the keeping of *detailed supporting records* in order to qualify the cost of meals provided for business associates as a deductible business expense. The most popular way to meet this requirement is to pay for such meals with a credit card and write down the names of those present at the meal and a brief description of the business discussed on the back of the customer's copy of the credit card receipt.

Rules concerning the deductibility of expenditures for *entertainment* of business clients are also set forth in the Code Sec. 274. The same requirement for deductibility that the expenditure must be *directly related to* or *associated with* the active conduct of the taxpayer's business, applies for expenses incurred for entertainment for clients as it does for meals provided for clients. However, in order to be eligible to take a business deduction for the cost of entertainment provided to clients, the taxpayer must pass a far more *stringent application* of the test to determine if an expense is either directly related to or associated with his or her business.

Treasury Regulation Sec. 1.274(c)(3) states that, in order for an expenditure for entertainment to be considered directly related to a taxpayer's trade or business, all four of the following requirements must be met.

- At the time of the entertainment expenditure, the taxpayer had to have an expectation of acquiring some specific trade or business, rather than merely developing goodwill.
- During the entertainment period, but either before or after the entertainment event, rather than during it, there must have been an active business meeting or transaction for the purpose of obtaining specific trade or business.
- The principal character or aspect of the activity must have been the active conduct of the taxpayer's trade or business.
- The cost of the activity must have been allocable to the taxpayer and the person or persons with whom was sought to actively conduct trade or business, rather than their companions or friends who were disinterested in business negotiations.

The Regulation goes on to say that it is required that activities engaged in that were in furtherance of the taxpayer's business during the entertainment activity had to have occurred in a *clear business setting*. Therefore, attempting to qualify entertainment expenditures as a business deduction by casually discussing business matters during the course of an actual entertainment event will not work.

Also, the Code Sec. 274(3) specifically disallows any deduction for payment of dues for membership in clubs that are *organized for business, pleasure, recreation, or other social purposes*. Even when expenditures for entertainment qualify for a business deduction, the Code Sec. 274(n) limits the deduction to 50% of the amount of the qualified expenditure.

EXAMPLE: Ron owned and operated a manufacturing facility in a small north Mississippi town. He wanted to hire Phil, a design engineer to work at his company. Ron persuaded Phil to come for an interview and provided him a room at a casino in Tunica, Mississippi. Upon his arrival, Ron and Phil met in Phil's room to discuss all the details of employment. At the conclusion of the discussion, Ron took Phil to dinner and a show at the casino during which he made several comments to Phil to the effect that, if he did take the job, he would have the benefit of a small town lifestyle but with entertainment more typical of large cities at the nearby casinos.

As long as the expenses incurred by Ron for the meal and entertainment were not lavish or extravagant, they should qualify for a business deduction since a bona fide business meeting clearly associated with Ron's trade or business was conducted in a clear business setting prior to the meal and entertainment. Had the meeting prior to the dinner and show not taken place, the deductibility of the expense would be questionable since it is likely that Ron's comments concerning the quality of life in the community that were made during dinner would probably not be considered sufficient to constitute a bona fide business discussion. None of the conversations between them during the show would qualify the expense for a business deduction, since they would not be regarded as having been held in a clear business setting.

Depreciation

If business assets are expected to have a useful life in excess of a year, the deduction for their cost must generally be spread out over their anticipated life and taken in the form of *depreciation*. Through the years, Congress has adjusted the law concerning depreciation in order to influence economic activity in the nation. When the law permits higher deductions for depreciation in the earliest years of an investment in depreciable assets, it tends to stimulate businesses to invest in such assets and, in turn, stimulate the economy. Requiring businesses to postpone deductions for depreciation makes expenditures for depreciable assets less appealing and tends to slow the economy down. However, such an action may be appropriate when the economy is suffering from excessive price inflation due to overstimulation.

In the most recent versions of the Internal Revenue Code, the provisions that address depreciation refer to it as *Asset Cost Recovery System* (ACRS). There is also a *Modified Asset Cost Recovery System* (MACRS).

Regardless of the name, the concept has remained the same. The amount of depreciation deduction that a party may take when an asset is used for business is determined by:

- depreciable value of the item;
- length of time over which the depreciation must be taken;
- method of depreciation used; and,
- time of year in which the asset was placed in service.

The depreciable value of *personalty*, such as equipment or automobiles used in business, is generally the *full purchase price paid* for it by the business. However, depreciation can be taken only for *improvements on realty*. Therefore, the cost of acquisition of realty must be reasonably allocated between the actual real estate and the improvements, such as buildings, and the value of the realty must be excluded from the basis upon which the depreciation is calculated.

The concept of depreciation is that deductions for the wear and tear of an asset that is expected to last more than one year should be spread out over the anticipated life of the asset. Recovery periods have been arbitrarily assigned by the Code Sec. 168(e)(3) to all the different varieties of business assets. These must be used in assigning an expected life to depreciable assets.

The method of depreciation and the recovery period assigned to an asset determine the rate of its depreciation. The most basic method of depreciation is *straight line*, which entails a pro rata allocation over the depreciable life of the asset. For example, if a taxpayer placed a piece of equipment that cost $10,000 in service at the beginning of the year with a five-year depreciable life and depreciated it using the straight line method, he or she would be able to take one-fifth of its value per year as a deduction for depreciation on the item.

Other methods of depreciation allow up to double the straight line rate for the first year in which the asset is placed in service. This kind of accelerated write off in the earlier years comes at the cost of offsetting reductions in depreciation for those assets in later years.

The time of year an asset is placed into service affects depreciation. The tax laws penalize parties who wait until the fourth quarter of the year before investing in business property. If more than 40% of an entity's investment in new business assets, excluding realty, occurs in the fourth quarter of its taxable year, it must use a *mid-quarter convention* to compute its cost recovery allowances for *all* such property placed in service for the taxable year. This means that, for depreciation purposes, such property is treated as having been placed in service at the mid-point of the quarter. If an entity does not place over 40% of its new business assets, exclusive of realty, in service during the last quarter of its taxable year, it uses a *half-year convention* (mid-year convention) to calculate its cost recovery allowances on such assets, resulting in such assets. This results in these assets being regarded, for depreciation purposes, as having been placed in service at the mid-point of the year in which they were placed in service.

Forcing a business entity to use the mid-quarter convention will usually result in less of a first year depreciation deduction than allowing it to use the mid-year convention. Therefore, businesses should view the last day of the third quarter of their taxable year as an investment decision deadline. They should consult with their tax advisors in advance of that date so they can time their investments to avoid any adverse consequences of inadvertently finding themselves forced to use the mid-quarter convention.

Small businesses, by virtue of the Code Sec. 179, may be allowed to *expense* the cost of some property that is actually a depreciable asset. Under provisions of the *Jobs and Growth Tax Relief Reconciliation Act of 2003* (JGTRRA), up to $100,000 of depreciable property placed in service between 2003 and 2005 may be expensed for the year. After 2005, the amount is reduced to the pre-JGTRRA level of $25,000. By expensing an asset, a taxpayer deducts the full amount paid for it in the year it is placed in service rather, than depreciating it.

If the taxpayer places over $400,000 worth of business assets in service in a taxable year, the amount eligible to be expensed begins to be phased out is evidence that this provision is aimed at small businesses. Moreover, parties may not use a Sec. 179 expense deduction to generate a loss from a trade or business. Also, some property, such as that used 50% or less in the taxpayer's trade or business, is ineligible to be expensed under the Code Sec. 179.

DEDUCTIBLE EMPLOYEES' EXPENSES

Workers who are considered to be employees of another party, rather than self-employed, are permitted, under Sec. 62 of the Code, to take a deduction for employee expenses. The tax treatment of these deductions depends on whether or not the employee business expenses are reimbursed by the employer.

Reimbursed Employee Business Expenses

If an employer has a policy of *reimbursing* employees for their employee business expenses, whether or not the reimbursement will be regarded as taxable income will depend on whether or not the employer has an *accountable plan* of reimbursement. If employee business expense reimbursements are made under an accountable plan, such reimbursements are regarded as *adjustments for adjusted gross income*, resulting in such reimbursements being totally excluded from the income reported on the employee's W-2. The employee is also allowed no deduction for the reimbursed expense. If the employer's plan for reimbursing employee business expenses is not an accountable plan, the reimbursements must be included in the employee's gross income and reported on the employee's W-2. The employee will then be allowed to take a deduction for the employee business expenses incurred.

Since employees who receive reimbursement in a plan that is not deemed to be an accountable plan are allowed to take deductions for the qualified employee business expenses that they incur, whereas recipients of reimbursements under terms of an accountable plan are allowed no such deductions, it may seem to the uninitiated that it would make no difference which type of reimbursement plan that an employer adopted. The fact is, by meeting the test for reimbursing employee business expenses so that an employer is deemed to have an *accountable plan*, an employer will help reduce employees' overall tax liability, as well as the employer's own liability for its share of Social Security and/or Medicare tax.

Generally, nearly all of an employee's earnings are subject to federal income tax and Medicare tax. Earnings up to a designated cut off amount are subject to Social Security tax, regardless of whether the earnings are labeled as *salary* or *wages*, or *supplemental earnings*. Additionally, employers must pay Social Security taxes and Medicare taxes on behalf of their employees in an amount equal to what the employees must pay. However, since employee business expense reimbursements paid by an employer under an accountable plan are excluded from the recipient's gross income, such reimbursements will not be subjected to income taxation, Social Security taxation, or Medicare taxation in the hands of the employee. The employer will also avoid having to pay a matching share to the degree that the employee avoids Social Security taxes and Medicare taxes. Including the reimbursements as income and allowing a deduction *from* adjusted gross income for the expenditure would *not* reduce liability for Social Security taxes or Medicare taxes at all, since such deductions are not allowed to reduce the amount of a taxpayer's income to which those taxes are applied.

In order for an employee business expense reimbursement plan to be considered as an *accountable plan*, the Code Sec. 62(c) provides that the recipient of the reimbursement must provide *substantiation* to the employer for the expenses that were reimbursed. The employee must be required to *return any amount received in excess* of the substantiated expenses and must *actually return the excess* within a reasonable time. An employee will generally be considered to have met the substantiation requirement if written, dated receipts or bills for bona fide business related expenses that were either paid or incurred in the furtherance of that employer's trade or business are supplied to the employer. A brief description of the specific business activity to which the expense was related should also be included, even if it is nothing more than a notation on each receipt or bill.

EXAMPLE: Bill, an employee of Mack's Tool & Die Co., Inc., represented his employer at a trade show 400 miles away. Bill charged his airfare and hotel room on his personal credit card. He paid a total of $114 for meals and $20 in cash for tips at those meals, obtaining a receipt for both the meals and tips. Upon returning home, he presented his employer with copies of his credit card charges of $600 for airfare and $250 for his hotel room along with copies of the cash receipts for meals and tips. Mack's Tool & Die Co., Inc. issued Bill a check for $984 as full reimbursement for these reasonable business expenses.

If these payments were made under a reimbursement program that is considered to be an accountable plan, none of the $984 will be included in Bill's adjusted gross income. Bill's employer will be allowed to take a deduction for the $984 in calculating its taxes, but Bill will not be allowed to deduct any of the reimbursement expenses.

Advances

Employer's are also allowed to establish reimbursement plans that are considered to be *accountable* even though they provide funds to employees in anticipation of their incurring business expenses, rather than after the expenses are paid or incurred. In order for a plan involving advance payments to be considered a *qualified plan*, it must require the employees who receive the advance payments to use the funds to cover the costs of expenses incurred while performing services in furtherance of the employer's trade or business. The employee must adequately account to the employer for the expenditures within a reasonable time and to return to the employer any excess payments received in advance for the expenses within a reasonable time.

Whether an employee will be considered to have acted within a reasonable time carrying out the requirements of an accountable plan will depend on the individual situation involved. However, there will be no question as to whether an employee acted timely if he or she incurs the expense for which funds were advanced within thirty days of receipt, adequately accounts for the expenses within sixty days after incurred, and returns any excess advances within 120 days after the expenses were incurred.

Alternatively, an employer may provide employees with a quarterly or more frequent statement requiring them to adequately account for advances for employee business expenses or else return them. Any employee who does so within 120 days will be considered to have acted within a reasonable time.

Similar to plans where payments by employers are actual reimbursements (rather than advances), in order for an employee who has received an advance payment against anticipated expenses to adequately account for business expenses, he or she must substantiate them with receipts, bills, or other documentation. However, it will not be necessary for an employee to provide actual proof of expenses in order to be considered to have adequately accounted for them if the employer reimburses him or her on the basis of miles driven or a per diem travel allowance. The payment rates cannot exceed those established by the federal government in Publication 1542.

Nonaccountable Plans

An employer will be deemed to have a nonaccountable employee business expense reimbursement plan if:

- ◆ employees fail to incur business expenses within a reasonable time after receiving advances for them;
- ◆ employees are not required to account for their business expenses;
- ◆ employees are required to account for their accrued business expenses, but fail to do so within a reasonable time;
- ◆ employees are not required to return unused advances for business expenses; or,
- ◆ employees are required to return unused advances but fail to do so within a reasonable time.

The consequences of an employer having a nonaccountable plan are that the employee must include the full amount of the employee business expense allowance received as part of his or her taxable income and the employer must deduct and withhold the appropriate federal income tax, Social Security tax, and Medicare tax. In addition, the employer must pay matching Social Security tax and Medicare tax on the payments.

There is an exception for plans based on mileage and per diem allowances. If such payments by the employer exceed the rates set by the federal government, only the *excess* must be included in the employee's taxable income. Only the amount included will result in liability for a matching share of Social Security tax and Medicare tax on the employer's part.

Convenience of the Employer Benefits

The tax treatment of certain benefits provided by employers to their employees is quite similar to the afforded reimbursements to employees in an accountable plan, although they are actually what are known as *payments in kind*. Earnings paid to an employee in kind (means other than in money) for work performed are generally fully taxable and are subject to income tax, Social Security tax, and Medicare tax. Typical of taxable payments in kind are paid vacations, country club memberships, and payment of an employee's living expenses by the employer. Employees who receive in kind compensation are taxed on it on the basis of its fair market value.

There are exceptions for some types of in kind compensation, such that the recipient will not be subject to federal taxation of any kind on it. Among the most common nontaxable types of in kind compensation are meals provided to workers for the employer's convenience on the employer's premises and lodging provided for the employer's convenience on the employer's premises and as a condition of employment.

EXAMPLE: Valley Forest Products conducts a logging operation in remote areas of the U.S. and Canada. On the sites, the company furnishes all its workers meals and provides living quarters in portable trailers, without charge for either. Due to the remoteness of the logging sites, if the company did not provide food and lodging, their workers would have to travel considerable distances to find motels and restaurants. That would make it difficult to hire people and far less likely that the workers would get to work on time. Although the meals and lodging provided by Valley clearly constitute earnings in kind to the workers, their value would qualify for exclusion from the workers' gross incomes since they are provided for the convenience of the employer on its premises and the workers are required, as a condition of employment, to live in the housing provided by the employer.

NONREIMBURSED, EMPLOYEE BUSINESS EXPENSES

Employees who incur business-related expenses during the course of conducting their trade or business are allowed a deduction from adjusted gross income for those expenses to the degree that they are ordinary and necessary. The deduction for employee business expenses is calculated on *Form 2106*. The form is devoted, to a large degree, to the calculation of travel expenses.

Although *Form 2106* does not devote lines to specific business deductions other than transportation expenses, travel expenses, and the cost of meals and entertainment, line 4 of Part I provides a line to enter all other qualified employee business expenses. Whether or not a given expenditure would qualify for an employee business expense deduction will have to be determined on a case-by-case basis depending on whether it is an ordinary, necessary business expense for the particular taxpayer in question. However, expenditures for *business gifts*, *business related professional services*, *trade association dues and publications*, *telephone service for business use*, *business supplies*, and *office space* are almost universally qualified for deduction as employee business expenses. (More details concerning the deductibility of employee business expenses are available in IRS Publications 463 and 529.)

Education Expenses

The Code and Regulations regarding taxability of education benefits provided by employers and deductibility of education expenses incurred by individuals are extensive. Employers may provide up to $5,250 per year in assistance for education to each of their employees and exclude it from the recipient's gross income under provision of Sec. 127.

The Code provides for a *tuition and fees deduction* available to taxpayers for qualified personal education expenses that they pay on their personal income tax return. That deduction is the only tax deduction for education expenses available to most taxpayers. A deduction for education expenses is limited to the personal tuition and fees deduction unless a taxpayer can pass the relatively stringent test set forth in Treasury Regulation Sec. 1.162-5 to qualify for a *business deduction.*

A party seeking to demonstrate that his or her education expenses qualify for a business expenses deduction must show that he or she obtained the education to either *maintain or improve skills required for employment* or to *meet requirements imposed by law or the employer in order to maintain employment at the party's current rank and pay rate.* But, even if one or both of the first two conditions are met—no business expense deduction for the education expense will be allowed if *either* the education is required for the taxpayer to meet *minimum educational requirements in order to qualify for the job* or the education *qualifies that party for a new trade or business.*

If the person who qualifies to take a business expense deduction for education expense is self-employed, the deduction will be taken on Schedule C of *Form 1040* as a deduction for adjusted gross income. This method avoids any federal taxation on the expenditure, whereas an employee must take the deduction on line 4 of Part I of *Form 2106* as a deduction from adjusted gross income. This may result in an income tax savings, but will not reduce Social Security tax or Medicare tax at all.

EXAMPLE: Julia, a CPA, is required by state law to take a minimum of thirty hours of continuing education courses per year in accounting or related subjects. In fulfillment of this requirement, Julia incurred expenses of $5,000 for a tax refresher course. Julia will be entitled to a business expense deduction for the cost of the course as well as associated expenses, such as the cost of travel to the site of the course and the cost of books and supplies for the course.

If Julia were self-employed, the deduction would be taken on Schedule C of *Form 1040* as a deduction from gross income, but if she is an employee, the deduction will be taken on Form 2106 as a deduction from adjusted gross income. Julia would certainly net more after-tax income if her employer were to pay for the cost of the course, thereby excluding its cost from her income altogether. Her employer could reduce any bonus she might have been paid by that amount, rather than paying a full bonus to her and having her pay her own education expenses.

Moving Expenses

The basic proposition is that the expense of moving from one residence to another is a personal expense for which no deduction is allowed. However, the Code Sec. 217 permits a deduction for moving expenses if the move is employment related and certain conditions are met. Some of those conditions are:

- ◆ employee has not previously been working and relocates in order to enter the job market;
- ◆ employee has been out of the job market;
- ◆ employee has been working only part-time for a substantial period and moves in order to reenter the work force;
- ◆ employee is transferred to a new location by a current employer; or,
- ◆ employee changes jobs.

The Distance Test

There are two major requirements that must be met in order to qualify a business-related move for a *Moving Expense* deduction. The first involves the *distance* of the employee's new place of employment from his or her former residence. The provisions of the Code Sec. 217(c)(1)(A) require that the taxpayer's new principal place of employment be at least fifty miles further from his or her former residence than his or her former principal place of employment was from his or her former residence.

The Time Test

Internal Revenue Code Sec. 217(c)(2) also imposes what is popularly known as the *time test*. It establishes the minimum amount of time that a taxpayer must be employed upon moving to a new location and still qualify for the moving expense deduction. There is a time test for employees and a different, more stringent time test for self-employed taxpayers.

For employees to meet the time test to qualify for the moving expense deduction, they must work full time for at least thirty-nine weeks of the first twelve months after moving to the location of a new job. The thirty-nine weeks of work does not have to be continuous, nor does it have to all be for the same employer. However, it must occur in the same general commuting area; must be considered full time for the type of work involved in the area where it is performed; and, cannot include periods of self-employment.

For self-employed taxpayers to qualify for the moving expense deduction, they must work full time for at least thirty-nine weeks of the first twenty-four months after moving *and* a total of at least seventy-eight weeks of the first twelve months after moving. Although the time requirements that a self-employed person must meet to qualify for the moving expense deduction are substantially more burdensome than those required of an employee, the work activity that qualifies to meet the requirement is not nearly as limited. All of the self-employed party's work must be done in the general commuting area to which he or she moved and it must be full time. However, the self-employed worker may count both the work performed as an employee and self-employed work toward the time test. Full-time work performed for any number of employers and in various trades during the first twenty-four months following relocation may be counted by the self-employed taxpayer to meet the time test.

Reimbursed Moving Expenses

Some employers, as a fringe benefit to their employees, will reimburse employees for the moving expenses that they incur in connection with relocation related to their employment. Although the Code Sec. 82 would normally cause such reimbursements to be included in the recipient's gross income, Sec. 132(a)(6) specifically excludes *qualified moving expense reimbursement* from gross income. Section 132(g) then defines qualified moving expense reimbursement as the amount paid to a taxpayer as either an advance or a reimbursement to cover moving expenses that a taxpayer would be eligible to take a deduction for under the Code Sec. 217 had he or she not been reimbursed for them.

Such reimbursements are not included in an employee's gross income, nor is he or she entitled to take a deduction for the reimbursed moving expenses. If an employee takes a moving expense deduction and is then reimbursed for the expenses, the reimbursement will be includible in gross income.

EXAMPLE: Skeeter's company transferred him from Duluth to New Orleans. He would qualify to take a deduction for moving expenses, but he did not have to pay any charges. His company has a policy of reimbursing its employees for moving expenses they incur when they accept a transfer. In fact, Skeeter's company not only reimbursed him for the cost of moving his and his family's household goods and their travel expenses, but it also reimbursed him for the real estate commission and closing costs that he incurred from the sale of his residence in Duluth. In addition, the company directly paid the closing costs on the purchase of his new residence in New Orleans.

Skeeter will not be required to recognize the reimbursements for the costs of moving his household goods and travel as gross income, nor will he be entitled to a deduction for those costs. However, Skeeter will have to recognize the reimbursements of real estate commission from the sale of his Duluth house as income and will also have to recognize the closing costs directly paid in his behalf by his employer for the house that he bought in New Orleans. It will be necessary for Skeeter to keep sufficiently detailed records to enable him to distinguish between the parts of his reimbursement that qualify for a Sec. 217 deduction (thereby being excluded) and those that do not.

Chapter 4
Home Office Expense

Taxpayers who rent office space are allowed a deduction for the rent that they pay. However, many taxpayers simply allocate space for an office in their homes and work from there. A deduction for the portion of a home that a taxpayer uses for an office or other permitted business use is provided for in the Code Sec. 280A, when certain conditions are met.

For the most part, taxpayers are not allowed to take a deduction for business use of part of their personal residence unless the part for which they are seeking the deduction is used *regularly and exclusively for qualifying business purposes*. In fact, Sec. 280A begins by setting forth the *general rule* that taxpayers will not be allowed to take deductions for expenses that they incur in connection with providing themselves with a personal residence. However, it then goes on to create exceptions that allow deductions for *interest*, *taxes*, and *casualty losses* without requiring that they be business related, followed by the business use exception.

QUALIFYING BUSINESS PURPOSES

Section 280A provides for three general categories of business use of a residence that qualify a taxpayer for a deduction. It also provides for two other more specific business uses of space in a taxpayer's residence that will qualify for a deduction.

Exclusive and Regular

As long as part of a taxpayer's residence is used *exclusively and regularly* for business, Sec. 280A(C)(1) permits a deduction if the use is:

- ♦ as the principal place of business for any trade or business of the taxpayer;
- ♦ as a place of business that is used by patients, clients, or customers in meeting or dealing with the taxpayer in the normal course of his or her trade or business; or,
- ♦ in the case of a separate structure that is not attached to the dwelling unit, in connection with the taxpayer's trade or business.

In order for a taxpayer who is an employee to qualify for a deduction for expenses related to a business use of his or her residence, not only must the use be exclusive and regular, but also for the *convenience of his or her employer*.

The requirement that a party must use some portion of his or her residence exclusively for business use in order to qualify for a deduction is a strict one. There is no tolerance and even minimal nonbusiness use will disqualify the expense for deduction.

EXAMPLE: Bert, an attorney, decided that, rather than provide legal services to the public, he would prefer to do legal research and prepare briefs and various documents for other attorneys. He set up his dining room as his office and usually kept the table covered with books and papers. On major holidays and a few other occasions during the year, Bert would clear off the table and use it to serve meals to his family and guests. Even though these nonbusiness uses of his dining room were very limited, they would disqualify him from taking a business deduction in connection with its business use.

It is not necessary to devote a separate room of a residence to business use as long as there is a definite area devoted to regular, exclusive business use. Congregating business-related furnishings and equipment into a single area rather than scattering them throughout various parts of the residence would likely be essential in establishing exclusive business use of a definite part of a residence.

Even if a taxpayer conducts more than one business in the part of his or her home set aside for business use, he or she may still take the appropriate deduction, provided that each business use would qualify. Employees who, in addition to their primary employment, also operate a business of their own from their residences must be especially careful in order to preserve their right to take a deduction for the business-related use of their residence. Otherwise, even if a taxpayer's use of his or her home would qualify for a deduction, if he or she also does work for his or her primary employer in the same area of the home that is set aside for self-employment activity, he or she will lose the right to take the deduction. Unless he or she can show that he or she was required to have business related space in the home for the convenience of the employer, he or she would lose that deduction. Without this proof, a taxpayer's use of space in his home to conduct business for his or her employer is regarded the same as personal use of the space.

EXAMPLE: Rob was employed as an interior decorator at a furniture store that sold furnishings to homeowners. He also started two of his own businesses—design consultant for small businesses and a computer consulting business. Rob operated both his design consultant business and his computer consulting business from the same office space in his home. The office space in Rob's home was used regularly and exclusively for his two businesses. The fact that Rob operates both a computer consulting firm and his design consulting firm for small businesses from the same space will not disqualify him from taking a business deduction for the space. However, if Rob works from his home office on estimates, plans, or any other material for the furniture store that employs him, that activity would disqualify him from taking any deduction for his home office.

Section 280A offers no guidance as to what constitutes *regular* use of a space for business purposes. Therefore, the term regular should be given its ordinary meaning, which would require a steady, ongoing, and frequent use, as opposed to a sporadic or occasional use, even if the total hours of sporadic use exceeded the total hours of ongoing use.

Principal Place of Business

In determining whether a taxpayer is using space in his or her residence as a *principal place of business* and thereby qualifies for a deduction for its use, IRS Publication 587 offers significant guidance. It states that a self-employed person who is regularly using part of his or her residence exclusively for an office in which he or she performs *administrative or management activities*, such as processing orders or bills in connection with a business, and who has no other fixed location from which a substantial part of the activities are performed, will be considered to have established a home office as his or her principal place of business. Even if a taxpayer also conducts business from a vehicle, motel rooms, or other places that are not fixed locations, he or she can still take a deduction for a home office if he or she otherwise qualifies for it.

EXAMPLE: Paul is a self-employed roofer who uses an office in his home regularly and exclusively to calculate and write payroll checks, pay bills and handle other administrative duties connected with his business. He has no other fixed site from which he operates. He usually meets customers at their homes and often works up estimates on the spot, either in the customer's home or in the cab of his truck. Paul will qualify for a deduction for his home office since he has no other fixed location that he uses for conducting his trade or business.

Patients, Clients, or Customers

Even if a self-employed person has his or her principal place of business at a fixed site away from the home, Sec. 280A still allows a deduction for that part of the home that a taxpayer regularly uses exclusively to meet or deal with patients, clients, or customers. Publication 587 states that *occasional meetings and telephone calls* in the taxpayer's home office are not enough to qualify for a deduction for use of the residence as a meeting place. For an employee to be entitled to such a deduction, he or she must show that he or she maintains the place in the residence to meet customers, clients, and patients for the convenience of his or her employer.

EXAMPLE: Serena makes custom curtains at her shop which is open Monday through Friday from 8:00 A.M. to 6:00 P.M. She also has an office in her home, complete with samples of material and pictures of work that she has done, which she uses exclusively for the purpose of meeting with customers by appointment on Saturdays. This enables her to get business from customers whose work schedules do not permit them to come to her shop during regular business hours without requiring her to open her shop on Saturdays. Serena will be entitled to take a deduction for her home office since she meets customers there as a regular part of her business and not merely occasionally.

Separate Structures

The third general deduction provision in Sec. 280A applies to business use of structures located on the premises of a taxpayer's residence, but that are not attached to his or her dwelling. Publication 587 explains that free standing structures such as a *studio, garage, or barn* would qualify for the deduction. The language of Publication 587 also indicates that the entire structure, rather than a mere part of it, must be used exclusively and regularly for the taxpayer's trade or business. However, Sec. 280A does not require that a separate structure located on the site of a taxpayer's residence be his or her primary place of business, nor does it require the meeting of patients, clients, or customers there in order to take a deduction for it, as long as it is used exclusively and regularly in his or her trade or business. An employee, once again, cannot take such a deduction unless he or she can show that he or she maintained the separate structure exclusively and regularly for use in trade or business for the convenience of the employer. Publication 587 offers the following example concerning business use of a separate structure.

EXAMPLE: John Berry operates a floral shop in town. He grows the plants for his shop in a greenhouse behind his home. He uses the greenhouse exclusively and regularly in his business, so he can deduct the expense for its use subject to the deduction limit.

REGULAR, BUT NOT EXCLUSIVE

A taxpayer whose business regularly uses some part of his or her residence to provide *day care* for children, care for people who are at least 65 years of age, or for individuals who are incapable of caring for themselves due to mental or physical incapacity is allowed by Sec. 280A to take a deduction for the part of the residence used for that business. It is not necessary that the part of the residence used for a day care be exclusively used for that purpose as long as the space is available for regular use in providing day care services and is used for that purpose more than merely occasionally. However, Sec. 280A provides that a deduction for use of a part of a residence as a day care will be denied if the party providing the care has not obtained the necessary authority under state law, such as a license, to legally provide such services or is exempt from such requirements.

The other deduction provided for in Sec. 280A that requires regular use of part of a residence for business purposes, but does not require exclusive use, is the one for allocation of space within a residence for the purpose of *storing inventory or product samples* in connection with the party's trade or business of selling products at either the retail or wholesale level. Although the area used for storage does not have to be exclusively used for that purpose in order for the taxpayer to be eligible for the deduction, Sec. 280A does require that the party's residence be *the sole fixed location of such trade or business,* in order to qualify for the deduction.

EXAMPLE: Burton, a manufacturer's representative, sells pocket knives. The sole fixed location of his business activity is his home. In addition to allocated office space in his home, Burton has set aside the smallest bedroom in his house to store samples of knives and some inventory with which to supply customers who put on special promotions and sometimes run low on merchandise. Burton also stores his sales brochures and display materials in the room, as well as an old baby bed.

To the degree to which Burton uses the room for storage of samples and inventory of his knives, he can take a deduction for that use. He is not entitled to a deduction for the part of the room used to store brochures and display materials, nor is he entitled to take a deduction for the part of the room used for storing the baby bed. However, the fact that the brochures, display materials, and baby bed are stored in the same room as the knives used as samples and inventory will not disqualify him from taking a deduction for the part of the room used to store the knives.

ALLOCATING PERCENTAGE OF USE

In calculating the deduction for a qualifying business use of a residence, the first step is to determine the appropriate percentage of the residence that qualifies for the deduction. Deductions for use of part of a residence as a primary place of business; a place to meet clients, patients, or customers; or for storage of samples or inventory are generally based on the percentage of square footage in the entire structure that is devoted to the qualifying business use.

EXAMPLE: Casey lives in a house containing 2000 square feet of habitable space. He has devoted a room of the house that is fifteen feet by twenty feet as his principal place of business from which he operates as a self-employed, management consultant. He uses the room exclusively and regularly for the purpose of conducting his business. By multiplying the length of the room, twenty feet, by its width, fifteen feet, Casey determined that he had allocated 300 square feet of his house to a qualifying business use. He then divided the amount of business use, 300 square feet, by the total number of square feet in his house, arriving at a figure of .15, or 15%.

Calculating the appropriate percentage of expenses to deduct for a qualifying business use of part of a residence is more difficult when the part used is a *free standing structure* than when it is actually part of the main residence. If the detached structure and the main residence are of similar quality and therefore of similar value to the user, it would still be appropriate to use a percentage-of-square-footage approach in order to calculate the business use deduction. However, when there is a significant difference in the nature of the square footage of the separate structure and that of the main dwelling, calculating the deduction on the basis of the percentage of overall square footage used for business is not appropriate.

Space in a barn or garage is simply not as valuable per square foot as space in the typical house, whereas, space in a specially designed and outfitted recording studio or research laboratory may be far more valuable than space used for living quarters in a house. In such cases, a deduction could be calculated by using the *fair rental value* of the separate structure or by still using the relative amount of square footage used for business. However, there must be an adjustment to reflect the relative value of the space in the separate structure compared to space in the main residence.

EXAMPLE: Dub lives in a house containing 4,000 square feet. There is a barn on the premises that also contains 4,000 square feet and he uses it exclusively and regularly as his only fixed business location for buying and selling Tennessee walking horses. The cost to construct such a barn would be only one fourth of the cost to construct the house. If Dub chooses to calculate his business deduction for the value of the barn on the basis of square footage, he must adjust the square footage of the barn to allow for its relative value compared to the value of the square footage of the house.

Therefore, since square footage of the barn is worth only one fourth as much as square footage in the house, he should take only one fourth of the total square footage of the barn and add that result to the total square footage of both properties. The result would be that Dub would add one fourth of the barn's 4,000 square feet (1,000) to the entire 4,000 square feet in his house, for a total of 5,000 square feet. He would then divide the 1,000 square feet allocated to the barn by the 5,000 square feet allocated to the total of both structures and the result would be a 20% allocation for the value of he barn.

Alternately, if Dub could show that the fair rental value of the barn would be $1,200 a month and the house and barn together are either currently renting for $5,000 a month or would have a fair rental value of that amount if the property is not actually being rented, he could calculate, differently. He could calculate the allocation for the barn for a business deduction by dividing the $1,200 fair rental value of the barn by the $5,000 total fair rental value—a 24% allocation.

Day Cares

Allocating the percentage of use of a residence devoted to a qualifying *day care* operation is the most complicated calculation among the deductible business uses of part of a residence. The calculation starts with a determination of the percentage of the residence that is available for regular use as a day care. Once that determination is made, if the area within the taxpayer's residence that is used to provide day care is used exclusively for that purpose, the percentage of square footage used for day care is calculated in the same manner as calculating the percentage of use for a principal business. However, since a deduction is available for the part of a residence used for day care even when the use is not exclusive, the taxpayer must then further adjust the percentage of the residence used to provide day care to reflect the amount of time that the space is devoted to personal use for the year.

EXAMPLE: Paula is licensed to operate a day care from her home. Of the 3,000 square feet in her home, 1,500 square feet are devoted to providing day care from the hours of 6:00 A.M. to 6:00 P.M., five days a week. At all times that she is not providing day care services, her entire house is used by her family for residential purposes. Paula uses 50% of her home for a day care, but only does so 12 hours a day for five days a week, a total of 60 hours weekly, or 3,120 hours annually. Since there are

8,760 hours in a year, her net percentage of use of her residence as a day care would be calculated as follows:

50% (percentage of house used for day care) x 3,120 (hours of day care operation) divided by 8,760 (total hours in a year) = 23.44%

ELIGIBLE EXPENSES

Once the percentage of business use of a residence is ascertained, the next step is to apply that percentage to the eligible general expenses associated with the residence. Included among those expenses are *insurance*, *property taxes*, *repairs*, *utilities*, *mortgage interest*, and the *cost of maintaining a security system*. If the taxpayer is renting the residence, the business use percentage should be applied to the *rental payments* to determine the deductible portion of them.

If the party who is qualified to take a deduction for business use of a part of the residence owns it, regardless of whether or not it is mortgaged, he or she is entitled to take a deduction for *depreciation* on the part of the residence used for business. The depreciation deduction is calculated by taking the lesser of the residence's adjusted basis or its fair market value, deducting the value of the land that it is on, dividing the remainder by thirty-nine, and applying the percentage of the residence that is devoted to a qualified business use. The depreciable value of the property is divided by thirty-nine because current law requires that non-residential real property be depreciated in even increments (known as the *straight line method*) over a period of thirty-nine years. Since the deduction is for business use of the property, the nonresidential rules for depreciation apply.

Adjusted basis of the residence is usually its acquisition cost plus the cost of the permanent improvements (such as additions or replacement of plumbing or electrical systems) less the past deductions for either depreciation or losses in value due to destruction (such as by fire or storm, not covered by insurance, known as casualty losses). Fair market value is the price for which the property would sell in an *arms length transaction* between a knowledgeable buyer and seller. The value of the land is deducted from the total value because land is not eligible for depreciation.

DRAWBACKS TO TAKING THE DEDUCTION

Although taking a deduction for depreciation for the part of a home used for business will likely result in a reduced tax liability, there is a down side to taking the deduction. Under the Code Sec. 121, if a taxpayer has owned his or her residence for at least two years and occupied it as his or her primary residence for at least two of the last five years, up to $250,000 of gain form its sale may be excluded from taxation. A married couple filing a joint return may exclude up to $500,000 of such gain from taxation. These are not mere postponements of taxation, but are permanent exclusions.

However, Sec. 121 does not permit exclusion of gain that was brought about due to any depreciation that was allowed on the property after May 6, 1997. Publication 587 states that only the gain attributable to the part of a taxpayer's residence devoted to personal use for the requisite period of time is eligible for exclusion from taxation under Sec. 121. However, Treasury Regulation Sec. 1.121-1 (e)(1) provides that only the gain that is attributable to that part of a taxpayer's dwelling used for business that is separate and detached from the main residence is ineligible for exclusion from taxation under Sec. 121. No such exclusion is mandated when parts of the main dwelling were used for business.

EXAMPLE: Jill's adjusted basis in her home is $230,000, of which $30,000 is attributable to the value of the lot. The fair market value of the house is $300,000, of which $50,000 is attributable to the lot. Jill uses 20% of her residence regularly and exclusively as her only fixed place of business as a self-employed personal fitness trainer. The depreciation that Jill is entitled to take on her business use of her residence is calculated as follows:

$230,000 (adjusted basis) less $30,000 (part of basis attributable to the land) = $200,000 (depreciable basis) x .20 (percentage of business usage) = $40,000 divided by 39 (number of years over which property must be depreciated) = $1,025.64 (allowable depreciation).

If after owning the house for five years, during which time she used 20% of it for business and deducted a total of $5128.20 in depreciation, Jill were to sell it for a net of $300,000, she would have a gain of $75,1258.20 ($300,000 net sales price less $224,871.80 adjusted basis), since the adjusted basis in her house must be reduced by any depreciation allowed. However, only $70,000 would qualify for exclusion under Sec. 121 and the $5,128.20 gain attributable to depreciation would be ineligible for such exclusion.

If the part of her residence that she used in connection with her business had been a detached, free standing studio, then the 20% portion of the $70,000 gain attributable to the studio ($14,000) would be ineligible for exclusion under Sec. 121. The $5,128.20 in gain brought about due to depreciation having been taken on the part of the residence used for business would be ineligible as well.

SPECIAL RULES

Although prorating costs based on square footage to determine the deduction for business use of a residence concludes calculation of the deduction in most instances, there are cases that call for further refinements. Normally, such expenses as the cost of utilities or security systems are allocated on the basis of square footage devoted to business, just as are rent or depreciation. However, if the business deduction is attributed to a barn, garage, or other free standing structure with so much different value per square foot than the main residence that the square footage of the separate structure had been adjusted to reflect the disparity in value, using square footage to allocate such expenses as utilities and the cost of a security system could be inappropriate. Also, to the degree that a taxpayer places equipment in use exclusively for business purposes, the entire cost should be treated as business related.

EXAMPLE: Nick owns and occupies a house that contains 1,500 square feet and has a detached garage containing 1,000 square feet. He decided to quit his job as a mechanic at a local automobile dealership and start his own auto repair business from his garage. He had the electrical wiring upgraded in the garage in order to be able to operate heavy equipment and installed a compressor and a lift. Once he started to operate the business from his garage, his utility bill doubled. The value of the space of Nick's garage is equal to one half of the value of the space in his house. For purposes of allocating depreciation, taxes, and other general expenses to the garage, Nick would have to figure the square footage of the garage at only 50% of its actual size since it is valued at only half as much as the square footage in his house. The allocation would be calculated as:

500 (square footage allowed for garage) divided by 2,000 (square footage allowed for garage + 1,500 actual footage of house) = .25 (25%)

But since Nick can show from his prior bills that his utility bill doubled upon opening his garage for business, he should be entitled to deduct half of his utility bill for business usage rather than merely 25%. Also, the compressor and lift that Nick installed are entirely business equipment and he will be entitled to take a depreciation deduction for them without regard to the percentage of square footage of his residential property that is devoted to business. Nick will not be entitled to deduct the cost of upgrading the electrical wiring in his garage since this is a permanent improvement to the property and will merely increase his basis in it. However, if Nick had merely been renting the property, he would be entitled to take a write off for the cost of the wiring.

Day Cares

Day care operators who devote part of their residence to their business may also be entitled to certain refinements of their business deductions associated with their residence. As previously discussed, if the part of a day care operator's home that is used to provide day care services is not exclusively used for that purpose, not only does that party have to allocate a percentage of the residence to day care in figuring the business deduction, but he or she must also further reduce that percentage to allow for the time that the part of the residence that is used for day care is also used for nonbusiness purposes. The net result is then applied to what are referred to as *indirect expenses*—those that apply to the entire house, such as utilities or general upkeep.

However, if expenses incurred in connection with the area devoted to day care are *direct expenses* (those that are specific to the space used for that operation), such as the cost of painting the area devoted to day care, then the only adjustment necessary to calculate the business deduction is to determine the percentage of time the space is used for business and apply that percentage to the expense.

EXAMPLE: Larry operates a day care in his residence. He uses 60% of the home for that purpose and is open 50% of each day, every day of the week. Last month, Larry spent $1,000 having the part of his house used for day care painted. His utility bill was $300. Since the cost of painting was a direct expense and the area that was painted is used for day care 50% of the time, he is allowed to take a business deduction of 50% of the painting cost. The utility bill is an indirect expense and this will limit Larry's deduction to 50% of 60% (30%) of the bill.

LIMITATIONS

A major potential limitation is placed on the availability of deductions for business use of residential space in the Code Sec. 280A(c)(5) that prohibits the deduction to the extent that it will produce a loss from the business. Therefore, despite the fact that a taxpayer may meet even the most stringent requirements of Sec. 280A and qualify for a deduction for business use of his or her residence, it cannot be taken if it results in a loss from the business involving the residence, even if there would have been no question about the deductibility of such expenses had the business been operated from a location other than the residence. However, the deductions may not be totally lost since taxpayers who cannot take deductions for business use of their residence due to the deductions generating a loss can carry the deductions forward and use them in subsequent years, provided they do not create a loss in those years.

Section 280A also prohibits any deduction for an employer for expenses incurred in connection with an employee renting any part of his or her residence to his or her employer for business use. Apparently, the potential for abuse in such cases outweighs the justification for allowing such deductions.

There are a few commonly committed errors in calculating deductions for business use of residential space. For example, when expenses, such as insurance premiums, are paid on an annual basis, it is not uncommon for taxpayers to use the entire premium in calculating the deductible portion allocated to their business. However, the degree to which a payment covers expenses attributable to the following tax year should be appropriately reduced to calculate the deductible expense for the current year. Also, taxpayers who itemize deductions for expenses such as home mortgage interest and real estate taxes must remember to reduce those deductions by the amount allocated and taken as a deduction for the business use of their residences.

EXAMPLE: Quirt, who files his taxes on a calendar year basis, paid his homeowners insurance of $600 on the first of July. His property taxes were $1,200 for the year. He began using 20% of his house for an office on the first of July under conditions that qualified him for a business deduction for its use. Since the insurance payment was for a full, twelve months, even though it was paid at mid year, Quirt can apply the 20% deduction to only half of the premium. He can use the remaining half the following year if he continues to use his home for a qualifying business purpose.

Since Quirt was in business for only half of the year, he can apply the 20% rate of business use to only half of his $1,200 property tax liability. If Quirt itemizes his personal deductions on Schedule A of *Form 1040,* his deduction for property taxes on his residence (which are 100% deductible by statute even if part of the property is used for business purposes) must be reduced by the $120 (20% x $600) that he took as a business deduction for the property taxes that he paid.

Chapter 5

Nonbusiness Deductions for the Self-Emloyed

There are several deductions that are available to self-employed taxpayers that do not result from direct business expenses. These deductions help self-employed parties overcome the inequity caused by the fact that they do not have employers providing benefits to them that are excludible from their gross incomes. These deductions are all *above-the-line* deductions for adjusted gross income, and are therefore quite likely to yield tax savings to those eligible to take them.

SELF-EMPLOYMENT TAX

Since self-employed taxpayers do not have employers to contribute a matching share of FICA taxes, they are left with having to pay self-employment taxes that have a nominal rate equal to both the employer's and employee's shares of Social Security taxes combined. Since an employer's share of FICA taxes paid on behalf of employees is not taxable to the employee, Congress saw fit to allow an equivalent adjustment for self-employed tax payers.

Self-employed taxpayers calculate their self-employment taxes on Schedule SE of *Form 1040*. On line 6 of the short Schedule SE and on line 13 of the long Schedule SE, a taxpayer who is required to pay self-employment taxes, is instructed to calculate 50% of the self-employment tax liability. The figure is transferred to *Form 1040* where it is then added into the total adjustments that are subtracted from total income to arrive at adjusted gross income. This is an adjustment for adjusted gross income, although it does not reduce the amount of self-employment income. Therefore, the adjustment will help reduce the taxable income of most self-employed taxpayers, regardless of whether or not they itemize deductions. This has an indirect effect on the impact of self-employment taxes, but it will not directly affect a taxpayer's self-employment tax rate.

HEALTH INSURANCE DEDUCTION

Taxpayers have long been allowed to take an itemized deduction for medical expenses on Schedule A of *Form 1040*. Included among medical expenses eligible for such deductions are medical insurance premiums paid by a party for medical insurance. However, under current U.S. tax law, the combined uninsured costs of medical and dental care, plus the medical insurance premiums paid by the taxpayer, are deductible only to the extent that the total exceeds 7.5% of adjusted gross income. Therefore, few taxpayers are actually entitled to a deduction for medical expenses on Schedule A.

Internal Revenue Code Sec. 162(1) provides special rules for self-employed individuals that permit them to deduct the health insurance premiums they pay as a deduction for adjusted gross income. Although in prior years self-employed individuals could only deduct a certain percentage of their medical insurance premiums under this provision, beginning in 2003 they were allowed a 100% deduction. However, self-employed taxpayers cannot take a medical insurance premium deduction in excess of their earned income from the self-employment trade or business that gave rise to establishment of the medical insurance plan. Also, neither the taxpayer nor the taxpayer's spouse can be eligible for participation in any subsidized healthcare plan provided by any employer and still qualify for the health insurance cost deduction for self-employed individuals.

For purposes of qualifying for the health insurance cost deduction for self-employed individuals, owners of more than 2% of an S corporation are considered to be eligible for the deduction. As with self-employed individuals, owners of over 2% of an S corporation cannot deduct premiums in excess of their earnings from the S corporation. Neither the taxpayer nor the taxpayer's spouse can be eligible for subsidized medical coverage from any employer and still be allowed to take the deduction.

To the degree that a party takes a deduction for medical insurance premiums under Sec. 162(1), he or she cannot use that same expense in calculating medical expense deduction on Schedule A. Also Sec. 162(1)(4) specifically states that the medical insurance premium deduction for self-employed individuals cannot be used to reduce an individual's net earnings for calculating self-employment taxes.

RETIREMENT PLANS

As an alternative to the qualified pension plans that many large corporations have established, Congress has established favorable tax treatment for two retirement plans that are both easy to establish and inexpensive to administer. Qualified payments into each of these plans by self-employed taxpayers are eligible for deductions for adjusted gross income.

Simplified Employee Pensions (SEP)

Section 408 of the Internal Revenue Code permits employers to establish an *individual retirement account* or *individual retirement annuity* for each of their employees and contribute to it the lesser of an amount equal to 25% of the employee's compensation for the year or $40,000. As long as employers meet the requirements of Sec. 408, they may deduct the payments that they make into each employee's *Simplified Employee Pension (SEP)*. At the same time, despite the fact that permitted contributions to a qualified SEP must immediately vest and be available for withdrawal by the employee whose IRA they were deposited in, the employee will not be taxed on the contribution until an actual or deemed withdrawal from the SEP-IRA is made. Self-employed taxpayers are considered to be their own employers and therefore qualify to establish a SEP-IRA, as do partners because each partner is considered to be employed by the partnership.

The deduction is taken out of adjusted gross income on *Form 1040.* However, contributions by a self-employed party to his or her own SEP-IRA will not reduce any earnings subject to self-employment tax, since they are not eligible for inclusion as a *pension and profit sharing* deduction on Schedule C of *Form 1040.*

Among the more stringent requirements that must be met in order for an IRA to qualify as a SEP under Sec. 408 are that the plan cannot discriminate in favor of highly compensated employees and there must be a written formula that specifies how the employer's overall contribution to the SEP program is to be divided among employees. Also, at least 50% of an employer's eligible employees must choose to participate in the SEP.

In the case of a self-employed sole proprietor who has no employees, other than him or herself, none of the requirements will present the slightest problem. However, there are several other provisions of Sec. 408 that must also be met. Banks, brokerage firms, and others who market SEP programs will usually offer guidance, at no additional charge, for meeting all of the requirements of Sec. 408.

SIMPLE Retirement Accounts

Employers with 100 or fewer employees whose earnings for the prior calendar year were at least $5,000 may establish a *Savings Incentive Match Plan for Employees (SIMPLE-IRA).* Self-employed individuals are considered to be their own employer and therefore qualify for such plans. SIMPLE retirement accounts can be set up so that the employer matches each employee's contribution to his or her SIMPLE-IRA up to an amount equal to 3% of the employee's compensation. Alternately, employers can choose to contribute an amount to each employee's SIMPLE-IRA equal to 2% of compensation without regard to the amount of contribution, if any, made by the employee.

Qualified contributions to SIMPLE-IRA's made by employers are deductible by them and are not includible in the income of the employee until the employee makes an actual or deemed withdrawal from the SIMPLE-IRA. Self-employed taxpayers who make contributions to such plans on their own behalf as their own employers are allowed to take their deductions for the contributions in the adjusted gross income section of *Form 1040*. Although the deduction is an adjustment for adjusted gross income, thereby reducing income for tax purposes even for those who do not itemize deductions on Schedule A of *Form 1040*, it cannot be used to offset earnings subject to self-employment tax. Such payments are not eligible for inclusion in the *pension and profit sharing* deduction on Schedule C of *Form 1040* to the extent that they are contributions made by a self-employed taxpayer on his or her own behalf.

Banks, brokerage houses, and others who market SIMPLE-IRA programs will usually gratuitously counsel prospective clients as to the requirements they must meet in order to comply with the Code Sec. 408(P) that establishes the favorable tax treatment for such programs.

Qualified Plans

There are a variety of retirement plans, other than the SEP-IRA or SIM-PLE-IRA available to employers, such as profit sharing plans and 401(k) plans. Self-employed taxpayers are eligible to participate in these plans, since they are regarded as their own employees. Typically, these plans are more complex and more difficult to administer than the SEP-IRA or SIMPLE-IRA, but generally offer greater flexibility and may offer larger contribution limits. To the degree that a self-employed taxpayer's contributions to a qualified plan are for his or her own direct benefit, he or she is permitted to take a tax deduction in the adjusted gross income section of *Form 1040*. This will reduce that portion of income that would otherwise be subject to income tax, but the deduction will not reduce any earnings subject to self-employment tax. Such contributions are not eligible for inclusion in the pension and profit sharing deduction on Schedule C of *Form 1040*, as such contributions are made on behalf of employees other than the employer.

Most small business owners will find it essential to engage the services of a professional to administer such plans to ensure the compliance necessary to qualify their plans for favorable tax treatment.

Chapter 6
Losses and Bad Debts

Businesses and individuals routinely sustain *losses for sale or exchange of property*, from *unprofitable business activity*, and from debts that are owed to them that become *uncollectible*. Some of these losses are deductible on a taxpayer's federal tax return and some of them are not.

LOSSES ON SALE OR EXCHANGE OF PROPERTY

Unless a loss on the sale or exchange of property is actually realized, it will definitely not be deductible. Therefore, no matter how much the value of an asset may decline, until the occurrence of a sale or exchange or an event that is the equivalent of a sale or exchange (such as a theft of an asset), there will be no tax consequences from the loss in value.

Held for Investment or Used in a Trade or Business

Losses sustained on the sale or exchange of assets used in a trade or business or held for investment are generally deductible. The issue that must be resolved in order to determine the extent of the deduction available for such losses is whether or not the asset that was sold or exchanged was a *capital asset*. Most assets are capital assets with the exception of *inven-*

tory, notes and accounts receivable, depreciable property used in a trade or business, or *land* used in a trade or business.

Losses on the sale of capital assets, known as capital losses, may be used by individuals and corporations alike to offset an unlimited amount of their capital gains. However, only $3,000 per year may be used by individuals to offset ordinary income. Corporations are not allowed to offset any of their ordinary income with capital losses. Losses from the sale of noncapital assets, such as inventory, are ordinary losses and may be used to offset ordinary income by both individuals and corporations. (For a more extensive discussion of deductions allowable for capital losses, see Chapter 2.)

Casualty and theft losses on property held for use in a trade or business are fully deductible without the limitations imposed on the casualty and theft deductions allowed for individuals.

CASUALTY AND THEFT LOSSES

The IRS defines a casualty loss as one that is caused by an identifiable event that is sudden, unexpected, and unusual. Among the more typical sources of deductible casualty losses are storms, fires, vandalism, and automobile accidents. The IRS considers theft to involve taking and removing another party's money or property with the intent that the rightful owner will be permanently deprived of it. In addition to such actions as burglary, robbery, and shoplifting, the IRS also recognizes blackmail, extortion, and kidnapping for ransom as forms of theft that qualify for the deduction, to the degree that it is allowed. Property that is misplaced does not qualify for the theft deduction. However, if it can be traced to a sudden, unexpected, and unusual identifiable event, the lost property may qualify for a deduction as a casualty loss.

Calculating the Deduction

If a person suffers a casualty loss or theft involving property used in performing services as an employee, the method for calculating the deduction is different than it is for calculating the casualty or theft loss deduction for personal property.

Calculating the amount of a casualty or theft loss starts with a determination of the taxpayer's *adjusted basis* in the property in question before it was the subject of a casualty or theft. The decrease in the fair market value of the property in question due to a casualty or theft must be determined next. The amount of the casualty loss or theft loss is then determined by subtracting any insurance or other reimbursement received (or expected) from the lesser of the taxpayer's adjusted basis in the property or the decline in the property's fair market value due to the casualty or theft.

When property is stolen and not recovered or totally destroyed by a casualty, the fair market value of the property after the loss is zero and the decline in the value of the property is equal to its fair market value. In determining the fair market value of property involved in a casualty of theft loss, no allowance can be included for the fact that replacement cost may exceed the property's fair market value, the fact that the property may hold sentimental value for the taxpayer, or the fact that the taxpayer incurred costs incidental to the loss, such as the need to temporarily obtain a rental car or the necessity to get medical treatment for injuries associated with the loss.

Once the amount of that loss is determined, it is then added to the employee's other job-related expenses and that total is added to the other *miscellaneous deductions* on Schedule A that must be reduced by 2% of the party's adjusted gross income to arrive at the deductible amount.

EXAMPLE: Bobby had a laptop computer that he used exclusively in connection with his job as a salesman. He had paid $1,500 for it. Before he owned it long enough to take any depreciation on it, it was stolen. At the time of the theft it would have brought $500 had he decided to sell it. Bobby's adjusted gross income for the year was $50,000 and he had job related expenses of $3,400. He had no other miscellaneous expenses.

Bobby's loss from the theft of the computer will be $500 since the decline in fair market value from $500 to zero is less than his adjusted basis of $1,500. This $500 theft loss will be fully added to his $3,400 of business-related expenses and the

$3,900 total will be reduced by $1,000 ($50,000 adjusted gross income x .02) to yield a net miscellaneous deduction of $2,900.

Deductions for casualty or theft losses on *business property* and *income producing property* are not subject to the 2% of adjusted gross income exclusion for miscellaneous deductions that personal property is. The amount of the loss on such property is still limited to the lesser of its fair market value or the owner's adjusted basis, but that amount is then fully deductible. Equipment owned by a self-employed individual to conduct his or her trade or business or an office building that is rented out, are examples of *business property.* Stocks, bonds, gold, notes, and works of art are all examples of *income-producing property.*

Reporting the Deduction

Casualty and theft loss deductions must be calculated on *Form 4684* that must be included with the taxpayer's tax return. Section A of the form is devoted to calculating casualty and theft losses for personal use property and Section B is for calculating a taxpayer's gain or loss from a casualty or theft involving business property, income producing property, and property used by an employee in carrying out his or her job.

The loss from casualty or theft of personal use property shown in Section A of *Form 4684* is to be transferred directly to the *Casualty and Theft Losses* section of Schedule A of *Form 1040.* If the insurance or other compensation that a taxpayer receives (or is eligible to receive) due to a casualty or theft loss exceeds his or her adjusted basis in the property, that amount must be reported as shown on *Form 4684* as gain on the appropriate line of Schedule D of *Form 1040.*

If a party's net gain or loss shown in Section B of *Form 4684* is attributable to business property, that figure must be entered in the *Net Gain or Loss from Form 4684* section of *Form 4797.* This section incorporates the figure with other items reported on the form. The total is then reported on the line on the front of *Form 1040* for individuals and *Form 1120* for corporations devoted to *Other Gains or (Losses).* If there would be no other entries on *Form 4797,* the figure may be entered directly on the

Other gains or (losses) line of *Form 1040* with the notation *Form 4684* next to that line. However, this procedure does not apply to S corporations and most partnerships that must report a net gain or loss that is attributable to business property on *Form 4684* on Schedule K of their tax returns.

The casualty or theft loss shown in Section B of *Form 4684* that is attributable to income producing property is to be entered in the *Other Miscellaneous Deductions* section of Schedule A of *Form 1040* for individuals. It is not subject to reduction by an amount equal to 2% of the taxpayer's adjusted gross income, as are most miscellaneous deductions. C corporations are to enter such losses on the *Other Deductions* line of the tax return, but S corporations and most partnerships must report the losses on Schedule K-1 of their returns. Net gains realized from settlements of casualty and theft losses from income producing property are to be reported on *Form 4797* for all entities except most partnerships. They must report the net gains on Schedule K-1 of their tax returns.

Postponing Recognition of Gain

Although the concept of realizing a gain from a casualty or theft loss may seem peculiar, it is actually relatively common. Most owners insure their property for its full, fair market value even though their adjusted basis in the property may be considerably less, due primarily to the property having appreciated in value or the owner's adjusted basis having been reduced due to depreciation taken on the property, or both. Since a taxpayer's casualty or theft loss, for tax purposes, is the lower of his or her basis in the damaged or stolen property or its decrease in fair market value due to the casualty or theft, it is not uncommon for insurance proceeds based on the fair market value of property to exceed losses based on the owner's adjusted basis in the property. In such cases, the taxpayer is expected to pay *capital gains tax* on the gain.

However, after paying the capital gains tax, the property owner would not be likely to have enough money from the insurance proceeds to replace the property. Therefore, taxpayers are allowed to *postpone recognition* of such gains if they reinvest an amount equal to the full amount of the insurance proceeds that they received for the property in similar property. Their basis in the new property, however, must be reduced by the amount of the deferred gain.

EXAMPLE: Natasha's delivery van that she used in her florist business was stolen and never recovered. She had depreciated the van to the point that her adjusted basis in it was $3,000. The fair market value of the van was $7,500 and she had it insured against theft for that amount. After subtracting her $500 deductible, the insurance company paid Natasha $7,000 as compensation for her stolen van. Natasha's deductible loss on the van as shown on *Form 4684* was $3,000 which, when netted against her insurance settlement of $7,000, left her with a $4,000 capital gain. If she spends at least $7,000 on a replacement van, she can defer recognition of the $4,000. Her basis in the first $7,000 of expenditure, however, would be only $3,000, since that was her basis in the property for which she received the $7,000.

If Natasha were to buy a van for $5,000, she could still defer recognition of $2,000 of the gain, but must recognize the $2,000 difference between what she collected in insurance and what she spent on the replacement van. If Natasha were to spend $10,000 on a new van, she could defer recognition of the full $4,000 gain. The extra $3,000 above the $7,000 insurance settlement would be added to the $3,000 basis that is attributable to the insurance settlement. This would bring the total of her basis in the replacement van to $6,000.

NOTE: *The property owner does not have to spend the actual insurance money that he or she receives in order to defer recognition of the gain. He or she can reinvest on credit, as long as he or she is obligated to make the payments.*

NET OPERATING LOSSES

When a taxpayer loses money from a business enterprise because business deductions exceed business income, it is referred to as a *net operating loss* (NOL). Section 172 of the Internal Revenue Code permits individuals, estates, trusts, and most C corporations with an NOL to use it to offset income earned in another year. Partnerships, S corporations, and personal holding companies are not allowed to carry NOL to other years.

An eligible taxpayer can carry an NOL *back* two years and *forward* for twenty years. Taxpayers may elect not to carry NOLs back at all but, if they do so, their carryforward period will still be only twenty years. However, taxpayers whose incomes were taxed in relatively low brackets in the previous two years may still want to save their NOLs for future years if they believe that the outlook for success warrants it.

If the taxpayer decides to carry an NOL back, he or she is required to apply the NOL back to the earlier of the last two years first, and then to the previous year if any of the NOL remains. Any unused NOL remaining after fulfilling the carryback requirement must be applied in future years in sequence starting with the very next year.

The *carryback provisions* will enable a taxpayer to claim a refund for taxes previously paid. The *carryforward provisions* will enable the party to reduce future taxable income, thereby reducing future tax liability. If a taxpayer has an NOL from more than one year that he or she is carrying forward, the earliest NOL must be used up first.

Since the object of allowing a taxpayer to utilize NOL to offset income in other years is to even out the impact of *business cycles*, the calculation of NOL is limited to determining the degree to which business related deductions exceed business income. Therefore, a party's net negative taxable income may not constitute NOL.

Net Income Adjustments

Certain adjustments must be made to net income to determine the taxpayer's NOL. Among the adjustments is that any NOL that had been carried forward and deducted to reduce that year's net loss must be added back to the taxpayer's net income for the year. This adjustment prevents NOL that had been carried forward and may be nearing expiration from generating fresh NOL that would have a new twenty-year life for carrying the loss forward. This adjustment must be made by all entities eligible to carry an NOL to another year.

Another adjustment is required of a few corporations in calculating their NOL. Corporations are allowed to deduct either 70%, 80%, or 100% of the dividends that they receive from other corporations, depending on the percentage they own of the corporation paying the dividend.

However, there are limitations that apply to the amount of those deductions. If taking the full deduction would generate an NOL for the corporation, it will be allowed to take the full deduction. Since most small C corporations are doing well to meet their own capital needs, few of them own stock in other corporations and the need for them to make this adjustment would be rare. (For a more detailed explanation of the limitation on corporate dividend deductions, see *Corporate Federal Income Taxes* in Chapter 8.)

In addition to adjusting taxable income by adding back any NOL taken from a prior year's carryover in order to calculate current NOL, an individual taxpayer must also add back several other items that may normally be excluded in calculating taxable income. He or she must add back any deduction taken for personal exemptions since the deduction for them is not business-related. An individual taxpayer must also add back nonbusiness deductions, such as a deduction for alimony payments, deduction for an IRA contribution, standard deduction, or itemized deductions on Schedule A of *Form 1040* (to the extent that they exceed nonbusiness income, such as interest, dividends, royalties, and income derived from annuities and endowments). Finally, individuals must add back any capital loss deduction that they took.

PASSIVE LOSSES

To curb the widespread use of *tax shelters*, Congress enacted Sec. 469 of the Internal Reveue Code. It created a new category of income and losses in the form of those attributable to a *passive activity*. Passive activity is defined as any activity:

   ♦ that involves the conduct of any trade or business and
   ♦ in which the taxpayer does not *materially* participate.

Section 469 also prohibits individuals, estates, trusts, closely held C corporations, partnerships, S corporations, and personal service corporations from using losses or credits generated by passive activity from being used to offset any income other than passive activity income.

In further clarification of what constitutes a passive activity, Sec. 469 provides that wages, salaries, bonuses, or other types of income derived from active participation in a trade or business shall be regarded as *active income*. It cannot be offset by passive losses.

Income derived from interest, dividends, royalties, and annuities, although often earned with little or no active involvement on the part of the taxpayer, are categorized as *portfolio income*, rather than passive activity income. Passive activity losses and credits cannot be used to offset that income or the tax levied on it.

Generally, whether a party's income from a given business operation is passive or active is not a question of the type of business involved, but a question of how involved the party was in the business. Section 469 requires that for a party's income from an activity to be considered active, he or she must have *materially participated in the activity*. Material participation is defined as that which is:

- ◆ regular;
- ◆ continuous; and,
- ◆ substantial.

Material Participation

Treasury Regulation Sec. 1.469-5T(a) provides guidance and certain *safe harbor* tests which, if met by the taxpayer, will establish material participation in an activity. The Regulation provides that a party will be considered to have materially participated in an activity if:

- ◆ he or she spent more than 500 hours in it during the year;
- ◆ the party spent over 100 hours in the activity during the taxable year; and,
   - ◆ that time was not less than the number of hours spent by anyone else in that activity or
   - ◆ participation in an activity was substantially all of the participation in that activity by anyone, regardless of how many hours were involved.

Regulation Sec. 1.469-5T(a) also provides that a party will be deemed to have materially participated in any activity that he or she had materially participated in for any five of the last ten years or in a personal service activity that he or she participated in for any three years preceding the taxable year.

EXAMPLE: Ray and Bob each owned a 50% interest in a corporation involved in the dry cleaning business. Ray worked in the business fifty hours a week, but Bob only dropped by for monthly meetings to review sales figures. Ray's income from the business is clearly active income. Any losses attributed to him from the business would be ordinary losses. Bob's income from the business is passive income. Any losses attributable to him would be passive.

Treasury Regulation Sec. 1.469-5T(a) also provides that a taxpayer may aggregate the time spent in somewhat related activities, known as *significant participation activities*, in order to reach the 500-hour level of participation in an activity. In order for an activity to be includible in the aggregation, the taxpayer must have spent more than 100 hours in that activity during the tax year. Taxpayers have been allowed considerable latitude in the types of activities that they have been permitted to group together for purposes of meeting this test. Different businesses in the same city have been aggregated, as have branches of the same business located in different cities.

EXAMPLE: Verbina opened a mens shoe store as well as a ladies dress shop in a local mall. She spends 300 hours per year in the operation of each store. Since the number of hours she spends between the two stores equals 600, she will have met the 500-hour test.

Rental Property

The most popular tax shelter used before the passive activity rules were passed was investment in rental real estate. By being able to depreciate rental properties at relatively rapid rates, investors were able to generate losses for tax purposes when they did not have actual out-of-pocket losses. The value of the rental property was actually increasing in value, rather than depreciating. As a result, Congress specifically categorized income and losses from rental activity as passive, regardless of whether or not a party who owns the property materially participated in the rental activity.

There are two exceptions concerning the income and losses from rental activity. The income and losses from rental real estate activity of someone in the real property business shall not be considered passive if the party meets the requirements of teh Code Sec. 469(c)(7)(B). Those requirements are that over half of the taxpayer's personal service performed in trades or businesses in which he or she materially participated must have been in real property trades or businesses. Also, the taxpayer must have performed over 750 hours of services in real property trades or businesses during the tax year. (Married couples who file joint returns are not allowed to add their hours of performance together in order to meet the test.)

Even individuals who are not in the real property business, but who actively participate in rental of property that they own may offset ordinary income of up to $25,000 (with net losses) from their rental activity. However, the $25,000 amount must be reduced by 50% of the amount by which the taxpayer's adjusted gross income for the taxable year exceeds $100,000. Therefore, this exception is completely phased out for a taxpayer with an adjusted gross income of $150,000 or more for the tax year.

Passive activity losses from any passive activity that are not used in any tax year may be carried forward indefinitely and used to offset subsequent passive activity income. If a taxpayer disposes of his or her entire interest in a passive activity and has unused passive activity losses that were being carried forward, the losses will no longer be considered attributable to a passive activity.

BAD DEBTS

When debts that are owed to taxpayers become *uncollectible*, a deduction is permitted for the bad debt under the Code Sec. 166, provided that certain criteria are met. No deduction will be allowed for any bad debt unless the debt is a *bona fide obligation*. For a debt to constitute a bona fide obligation, Treasury Regulation Sec. 1.166-1(c) provides that it must arise *from a debtor-creditor relationship based upon a valid and enforceable obligation to pay a fixed or determinable sum of money.*

A further requirement is that the taxpayer must have had a *basis* in the debt. To the degree that a party surrenders cash or goods in exchange for the indebtedness, his or her basis in the debt will be equal to the basis in what was given up. However, a debt that was incurred for services that the taxpayer never reported the income from or which arose from an unpaid judgment from a situation in which the taxpayer was not seeking to recover an actual economic loss sustained, will not entitle a party to a bad debt deduction in the event of default.

EXAMPLE: Antwon, a cash basis taxpayer, did construction work for a week and was to be paid $1,000 for his work. But the company that he had worked for became insolvent and could not pay him. Antwon cannot take a bad debt deduction for the unpaid wages since he had never recognized them as income on a tax return. Had he been an accrual basis taxpayer and had already recognized the income, he would be allowed to take a bad debt deduction.

Deductions of Bad Debts

Once it has been established that a taxpayer is entitled to a bad debt deduction, it must be determined *when* the debt became uncollectible. Section 166 restricts deductibility of bad debts to the year in which they became worthless. This prevents taxpayers with uncollectible debts from waiting to declare them uncollectible in a year in which their incomes are being taxed in relatively high brackets.

How a taxpayer is allowed to take a bad debt deduction depends on whether or not the taxpayer is a corporation and whether the debt is a business or nonbusiness bad debt. Corporations may deduct any of their bad debts that qualify for deduction as a *deduction against ordinary income*. Taxpayers, other than corporations, may deduct their qualified business bad debts in the same manner as corporations but must treat their nonbusiness bad debts as if they were *short-term capital losses*. This can be a severe restriction on the deduction of nonbusiness bad debts for taxpayers other than corporations since only $3,000 of capital losses may be used by them to offset ordinary income in any one tax year. Taxpayers are permitted to take a deduction for partially worthless business bad debts.

However, they are not allowed to do so for partially worthless nonbusiness bad debts until final settlement of the debt at less than full value has occurred.

The IRS is particularly suspicious of taxpayers who take bad debt deductions for loans to relatives, partnerships, and/or corporations in which they have an ownership interest. It may appear that transfers to such parties were gifts or investments that the taxpayer later decided to try and pass off as loans that became uncollectible. Therefore, it is *imperative* that parties who lend money to such borrowers have them execute promissory notes that provide details for repayment and other terms of the loan. It is also advisable for the lender to take a security interest in any collateral pledged to secure the loan and to record that security interest in the public records.

Chapter 7
Taxable Income

After determining adjusted gross income, the next step in arriving at a party's tax liability is to calculate his or her *taxable income*. The definition of taxable income, provided in Sec. 63 of the Internal Revenue Code, is gross income minus *allowable deductions* (other than the standard deduction).

CATEGORIES OF DEDUCTIONS

Allowable deductions include the *itemized deductions* specifically set forth in the Internal Revenue Code in various sections, and the deduction for *personal exemptions* provided for in the Code Sec. 151. For those who do not itemize deduction, Sec. 63 defines taxable income as *adjusted gross income* minus (1) the *standard deduction* and (2) the deduction for *personal exemptions* provided for in Sec. 151.

The Standard Deduction

The approach to the standard deduction taken by Congress, as reflected by Sec. 63, was to establish some base amount of income necessary for individuals to meet their needs and exclude that amount from federal income taxation. Section 63 provides that the standard deduction base is to be adjusted to reflect increases in the *cost of living*, but rounded down to the nearest $50 increment. A certain percentage of the base amount of the standard deduction is then taken to establish the standard deduction for each taxpayer based on the party's filing status.

Individual Itemized Deductions

Congress has seen fit to allow individual taxpayers to deduct certain expenditures from their adjusted gross incomes in lieu of the standard deduction. Unlike the *business expense deduction* (the Code Sec. 162) that permits the deduction of any reasonable business expense that can be shown to be *ordinary and necessary* for the specific taxpayer in question, the expenses that *individuals* are permitted to deduct are very specific. The possible exceptions to this are certain *other expenses* provided for on Schedule A of *Form 1040*. Also, rather than authorizing the deduction of various expenses for individuals in a single Code section, the various expenses are made deductible through a series of individual Code sections.

The itemized deductions available to individuals are deductions *from* adjusted gross income. The importance of this distinction is repeatedly brought to light in calculating total itemized deductions. Some of the deductions from adjusted gross income can be deducted only to the extent that they exceed a set *percentage* of the taxpayer's adjusted gross income. Even after a determination is made that part of a taxpayer's expenditures qualify as a deduction from adjusted gross income, his or her total must exceed the party's allowable standard deduction. If this is not the case, the taxpayer would be better off not to itemize deductions. The fact that he or she was allowed to take a deduction for certain expenditures would offer no tax savings at all. However, deductions *for* adjusted gross income, which are subtracted from gross income in calculating adjusted gross income, are allowed *in addition* to the standard deduction.

Those who earn relatively high incomes face still another obstacle to using their itemized deductions to reduce their taxable income. At certain levels (which vary based on filing status and are adjusted annually for inflation) a taxpayer must begin to *reduce* the amount of itemized deductions that are available to him or her as a deduction from adjusted gross income. Schedule A of *Form 1040*, which is used to calculate itemized deductions and must be filed with the *Form 1040* if a taxpayer itemizes deductions, concludes by directing those with over certain levels of adjusted gross income to a worksheet. This worksheet is used to calculate the portion of the party's itemized deductions that he or she will be allowed to deduct.

ITEMIZED DEDUCTIONS

Many of the itemized deductions that taxpayers are permitted to take are purely *personal expenditures*. Among them are part of a taxpayer's *medical and dental expense*. These expenses include not only payments for prevention, diagnosis, treatment, or cure of disease, but also include the cost of transportation to receive the medical care, health insurance premiums paid, and the cost of long-term care prescribed by a licensed, healthcare practitioner for a chronically ill individual. Drugs are considered to be a deductible medical expense only if they are prescribed by a physician.

However, it is rare for taxpayers to actually take a deduction for medical expenses. Since medical expenses that are paid or reimbursed by insurance do not qualify for deduction, those who have medical insurance coverage or other plans usually have relatively little uninsured medical expenses. Even though medical insurance premiums are a deductible medical expense (to the degree that an employer pays them or a self-employed person pays them and takes a deduction for adjusted gross income for them elsewhere on *Form 1040*) they are not deductible as a medical expense on a taxpayer's Schedule A. Finally, even a taxpayer who has medical expenses that qualify for deduction may take a deduction for those expenses only to the extent that they exceed 7.5% of adjusted gross income.

In light of these restrictions, a self-employed individual would likely be able to reduce his or her income tax liability by purchasing a health insurance policy with greater insurance coverage, despite higher premiums, rather than limited coverage and relatively low premiums. Such a choice would give a deduction for the higher premium and reduce the uninsured medical expenses for which he or she is unlikely to be entitled to take an itemized deduction.

EXAMPLE: Clay is a self-employed, automobile stereo designer and installer. His annual adjusted gross income has averaged $110,000 for the last few years and is likely to remain about the same. His medical insurance provider has offered him a choice. Clay can purchase the *Platinum Plan* for $750 per month that pays all but $10.00 of each visit to a doctor's office, all but $10.00 for each prescription, and all but $50.00 for each hospital stay, or he can keep the *Iron Plan* for $300 per month which pays nothing for routine office visits, covers the cost of each prescription in excess of $50.00, and pays 80% of the cost of treatment either in or out of the hospital after the total cost exceeds $1,500 per person. The extra $5,400 in annual insurance premiums to get the Platinum, rather than the Iron coverage, seems excessive to Clay.

He analyzed his family's medical expenses for the last year and found that if he had been covered by the Platinum Plan, he would have paid out $4,900 less in uninsured medical costs than he did under the Iron Plan. Since only the part of Clay's itemized medical expenses that exceeds 7.5% of his $110,000 adjusted gross income (a total of $8,250) will qualify for a medical expense deduction on his Schedule A, he will likely get no medical expense deduction for his uninsured medical expenses if he remains with the Iron Plan and his family's medical expenses remain about the same. However, if he selects the Platinum Plan, he will be allowed to fully deduct his entire self-employed health care premium as a deduction for adjusted gross income on the front of his *Form 1040* and realize tax savings from the additional $5,400 premium (which would most likely be $1,350, since he would almost certainly be in the 25% marginal tax bracket).

NOTE: *There are several personal deductions that are generated by taxpayers' business activities. Some deductions are allowed for both individuals and businesses. The rules for taking such deductions are often the same for businesses and individuals, as the rules for taking the business deduction are merely a modified version of the rules for taking the deduction as an individual.*

Interest and Taxes Paid

A personal deduction is allowed for interest paid on a second mortgage, line of credit, or home equity loan if they are secured by a mortgage on a main or second home. To qualify for this deduction, the combined amount cannot exceed $100,000 on the party's primary and second home. Also, the combined total indebtedness on the properties does not exceed their fair market value.

Taxpayers are also allowed a deduction for student loan interest. However, eligibility for this deduction is phased out at relatively high income levels.

Section 164 of the Internal Revenue Code permits taxpayers to take an itemized deduction for some types of taxes that are imposed on them and paid during the year. State, local, and foreign income taxes are eligible to be taken as itemized deductions on Schedule A of *Form 1040*. Although those who pay foreign income taxes have the option of taking a tax credit for those taxes rather than a deduction, the credit is often the better choice. Paid state, local, and foreign real estate taxes are also eligible for deduction on Schedule A of *Form 1040*, even when they are paid indirectly through payments to a cooperative housing corporation that then pays the taxes. State and local taxes on personal property are deductible on Schedule A, as well.

Section 164 also permits the deduction of taxes that are part of the cost of conducting a trade or business or that are incurred in producing rents, royalties, or other income. However, these all generally qualify as business deductions for adjusted gross income that can be used to offset earnings subject to self-employment tax. (These would generally better serve a taxpayer when taken as a *business deduction* rather than an itemized deduction on Schedule A.)

A deduction for one half of *self-employment tax* is also provided for in Sec. 164 as a deduction for adjusted gross income on the front of *Form 1040*. This benefits even those taxpayers who do not have sufficient itemized deductions to exceed the standard deduction, although it cannot be used to offset any part of the party's earnings that are subject to self-employment tax.

Among the more notable taxes that individuals are *not* eligible to take as an itemized deduction are federal income taxes, sales taxes, FICA taxes, estate and gift taxes, and any payments to governmental entities for which goods, services, or personal privileges are received in return. However, to the degree that such taxes are an ordinary and necessary business expense, they not only are deductible against income subject to income taxation, but also offset earnings subject to self-employment taxes.

EXAMPLE 1: The state of Arkansas held a lottery that permitted winners to purchase one of 1,000 licenses to hunt Ozark black bears. Christine was a winner and bought the license from the state for $500. She will not be allowed to take an itemized deduction on her Schedule A as a deductible tax for the cost of the license, since she is not in the business of hunting and she got something in return for the payment to the state.

EXAMPLE 2: Don is a professional fishing guide. The state in which he resides requires that he buy a professional fisherman's license in order to engage in his occupation. The annual cost of the license is $1,000. Don will be allowed to deduct the cost of the license as a business expense on Schedule C of his *Form 1040*.

EXAMPLE 3: In order to conduct his business as a professional fishing guide, Don purchased a boat, motor, and trailer at a cost of $10,000. He was charged $800 in sales tax on the purchase. Don cannot deduct the sales tax as an itemized deduction on Schedule A of *Form 1040*, but he can add it to the cost of the boat and increase his basis for purposes of calculating depreciation. If he prefers *and* he is eligible, he can expense the cost of the boat in the year of acquisition, as provided for in the Code Sec. 179.

Investment Interest

Taxpayers are allowed to deduct the interest they pay on most indebtedness attributable to property held as an investment. *Investment property* is that which generates gross income from interest, dividends, annuities, or royalties not derived in the course of a trade or business. The *investment interest deduction* is authorized by the Code Sec. 163(d)(5). Congress has prohibited the deduction of investment interest to the extent that it exceeds a party's net investment income.

No investment interest expense deduction is permitted for interest incurred on investments that generate *tax-exempt income,* investments regarded as *passive activities* (defined as conduct of a trade or business in which a taxpayer did not materially participate), or interest incurred on *straddles* (a rather sophisticated investment strategy involving taking simultaneous long and short positions in the same security).

Net investment income is the total of interest, dividends, annuities, royalties, or other such income, less investment expenses other than interest, such as fees paid to a financial planner or the cost of publications for investors. Commissions charged by brokers to execute a transaction are not regarded as an investment expense, but merely increase the cost of acquisition on purchases and they reduce the net proceeds upon sale.

Investment expenses themselves are deductible on Schedule A as a *Miscellaneous Itemized Deduction* to the extent that the total of such deduction exceeds 2% of the taxpayer's adjusted gross income for the year. To the extent that no deduction is allowed for these expenses due to failure of the total miscellaneous itemized deductions to exceed 2% of a party's adjusted gross income, he or she will not be required to reduce his or her investment income by the amount of those expenses.

However, in calculating a party's miscellaneous itemized deduction, all such expenses, other than investment expenses, are applied against the 2% of adjusted gross income limitation first. To the extent that the limitation is exceeded by noninterest investment expenses for which a miscellaneous itemized deduction is then allowed, those expenses must be deducted from the party's gross investment income to determine net investment income.

To the extent that a taxpayer has insufficient net investment income to fully deduct his or her investment interest, the interest deduction may be carried over to the next tax year. Normally, net investment income does not include net gains from the sale of investment property, but taxpayers may elect to include it in order to raise their investment incomes and permit them to fully deduct their investment interest expenses.

However, if such an election is made, the gain that was realized must then be taxed as ordinary income, whereas it may have otherwise qualified to be taxed as long-term, capital gain, which is subject to a maximum tax rate of only 15%. Therefore, the taxpayer making an election to treat long-term, capital gain as investment income would be using his or her investment interest deduction to offset capital gain that would have been taxed at only 15%. This would occur rather than carrying the deduction forward and using it to offset ordinary income that could be subject to as much as a 35% rate of taxation, depending on the taxpayer's income and filing status.

EXAMPLE: Rusty, whose adjusted gross income for the year was $45,000, earned dividend income of $2,000 from stock he had bought partially on credit through what is known as a *margin account*. The interest on his margin account was $2,200 for the year. His only investment expense was a subscription to an investment information service that cost $400 per year. Rusty had other miscellaneous itemized deductions subject to the 2% of adjusted gross income limit that totaled $800. He will be entitled to take an investment interest deduction of $1,700 and must carry over the remaining $500 of investment interest expense to the next year for possible deduction.

Rusty's investment interest deduction is calculated by first subtracting 2% of his adjusted gross income (.02 x $45.000), which is $900, from his miscellaneous itemized deductions subject to the 2% of adjusted gross income limit ($800 of noninvestment related deductions plus $400 of noninterest investment related deductions), which is $1,200, leaving a total deductible amount of $300. Since noninvestment related, miscellaneous itemized deductions must be offset by the 2% adjusted gross income deduction first in calculating the net deduction, the full $800 of Rusty's deductions in this category is entirely offset, as is $100 of his noninterest investment expense.

Therefore, the full $300 of miscellaneous itemized deductions remaining after the 2% of adjusted gross income limitation is applied and Rusty is eligible to take on his Schedule A. The itemized deductions are attributable to noninterest investment expenses that must be deducted from his investment income ($2,000 - $300) to arrive at his net investment income of $1,700. Since Sec. 163 prohibits a taxpayer from taking an investment interest deduction in excess of his investment income, Rusty will be allowed to take a deduction of only $1,700, leaving the $500 difference in his investment interest expense. The net investment income ($2,200 - $1,700) will be carried forward to the next tax year for deduction.

If an individual has investment interest expense in excess of interest income, has deductible investment expenses other than interest, or has investment interest expenses that were carried over from a prior year, *Form 4952* must be used to calculate his or her investment interest expense deduction and then the deduction must be transferred over to Schedule A. Otherwise, individuals may deduct their investment interest expense directly on Schedule A without having to file *Form 4952*.

Interest Incurred to Produce Rents or Royalties

The full amount of interest expense allocable to rental activities and properly attributable to the tax year in question is generally fully deductible on an individual's Schedule E of *Form 1040*. Taxpayers must keep records to show that the proceeds of the debt on each property were used for the purpose of producing rent or royalty income, thereby qualifying interest payments on the debts for deductions associated with production of rent or royalty income. If a party is obligated for only part of the indebtedness on property producing rent or royalty income, he or she may take a deduction for only the obligated part.

Financial institutions are required to send out a *Form 1098* reporting the amount of deductible interest paid for the year by a mortgagor. The figures on the combined *Form 1098* for each rent or royalty producing property are to be reported on the *Mortgage Interest Paid to Banks, etc.* line of Schedule E. Interest paid on property held for the production of rent or royalty income, but not reported on a *Form 1098*, should be reported on the *Other Interest* line of Schedule E.

There is no direct limitation on the amount of interest expense deduction that can be taken for indebtedness on property held for the production of rent or royalty income. However, since rental of real or personal property is generally considered to be a *passive activity* from which losses can be used to offset a maximum of only $25,000 of ordinary income (such as wages or interest income). Interest deductions are indirectly limited on rental property to the degree that they contribute to losses in excess of $25,000 for taxpayers without passive activity income.

Business Interest

Since the interest expense incurred on loans related to a party's trade or business usually qualifies as an ordinary, necessary business expense, it would be deductible under the provisions of the Code Sec. 162 even if the deduction were not specifically allowed under the Code Sec. 163. In order to qualify for a *business interest deduction*, a taxpayer must use the proceeds of the loan in his or her trade or business and be held legally liable on the debt. Both the debtor and creditor must intend that the debt be repaid and there must be a true debtor-creditor relationship between the parties.

The governing factor on whether or not a party may deduct interest as a business expense is how the loan proceeds are used. Even if personal property were pledged as collateral for a loan, but the proceeds were used in the debtor's trade or business, the interest on the loan would be deductible as a business expense. Likewise, if business property is pledged as collateral for a loan, but the proceeds are used for nonbusiness purposes, the interest on the loan would not be deductible as a business expense.

A debtor will virtually always be better off taking interest expense as a business deduction rather than by taking the deduction in any other way. By taking a business deduction for interest expense, a debtor does not have to be concerned with whether or not his or her itemized deductions will exceed the standard deduction, since it will be a deduction *for* adjusted gross income. Moreover, the business interest deduction that is taken on Schedule C of *Form 1040* by self-employed individuals, will reduce the individual's earnings that are subject to self-employment tax, as well as income tax.

Mortgages

In an effort to acquire loans for business purposes at favorable rates, many owners of small businesses take out mortgages on their homes. By pledging their homes as collateral for the loans, the business owners are entitled to take a deduction for home mortgage interest expense, unless the loan amounts have exceeded the deductible limits, despite the fact that the loan proceeds are used for business purposes. To the extent that the loan amount exceeds the deductible limits, the interest attributable to the excess is deductible on Schedule C on the *other* line under the space given for the deduction of interest, provided that the loan proceeds were used in the debtor's trade or business.

In fact, a debtor who secures a loan in the form of a home mortgage that qualifies for the home mortgage interest deduction, but uses the loan proceeds in his or her trade or business, may choose to take the interest payments on the loan as a business interest deduction, rather than a home mortgage interest deduction. This option is provided for in Treasury Regulation Sec. 1.163-10T(o)(5).

Once the election is made to treat a loan that is secured by a qualified residence as if it were not secured by a qualified residence, the election will be effective not only for the year in which it was initially made, but also for all future taxable years, unless the Commissioner of the IRS consents to the revocation of the election. Therefore, if a taxpayer elects to treat a loan that is secured by a qualified residence as if it were not secured by a qualified residence, and then discontinues the business still owing money on the loan, he or she will not be allowed to take a home mortgage interest deduction.

Unless interest rates have moved upward substantially or the debtor's credit rating has suffered due to his or her business reversals, it may be possible for a debtor who cannot take a deduction for home mortgage interest (due to having elected to treat the loan as not secured by a qualified residence) to alleviate the problem. This is accomplished by refinancing the debt and replacing the nonqualifying loan with one that qualifies for the home mortgage interest deduction.

EXAMPLE: Doe opened a gift shop. In order to obtain capital for her store, she took out a $90,000 home equity loan, securing the loan with a mortgage on her main residence that already had a $100,000 first mortgage on it and has a fair market value of $200,000. She elected to treat her home equity loan as not being secured by a qualified residence. She will be allowed to take a deduction for the interest on her home equity loan as a business deduction on her Schedule C.

After eighteen months, poor sales forced Doe to close her gift shop. The money that she had obtained on her home equity loan had been used to pay wages, rent, and other expenses and was not available to pay back the loan. She was unable to refinance the loan due to delinquent indebtedness in connection with her business. Doe will not be allowed to deduct the interest on her home equity loan as home mortgage interest due to her previous election, unless she can obtain the consent of the Commissioner of the IRS to revoke the election. She can no longer take a business deduction for the interest since she is no longer operating a business.

If the fair market value of Doe's home had been only $150,000, she could have taken a home mortgage interest deduction for the interest attributable to only the first $50,000 of her home equity loan. The amount of her home equity loan plus her first mortgage of $100,000 would equal the $150,000 fair market value of her home. She could still have taken a business deduction for the interest attributable to the remaining $40,000 of her home equity loan. In the case that she closed her business, she would lose her right to continue taking the business expense deduction on the $40,000 part of her home equity loan in excess of the fair market value of her home. However, she could continue to deduct the interest payments on the first $50,000 of the home equity loan, as a home mortgage interest deduction.

Gifts to Charity

A taxpayer who makes eligible gifts to qualified organizations is permitted to take an itemized deduction for those gifts on Schedule A on *Form 1040*. However, the Code Sec. 170 and the corresponding Treasury Regulations impose a number of restrictions on the deductibility of gifts to charity. Contributions are capped at a certain percentage of adjusted gross income.

Cash contributions and the fair market value of contributions of property made to qualified organizations can be deducted up to an amount equal to 50% of the individual donor's adjusted gross income.

If a taxpayer makes gifts to a charity that does not qualify as a 50% limit organization or if he or she donates property on which he or she has a *long-term capital gain* and bases the deduction on the *fair market value of the appreciated property*, the total itemized deduction for those contributions for the year is limited to 30% of his or her adjusted gross income for the year. A party who donates such *appreciated property* to a charity that is not a 50% limit organization is not permitted to take a total itemized deduction for those contributions in excess of 20% of his or her adjusted gross income.

The charitable organization to which a donation is made should be able to inform its donors whether or not it is a 50% limit organization. Donors can also obtain that information by calling the *Tax Exempt/Government Entities Customer Service Department* of the IRS at 877-829-5500. Any charitable contributions that cannot be taken because they exceed the limit for such deductions may be carried over and deducted in a later year for up to five years, but no further.

Contributions of Services

No deduction is available for the *contribution of an individual's time or service*, even when the contribution is made to a qualified organization. However, *out-of-pocket expenses* associated with contributed services, such as the cost of transportation or the cost of buying and cleaning uniforms, are deductible. An exception to this is the cost of child care necessary to permit a person to perform volunteer work. This is not a deductible expense as a charitable contribution.

EXAMPLE: Robert drove to the Red Cross office in order to give a blood donation. He had to pay his babysitter an extra $10.00 to stay with his children longer than usual so he could give the blood donation. Robert can take no deduction for the blood that he donated or the extra $10.00 that he paid the babysitter, but he can deduct the cost of transportation to the Red Cross office as a charitable deduction. A cents-per-mile deduction is provided for in the instructions to Schedule A for those who do not wish to keep up with the actual cost of transportation for charitable purposes.

Cash Contributions

The type of records that must be generated and maintained in order to substantiate a charitable contribution depends on the amount of the contribution and on whether the contribution was in cash or property. In general, the higher the amount of the contribution, the more extensive the records that must be kept to support the deduction.

If a donor makes an individual cash contribution of less than $250, even if other contributions to the same recipient would put the combined total of those contributions well over $250, the only records required to support the deduction would be canceled checks or account statements showing the amount of the donation, the date it was made, and the charity that received it. A receipt from the recipient with similar information would also be sufficient proof to support a deduction for a cash contribution that is less than $250.

A party taking a contribution for auto expenses in connection with charitable service can support the deduction claimed with a written record of the date, the amount of mileage driven, and the identity of the charity served.

Deductions for cash contributions (other than by payroll deduction) in excess of $250 each, must be supported by a written acknowledgment from the qualified organization receiving them, stating the amount of the contributions and the value of goods or services, if any, that were received as a result of the contributions. This acknowledgment must be received by the taxpayer on or before the earlier of the dates the taxpayer files his or her return for the year in which the contribution was made or the due date for such return, including extensions. If a donor makes multiple cash contributions in excess of $250 to the same donee and does not make them by payroll deduction, the deduction of the contributions may be supported by a single acknowledgment showing the party's total contributions or by a separate acknowledgment for each contribution.

Noncash Contributions

Noncash contributions require the most stringent documentation to support a charitable contribution deduction. There are four different categories of noncash contributions that have separate requirements for supporting a deduction. The categories are determined by the fair market value of each contribution.

1. Noncash contributions of less than $250 require a receipt from the recipient showing its name and location, the date of the gift, and a reasonably detailed description of the property that is donated. Additionally, for each donated item, the donor must maintain his or her own records that contain:
   - the name and address of the donee;
   - the date of the gift;
   - a reasonably detailed description of the property;
   - the value of the contribution and how it was determined; and,
   - any terms or conditions attached to the gift.

2. A taxpayer who takes a charitable gift deduction for noncash donations of items valued at $250 to $500 must obtain and keep a written acknowledgment of the contribution from the recipient. The acknowledgment must show the name and address of the donee, the date of the gift, a reasonably detailed description of the property, and whether goods or services were given to the donor as a result of the contribution and, if so, the estimated fair market value of them. The taxpayer must also maintain his or her own records with the same information as the records for noncash gifts valued at less than $250.

3. Deductions for donations of noncash property valued at more than $500, but not over $5,000, must be supported by the

same information as for gifts valued between $250 and $500, with the taxpayer keeping additional information as to how and when the donor got the property, and the donor's cost or other basis in the donated property.

4. Those who take deductions for noncash property valued in excess of $5,000 must meet all of the requirements for supporting a deduction for noncash contributions valued at over $500 but not over $5,000, plus they must obtain a *qualified written appraisal* of the donated property. For purposes of determining whether the value of noncash donations exceeds $5,000, taxpayers must combine all similar items donated to all donees during the taxable year. (The appraisal requirement does not apply to donations of publicly traded securities.)

Reporting

Most taxpayers are permitted to take their charitable contributions on Schedule A of *Form 1040*. However, taxpayers who take deductions for total noncash contributions of over $500 must also file *Form 8283*. This form requires extensive information concerning donated property, an acknowledgment by the donee, and an attachment of appraisals when necessary.

EXAMPLE: In June, Igor donated $2,500 worth of collectible stamps to his local library, $3,500 worth of collectible stamps to the college he attended, and $1,500 worth of collectible stamps to his church. Since all of the stamps are of a single category of collateral and their total combined value for the taxable year exceeds $5,000, Igor must get the stamps appraised by a qualified appraiser of stamps. He must also file a *Form 8283* with a copy of the appraisal attached in order to substantiate his deduction.

Contributions by Businesses

Corporations that are taxed under subchapter C of the Internal Revenue Code, known as C corporations, are allowed to take deductions for charitable contributions. The rules concerning the deductibility of corporate charitable contributions are much the same as those for allowing individuals to take deductions for contributions. However, there are three significant differences between corporate and individual deductions for contributions.

Individuals cannot take a deduction for a contribution that has merely been *pledged*. The deduction is available only when the contribution is actually paid. C corporations that are on the accrual method of accounting are allowed to take a charitable deduction for the year in which it is authorized by the board of directors, as long as it is actually paid by the 15th day of the third month following the end of the corporation's taxable year.

While, in most cases, individuals are allowed to take deductions for charitable contributions up to an amount equal to 50% of their adjusted gross income, C corporations cannot take deductions in excess of 10% of their adjusted taxable income for the year. Corporate adjusted taxable income is merely taxable income before allowances are made for the charitable contribution, loss carrybacks, and the dividends-received deduction. Corporations that are unable to fully deduct their contributions due to this limitation may carry them forward for up to five years.

The deduction for noncash contributions of appreciated tangible personal property by a C corporation is limited to the fair market value of the gift, less the long-term capital gain that would have been realized had the property been sold. An exception is if the gift is for a use related to the recipient's tax exempt purpose and the recipient is not a private nonoperating foundation, in which case the corporation is entitled to deduct the full fair market value of the gift.

C corporations that donate inventory used to care for the ill, needy, or infants, scientific research property or computer technology, and equipment to qualified educational institutions may take a charitable deduction equal to the corporation's basis in the property plus one half of the difference in its basis and the fair market value of the donated property. This deduction is limited to a maximum equal to twice the donor's basis in the property.

Partnerships and business entities that are taxed as partnerships are not allowed to deduct charitable contributions in calculating their incomes. Charitable contributions made by such organizations are reported in amounts proportionate to each owner's share of the organiza-

tion on his or her annual *Form K-1*. The owners then must take the figures from *Form K-1* and put them on either *Form 8283* or directly on
Schedule A, depending on which is appropriate. They must use their
share of the organization's charitable contributions to calculate their personal itemized deductions. Therefore, the owners of business entities that
are taxed as partnerships are unable to convert charitable contributions
into deductions for adjusted gross income by causing the contributions
to be made at the business entity level, rather than individually.

EXAMPLE: Ben and Jerry owned a partnership that was on course to make
a profit of $500,000 for the year. Each of them wanted to
make a $5,000 contribution to St. Jude Children's Research
Hospital. Since neither of them had significant itemized
deductions to take and would therefore realize no benefit from
an individual deduction for the contribution, they decided to
have the partnership make the contribution and reduce the
amount of income that it would generate for each of them.

Their plan will not work. Rather than their partnership
reducing its income due to the contribution, the organization's income will remain the same and each of them will get
a *K-1* that shows a $5,000 contribution that each one is enti-
tled to deduct on each person's Schedule A.

Job Expenses

An employee who incurs expenses that are related to his or her job is
entitled to take a deduction for those expenses to the extent that they
have not been reimbursed by his or her employer. Typical of these
expenses are *travel* and *transportation costs*, *meals* and *entertainment expenses*,
and various other business-related expenses that are *ordinary and necessary*
in carrying on the employee's business, such as *office expenses*, *job-related
education*, and the *cost of promotional materials* and *postage*.

Employee job expenses must be reported on a *Form 2106*. The total
amount of a taxpayer's *unreimbursed employee business expenses* shown on
Form 2106 is then transferred to the *Job Expenses and Most Other
Miscellaneous Deductions* section of Schedule A. A comparison of the tax
benefits offered by deductions of employee business expenses to the ben-

efits from business expense deductions of self-employed parties and various business entities vividly illustrates the considerable advantage that deductions *for* adjusted gross income offer over adjustments *from* adjusted gross income.

Business expenses deducted by the self-employed and various business entities reduce the taxpayer's income *dollar for dollar*. These deductions are allowed in addition to an individual's itemized deductions or standard deduction, so there is no set amount that the deduction must exceed before it will benefit a taxpayer. Moreover, business expenses deducted by the self-employed and business entities are not subject to being partially offset by some percentage of a taxpayer's gross income. The fact that such deductions reduce the earnings of self-employed taxpayers and some business owners that are subject to self-employment tax is particularly beneficial.

On the other hand, deductions for job-related, business expenses of employees are added to most of the taxpayer's other miscellaneous deductions. The total is then reduced by an amount equal to 2% of the party's adjusted gross income. The remainder is then added to the taxpayer's other itemized deductions to determine if their total exceeds the standard deduction available to the party. Since most people do not have a significant amount of miscellaneous deductions, a party who has job-related expenses will likely lose the benefit of the deduction for those expenses in an amount equal to 2% of adjusted gross income, even if itemized deductions exceed the standard deduction. If a taxpayer's standard deduction exceeds his or her itemized deduction, no tax benefit will be received from the itemized deductions even if part of those deductions were attributable to job-related expenses incurred in earning his or her taxable income.

Furthermore, even if a taxpayer's itemized deductions exceed his or her standard deduction, all or part of the benefit of having itemized his or her deductions may still be lost. This is due to the provisions of the Code Sec. 68 that reduce some of the itemized deductions for those who earn relatively high incomes. The instructions to Schedule A provide a worksheet for calculating the portion of itemized deductions that will be available as an offset of adjusted gross income in determining taxable income.

Regardless of how much of an itemized deduction may be generated by a taxpayer's job expenses, the deduction will not reduce self-employment tax liability whatsoever. This is due to the fact that, unlike the deductible business expenses of self-employed people and owners of some types of businesses, (which are not only deductions for gross income, but are also deductible from income subject to self-employment tax), job expenses are strictly a deduction from adjusted gross income. That type of deduction can never be used to offset earnings subject to self-employment tax.

EXAMPLE 1: Martin is a self-employed manufacturer's representative who sells ingredients to commercial bakeries. His gross income for his most recent tax year was $48,000. His gross income was reduced by $4,400 in business expenses that were primarily due to job related travel. He had some itemized deductions available to him, which he took. Martin's $4,400 business expense deduction will reduce both the amount of his income subject to self-employment taxes and the amount subject to income tax by the full $4,400. He will be allowed to take the full standard deduction for his filing status, as well, as a further reduction in his earnings that are subject to income tax.

EXAMPLE 2: Lewis, an acquaintance of Martin, works for a competitor as an employee. Last year, Lewis had job-related expenses of $4,300 and was paid $44,000 as his adjusted gross income. His itemized deductions, consisting in large part of his job-related expenses, less 2% of his adjusted gross income, were $210 less than the standard deduction that he took on his tax return.

Since Lewis' job-related expenses were deductions from his adjusted gross income, they were not permitted to offset any of his earnings subject to FICA taxes. Since his standard deduction exceeded his itemized deductions, his job-related expenses did not offset any of his income subject to income taxes whatsoever.

Miscellaneous Deductions not Subject to Reduction

The final category of itemized deductions on Schedule A is *Other Miscellaneous Deductions*. The miscellaneous deductions in this category differ from those in the category that includes job expenses in that their total is not reduced by an amount equal to 2% of the taxpayer's adjusted gross income. There are very few items that qualify for this type of deduction. Those that do are specifically listed in the Schedule A instructions. Among the more common ones are:

- casualty and theft losses from income producing property (discussed in Chapter 6);
- gambling losses up to the amount of the taxpayer's reported gambling winnings;
- expenses incurred by a disabled person that are related to his or her work and necessitated by the disability; and,
- federal estate tax paid on inheritances consisting of wages that the deceased had earned, but not received, and were included in the heirs' earnings for income tax purposes, known as *income in respect of a decedent.*

Total Itemized Deductions

The final step in calculating the total amount of itemized deductions available to a taxpayer is to add the totals of the various allowable deductions entered in each category of Schedule A. It is at this stage that those with incomes in excess of a specified amount must use the worksheet in the Schedule A instructions to determine whether some of their total itemized deductions will be disallowed. The income level at which a party's itemized deductions will be reduced is subject to annual adjustments to reflect inflation as provided for in the Code Sec. 68(b)(2).

EXEMPTIONS

In calculating taxable income, a taxpayer is allowed to reduce adjusted gross income by not only the larger of his or her standard deduction or allowable itemized deductions, but also by his or her allowance for *exemptions,* as well. The amount of the *exemption deduction*, stated on the line that is designated on *Form 1040* for the total exemption deduction to be taken, is adjusted annually, as provided for in the Code Sec. 151(d)(4). The exemptions that are available are *personal exemptions* and exemptions for *dependants*. The instructions to *Form 1040* generally offer a relatively comprehensive explanation of the requirements that must be met in order to qualify to take an exemption deduction.

Chapter 8
Taxes

Most small businesses are not taxable entities. Various forms of partnerships and organizations that choose to be taxed as partnerships, such as corporations that have chosen to be taxed under subchapter S of the Internal Revenue Code, as well as limited liability companies that have chosen to be taxed as partnerships, must file tax returns that show their profits and losses and the amount attributed to each owner. However, the income of such organizations is deemed to *pass through* the company to the owners. The organization will have no liability for taxes on the income. Each owner's share of income from such entities is reported to him or her and to the IRS on a *Form K-1*. The owner must then report those earnings on the appropriate Schedule of *Form 1040*. Therefore, the income generated by most small businesses is simply a part of each individual owner's personal income.

Corporations that do not choose to be taxed under subchapter S of the Internal Revenue Code are taxed under subchapter C. These *C corporations* are taxed on their *net earnings* and, if the corporation makes payments from its net profits to its shareholders, they must then report those dividends as income on their individual returns and pay tax of up to 15% on them. In order to avoid this double taxation, most owners of small C corporations simply pay themselves high enough salaries and bonuses that are a deductible expense to the corporation, to leave little, if any, profit at the corporate level. Of course, the compensation taken from the corporation by the owner/employee must be reported on his or her personal tax return as wages on *Form 1040* which, once again, causes the incidence of taxation of small business income to occur at the individual level, rather than the company level.

In light of the fact that most small business profits are actually taxed as some form of individual income, an analysis of U.S. taxation of small businesses should center on taxation of individuals. Although basic federal income taxes are probably what most people think of when the topic of federal taxation arises, it is not the only federal tax affecting most taxpayers. In fact, many U.S. taxpayers pay considerably less in income taxes than they do in other federal taxes.

INDIVIDUAL FEDERAL INCOME TAXES

Once a taxpayer has done the necessary calculations to determine taxable income, he or she must merely apply the appropriate tax rate to his or her taxable income in order to determine his or her *federal income tax liability*. The U.S. federal income tax is considered to be a *progressive tax* because the rates of taxation increase as taxpayer's taxable incomes increase. This progressiveness is accomplished in the U.S. by establishing income segments, known as *tax brackets*, and applying higher tax rates to higher segments of a taxpayer's income. As a taxpayer's income rises and enters higher tax brackets, the higher rates will apply only to the income in the higher bracket. Therefore, *contrary to popular belief,* an increase in income cannot cause a taxpayer to incur an increase in tax liability that exceeds his or her increase in income.

Tax brackets vary on the basis of filing status. The bracket that is subject to the lowest tax rate (10%) is the first $7,000 of taxable income for taxpayers filing single in either 2003 or 2004, the first $14,000 for married taxpayers filing joint returns, and $10,000 for those filing as head of household. Because the *Jobs and Growth Tax Relief Reconciliation Act of 2003* temporarily increased the 10% bracket in 2003 and 2004 by $1,000 for single taxpayers and $2,000 for those who are married and filing jointly (in an effort to stimulate the economy), the brackets will shrink back to $6,000 and $12,000 respectively for 2005 through 2007.

The brackets will then be restored to their 2003-2004 levels in 2008. There are provisions for some adjustments in the bracket size to reflect inflation. There are also brackets of 15%, 25%, 28%, 33%, and 35%.

The instructions to *Form 1040* contain a tax table that shows the tax liability for each filing status at various levels of annual ordinary income up to $100,000. Those who make in excess of $100,000 in ordinary income for the year must use the *Tax Rate Schedules* provided in the *Form 1040* instructions to calculate their tax liability. Taxpayers who have some income in the form of long-term capital gains must calculate their tax liability on Schedule D of *Form 1040* in order to prevent those gains from being taxed in excess of the maximum 15% capital gains tax rate.

ALTERNATIVE MINIMUM TAX

Some taxpayers with relatively substantial incomes have greatly reduced federal income tax liabilities or even no federal income tax liability at all, due to collecting income from sources that are given special tax treatment and using tax deductions and credits. Congress established the *Alternative Maximum Tax (AMT)* to prevent these taxpayers from avoiding the payment of at least some minimum amount of federal income tax.

The AMT, which is calculated on *Form 6251*, accomplishes its purpose by requiring taxpayers to determine the alternative minimum taxable incomes, subtracting the AMT exemption, and then applying the AMT rate to the remainder. If a taxpayer's AMT on *Form 6251* exceeds his or her regular federal income tax liability, the excess of the AMT must be reported on *Form 1040*.

Calculating Alternative Minimum Taxable Income

The calculation of *alternative minimum taxable income* (AMTI) is accomplished in Part I of *Form 6251* and begins with the taxpayer's adjusted gross income. If a taxpayer itemized deductions, he or she is allowed to subtract his or her allowance for itemized deductions, as shown on Schedule A, from adjusted gross income, but must add back part or all of some of the deductions. Among the deductions that must be added back are:

◆ any deductions taken for property taxes or any other state and local taxes;

◆ all miscellaneous deductions, including those for employee business expenses;

◆ any deduction taken for interest on a home mortgage that was not taken out to buy, build, or improve a primary residence or second home; and,

◆ part of the deduction taken for medical and dental expenses.

A party who takes the standard deduction in calculating his or her regular federal income tax does not get to take a standard deduction in calculating AMT, therefore, there is no need to make any adjustment for deductions. The process of making adjustments to determine AMTI begins with his or her adjusted gross income.

The next adjustment to be made in determining AMTI is to subtract the amount of tax refunds and credits associated with state and local taxes that were included in the taxpayer's income on *Form 1040*. Since no write off is allowed for payment of state and local taxes in computing AMTI, it is appropriate in calculating AMTI to offset refunds and credits from such taxes to the degree that they were included in the taxpayer's adjusted gross income.

Form 6251 then requires adjustments to add back all, or part, of certain exclusions, called *tax preference items*, that were permitted in calculating the taxpayer's regular federal income tax liability. The deduction allowed for such items as investment interest expense, depletion, depreciation on certain assets, and research and experimental costs in calculating regular income taxes are larger than the deduction allowed for those items in determining AMTI, and, in situations involving those types of items, the adjustment involves merely adding back the difference in the two allowances. Other items, such as the exclusion of interest from tax exempt private activity bonds, exclusion of part of the gain from the sale of small business stock, and intangible drilling cost preferences have no allowance for any exclusion in calculating AMTI and must be fully added back in when making the calculation. Any deduction for net operating losses taken on *Form 1040* must be fully added back, but a somewhat limited net operating loss is allowed as a separate item in calculating AMTI.

Calculating and Applying the Alternative Minimum Tax Exemption

Once the AMTI has been determined, a taxpayer is then allowed to reduce it by his or her AMT exemption, which is determined by filing status and AMTI. The *Jobs and Growth Tax Relief Reconciliation Act of 2003* (JGTRRA) raised the AMT exemption to $58,000 for married taxpayers filing joint returns and surviving spouses, $40,250 for unmarried taxpayers, and $29,000 for married taxpayers who file separate returns. However, these increases apply only for years beginning in 2003 and 2004. After those two years, JGTRRA provides that the AMT exemption will revert to its pre-2003 levels of $45,000 for married taxpayers filing joint returns and surviving spouses, $33,750 for unmarried taxpayers and $22,500 for married taxpayers who file separate returns. The provision that established the AMT, the Code Sec. 55, does not provide for adjustments in the amount of the AMT exemptions to allow for inflation. Nevertheless, whether the applicable AMT exemption is the increased amount provided for in JGTRRA or the lower amount scheduled for reinstatement after 2004, it is actually a tentative exemption that is subject to reduction or even elimination, based on the taxpayer's AMTI.

As long as their AMTI's do not exceed $150,000, the full AMT exemption is available to married couples who file jointly and to qualifying widows and widowers. An unmarried taxpayer may take the full exemption if his or her AMTI does not exceed $112,500. Married parties who file separately can have no more than $75,000 in AMTI for the full exemption. There is no provision to change the limits automatically to reflect inflation. Congress has not seen fit to alter them since the inception of the AMT in 1994.

If a party's AMTI exceeds the maximum level permitted for deduction of the full AMT exemption, the exemption must be reduced by an amount equal to 25% of the amount that his or her AMTI exceeds the maximum level permitted for full deduction. Therefore, a married couple with $382,000 or more of AMTI in 2003 or 2004 would lose their AMT exemption entirely. The same would happen to an unmarried taxpayer with AMTI of $273,500 or more, or a married taxpayer filing separately with AMTI of at least $192,000.

EXAMPLE: Siegfried and his wife, Jane, had an adjusted gross income in 2003 of $175,000. They also had tax exempt interest of $25,000 from bonds issued by their city to raise funds to lend to a company to construct a nursing home. Siegfried and Jane took the standard deduction on their joint return. Assuming that they had no income from tax preference items except the interest on the tax exempt bonds, the couple's AMTI would be $200,000. Their AMTI consisted of their adjusted gross income of $175,000 plus their $25,000 of interest from the bonds. Since the couple's AMTI exceeds the $150,000 maximum permitted for taking the full exemption by $50,000, their exemption must be reduced by 25% of the $50,000. This is a reduction of $12,500, leaving them with a deductible exemption of $45,500 of their initial $58,000.

Determining the Alternative Minimum Tax

Once the AMTI is reduced by a party's allowable AMT exemption, the remainder is taxed at the rate of 26% on the first $175,000 ($87,500 for married taxpayers filing separately) and 28% on all over that amount. This calculation yields a result that is further adjusted by deducting foreign tax credits to the degree permitted, which produces a balance referred to as the party's *tentative minimum tax*. The final step in calculating AMT is to deduct the taxpayer's federal tax liability, less foreign tax credits and taxes paid on lump sum distributions from qualified plans from *Form 4972*, from his or her tentative minimum tax. The balance, if any, is the party's AMT. If a taxpayer had long-term capital gains, part III of *Form 6251* takes the capital gains rates into consideration in calculating AMT.

In addition to applying to individuals, the AMT also applies to C corporations, estates, and trusts. The degree to which partnerships, S corporations, and other entities taxed as partnerships are able to reduce their incomes by tax preference items or other items includible in determining AMTI should be reported by those entities on each owner's *Form K-1*. Any reductions of income must be picked up by the individual taxpayer in determining his or her AMT.

FICA TAXES—
SOCIAL SECURITY AND MEDICARE TAXES

Employees are required to pay taxes under provisions of the *Federal Insurance Contributions Act* (FICA). It is comprised of payments for old age, survivors, and disability insurance (OASDI), generally referred to as Social Security tax. The Social Security tax is 6.2% of the income subject to the tax. It also consists of hospital insurance, *Medicare*, that is 1.45% of the income subject to tax.

The portion of the tax that goes to OASDI is used to fund Social Security programs such as retirement benefits paid to those who have reached the requisite age with sufficient years of participation in the program or who have become disabled prior to reaching retirement age, but with the necessary years of participation in the program to qualify for disability benefits. It is also used to provide benefits for eligible spouses and dependent children of qualified deceased, disabled, or retired taxpayers. The Medicare portion of the FICA tax is used to finance the Medicare program that provides health care benefits primarily to elderly retirees.

The OASDI portion of FICA taxes is imposed on only a specified amount of a taxpayer's income. In 2003, that amount was $87,000. The amount of income on which the OASDI portion of FICA taxes is levied is indexed such that it is changed each year to the same degree as the percentage of change in average income in the U.S. There is no cap on the level of a taxpayer's earnings that are subject to the Medicare portion of FICA taxes.

Employers are required to pay FICA taxes equal to the amount that their employees must pay on behalf of their employees. As a result, both the employer and employee will be required to pay a total of 7.65%, each, on the amount of the employee's earnings that are subject to both the OASDI and Medicare components of FICA taxes—a combined total of 15.3%. Their combined Medicare tax payments on income in excess of the earnings subject to OASDI is 2.9%.

The Social Security portion of FICA taxes is applied only to the specified base amount of income, such as the $87,000 base that was in effect for 2003, regardless of how many different jobs a taxpayer may have had in order to earn it. However, each employer is required to withhold both Social Security and the Medicare portion of FICA taxes on each employee's earnings up to the full base amount. Therefore, it is possible for taxpayers who have worked more than one job during the year to have overpaid their Social Security taxes.

In such cases, an employee is entitled to claim a refund for the excess payment by subtracting the amount of Social Security taxes that he or she should have paid from the combined Social Security payments actually paid through withholdings by various employers. The employee then enters the amount of the overpayment on the line provided for excess Social Security payments in the *Payments* section of *Form 1040*. However, if a single employer withholds too much in Social Security taxes from an employee's earnings, the employee must seek reimbursement directly from the employer and is not allowed to claim a refund for the excess on *Form 1040*.

EXAMPLE: Rodney is a mechanic at a new car dealership. In 2003, he made $80,000 as a mechanic and his employer withheld both OASDI and Medicare portions of FICA taxes on his full earnings. On weekends, he worked as a bouncer at a local show club and earned $25,000 in wages there, from which his employer withheld OASDI and Medicare portions of FICA taxes from his full earnings. As a result, Rodney paid the 6.2% OASDI tax rate on $105,000 in 2003, when the maximum amount of earnings subject to the tax was $87,000. He will be entitled to a refund of the excess OASDI tax, 6.2% of $18,000, that was withheld from his earnings.

SELF-EMPLOYMENT TAX

Self-employed taxpayers are required to pay *self-employment taxes* in lieu of FICA taxes. Since there is no employer to pay a matching share, the rate for self-employment taxes is set at the total of the combined employer's and employee's shares of FICA taxes. The tax is especially burdensome due to the fact that, rather than being a progressive tax (that starts out at low rates and increases the rate as taxable income increases), it starts out at the highest rate on the very first dollar that is subject to the tax. In fact, the tax is actually a *regressive tax* since it drops dramatically once a self-employed taxpayer's self-employment income reaches a relatively high level.

Other factors that make self-employment taxes such a burden are the lack of nonbusiness deductions, such as the itemized or standard deduction and the lack of any allowance for exemptions for dependents, to reduce the amount of earnings to which the tax rate is applied. However, self-employed taxpayers are allowed to use business related deductions to reduce their self-employment incomes and thereby reduce their self-employment tax liability. It is for this reason that it is so important that self-employed taxpayers need to qualify as many of their deductions as they can for treatment as deductions *for* adjusted gross income. This will exclude the amount of the deduction from self-employment tax, rather than deductions *from* adjusted gross income, that will not offset earnings subject to self-employment tax.

EXAMPLE: Suzanne started a business designing decorative rubber stamps and selling them over the Internet. She needed some working capital to acquire inventory and to take out ads in some magazines. A local bank was willing to make her a home equity loan against the equity in her house at a rate of 5.5% per annum. The banker said that the interest that she would pay on the loan would be deductible since her home equity loan would qualify as an itemized deduction on Schedule A of her *Form 1040.* Even though the banker is right, the fact that she used the loan for her business will entitle her to take a business deduction for the interest that she pays on the loan. This would be a far better choice, since it would be a deduction for adjusted gross income, thereby reducing Suzanne's net earnings that are subject to both self-employment tax and income tax.

Many self-employed taxpayers pay larger amounts of self-employment taxes than income taxes. This is attributable to the fact that, although income tax rates reach the much larger maximum of 35% (compared to the 15.3% maximum self-employment tax rate), much of the typical taxpayer's earnings are excluded from income taxation due to deductions and exemptions. This is not true with self-employment taxes. Also, once a party's taxable income is determined, part of it is taxed in a 10% income tax bracket, followed by a 15% bracket, before rates in excess of the self-employment tax rate are applied.

EXAMPLE: Leonardo is an artist who specializes in painting portraits. His gross receipts for 2003 were $72,000, but his art supplies, auto expenses for business use, advertising, and other business expenses deductible on his Schedule C of *Form 1040* totaled $38,000, leaving him with a net profit from self-employment of $34,000. This is the amount that will be subject to both income tax and self-employment tax.

If Leonardo were married, filing a joint return, and claiming himself and the couple's two minor children as dependents, his income tax liability would be less than $1,500, even if he merely took the standard deduction. This is true because over $20,000 of his income would be spared from income taxation due to his exemptions and deductions, leaving a balance that would be taxed almost entirely at the 10% rate. In fact, the child credit available to Leonardo and his wife would more than offset their income tax liability.

Were Leonardo required to pay a straight 15.3% of his net earnings in self-employment taxes, his liability for those taxes would be $5,202.

Realizing what a burden self-employment taxes have become for self-employed taxpayers, who constitute over two thirds of the small businesses in the U.S., Congress has enacted measures that soften the blow of these taxes. For example, rather than impose self-employment taxes on a taxpayer's self-employment income independent of income also earned as an employee, the specified base amount of earned income from all sources combined for the tax year is all that will be subject to the full Social Security tax rates. If a taxpayer has salary or wages from a source that was not self-employment income that had already been subjected to Social Security taxes, half of which were paid by the employer, then the amount of those earnings will be deducted from the base amount of earnings subject to Social Security part of FICA taxes. Only the balance will be subject to the full self-employment tax.

EXAMPLE: Justin is a manager of a transmission shop. His salary for 2003 was $80,000, which was subject to FICA taxes. His part was withheld from his paycheck and his employer paid a matching share. On weekends Justin repaired cars in his garage at his home. He earned $32,000 in self-employment income from his weekend work. The amount of self-employment income subject to Social Security tax in 2003 was $87,000. However, since Justin also had earnings of $80,000 as an employee, which had been subject to Social Security tax, he is allowed to subtract the $80,000 from the earnings limit for self-employment income subject to Social Security tax, leaving only $7,000 that will be taxed at the full self-employment tax rate. The remaining $25,000 of his self-employment income will be subject only to the Medicare portion of self-employment taxes (but still subject to income tax).

Taxpayers who are regarded as employees have the benefit of an employer paying half of the FICA taxes paid on their behalf. They also enjoy the advantage of not having to pay either income tax or FICA taxes on the employer's matching share paid on their earnings. Line 4 of Schedule SE of *Form 1040*, which is the Schedule for calculating self-employment taxes, provides for an adjustment that permits a reduction in the amount of a taxpayer's self-employment income that is subject to self-employment taxes. This reduction is equivalent to an employer's share of FICA taxes to the extent that the taxpayer's self-employment income does not exceed the maximum amount of income subject to the Social Security portion of FICA taxes.

This is accomplished by multiplying the self-employment income by 92.35% (.9235) before applying the self-employment tax rate. The impact of this adjustment is the same as if 92.35% of 15.3% were applied to the full taxable self-employment income. It yields an effective tax rate of 14.13% rather than 15.3%, as long as the total of the taxpayer's income subject to FICA taxes combined with income subject to self-employment taxes does not exceed the maximum amount of income that is subject to the Social Security portion of FICA taxes.

EXAMPLE: Salinda is a beautician who works as a self-employed, independent contractor at a shop under an arrangement where she gets 65% of the revenue that she generates. The shop owner gets 35% of the revenue. Her net income for 2003, that is subject to self-employment tax, was $41,000. She earned no income as an employee or from other self-employment. In calculating her self-employment taxes, she will multiply her $41,000 self-employment earnings by .9235 leaving a balance of $37,863.50 which will be subject to the 15.3% tax. Her self-employment tax liability, calculated by multiplying .153 times $37,863.50, would be $5,793.12. This total self-employment tax liability, when divided by her $41,000 net self-employment income works out to an effective rate of approximately 14.13%.

However, if Salinda's self-employment income had been $100,000, which was then multiplied by .9235 leaving a balance of $92,350 subject to application of the self-employment tax, $87,000 would have still been subject to the full 15.3% self-employment tax rate. $5,350 would have been subject to only the 2.9% Medicare portion of the self-employment tax and $7,650 would escape self-employment taxation that would otherwise have also been subjected to only the 2.9% Medicare portion of the self-employment taxes.

In addition to the adjustment in the amount of self-employment income to which self-employment tax rates are applied, taxpayers who pay self-employment taxes are also permitted to deduct one half of their self-employment tax liability from their total income in order to calculate their adjusted gross income and avoid paying income tax on that amount of their income. Although this adjustment reduces part of the self-employed party's income that is subject to federal income tax, it does not reduce any part of income that is subject to self-employment taxes. However, since most taxpayers are in the 25% tax bracket, the net effect of this adjustment is a savings of 25% of one half of the effective self-employment tax rate.

CORPORATE FEDERAL INCOME TAXES

Most corporations with no more than seventy-five shareholders are eligible to elect to be taxed as partnerships under the provisions of subchapter S of the Internal Revenue Code. The corporations that make such an election, known as *S corporations*, must file annual tax returns, but are not required to pay taxes on their earnings. Income tax returns of S corporations, filed on *Form 1065*, take the traditional approach of revenue minus ordinary and necessary business expenses, in calculating the income of the corporation.

Rather than applying tax rates to the corporation's income and calculating a tax liability for it, the income or loss of the corporation is simply allocated to the various owners of the company on the basis of their respective ownership shares and reported to them and to the IRS on a *Form K-1*. The shareholders must then report their income or loss from the S corporation on their individual returns. Partnerships and limited liability companies whose members have chosen to be taxed as partnerships are treated in the same way regarding their U.S. federal income tax returns.

Corporations whose owners are ineligible to make a subchapter S election or who choose not to make such an election, will be taxed under subchapter C of the Internal Revenue Code. These companies are known as C corporations. Unlike S corporations, C corporations are subject to income taxation at the corporate level. Tax returns for C corporations and limited liability companies whose members choose to be taxed as C corporations are filed on *Form 1120*.

The approach to determining taxable income for corporations is not appreciably different from the basic approach to calculating taxable income for individuals. The calculation of corporate income starts off with inclusion of gross income from various sources and is followed by the deduction of ordinary and necessary business expenses to arrive at taxable income. (The deduction for charitable contributions for C corporations is much more limited than that allowed for individuals.) However, a distinction that does exist between individual and corporate tax calculations is the fact that corporations do not have the equivalent of a standard deduction. However, none of a corporation's deductions are subject to being reduced by some percentage of its income, as are individuals' deductions for medical expenses, casualty losses, and miscellaneous deductions.

Dividends

Still another distinction, and perhaps the most striking difference between the way in which individual taxable income and corporate taxable income are calculated, is the way divedends are taxed. Dividends received by individuals are fully taxed, although at a lower rate than other ordinary income. Corporations, however, are permitted to exclude most, if not all, of the dividends that they receive.

Section 243 of the Internal Revenue Code provides that C corporations that own less than 20% of another domestic corporation that is subject to U.S. taxation (or certain foreign corporations subject to U.S. taxation) may exclude 70% of the dividends that they receive from such companies from their income for purposes of calculating their taxable incomes. Additionally, corporations that own 20% or more of another such corporation may exclude 80% of the dividends that they receive from that company from their taxable incomes. And, if the recipient of the dividend and the company paying it are considered to be part of the same affiliated group, the recipient may exclude 100% of such dividends from its taxable income. An *affiliated group*, for purposes of Sec. 243, must meet the definition set out in the Code Sec. 1504. It requires that a *parent corporation* must own at least 80% of the value of the outstanding stock of a corporation and possess at least 80% of the voting power of that corporation's stock.

There are some limitations on a corporation's right to deduct part or all of the dividends that it receives from other corporations from its own taxable income. In particular, a corporation will not be allowed a dividend deduction for dividends received from corporations whose stock it has not owned for forty-six days or more during the ninety day period beginning on the date that is forty-five days before the date that the shares of stock become *ex-dividend*. The ex-dividend date on stock is the first date upon which a party who buys the stock will not receive the most recently declared dividend. This rule is designed to prevent corporations from buying stock just before it goes ex-dividend and then selling it right after. If such a restriction did not exist, corporations could deduct most of their dividends from that type of transaction from taxable income but write off the loss on the sale of the stock in full, since stock prices usually fall in an amount equal to dividends that they have just paid.

There is also a limitation in the Code Sec. 246A that disallows the *dividends-received deduction* on stock that is debt financed. This prevents companies from taking a write off for interest paid on the debt that was incurred to acquire the stock, but excluding their dividend income from the stock from taxation.

Another provision in Sec. 246A limits the dividends-received deduction to the lesser of the percentage of deduction allowed, based on the recipient's ownership interest in the company paying the dividend. The same percentage applied to the recipient's taxable income computed without regard to any net operating loss deduction, capital loss carryback, or dividends-received deduction. However, this limitation does not apply when a C corporation takes the full dividends-received deduction.

EXAMPLE: Axton Corp. had gross income of $500,000, of which $150,000 was dividends from corporations in which it owned less than a 1% interest. The stocks had not been bought on credit and it had owned the stocks for the entire year. Axton had deductible expenses of $200,000. Since Axton owned less than 20% of the corporations that paid dividends to it, Axton is entitled to deduct the lesser of 70% of its dividends received or 70% of its income without the dividends-received deduction. Since 70% of the dividends received (.70 x $150,000 = $105,000) is less than 70% of Axton's taxable income before taking the dividend-received deduction (.70 x $300,000 = $210,000), it will be allowed a dividend-received deduction of $105,000.

If Axton's deductible expenses for the year had been $375,000, its $105,000 dividends-received deduction would have exceeded 70% of its taxable income without regard to the dividend-received deduction. Axton's income limitation is calculated by subtracting the company's deductible expenses of $375,000 from the gross income of $500,000 to yield a result of $125,000. That result is then multiplied by 70%, resulting in an amount of $87,500. That will be the maximum amount of its dividends-received exclusion that Axton will be entitled to take for the year. The disqualified portion of Axton's dividend-received deduction will be lost.

If Axton's deductible expenses had been $400,000, it would still be allowed to take its full dividends-received deduction, despite the fact that the $105,000 deduction would have exceeded 70% of its $100,000 taxable income ($500,000 gross income – $400,000 deductible expenses). This would be allowed because deducting the full $105,000 from its $100,000 income would have resulted in a net operating loss of $5,000.

Clearly, C corporations with dividend income should be careful to incur expenses and time their transactions so that they will realize sufficient income or losses to enable them to fully utilize their dividends-received deduction.

Corporate Tax Rate

Once a C corporation's taxable income has been determined, its filing status will be the same as other C corporations. They will all be subject to the same tax rates, with the exception of personal service corporations. The basic income tax rates for C corporations are 15% for the first $50,000 of taxable income, 25% for the next $25,000, 34% for taxable income in excess of $75,000 up to $10,000,000, and 35% for taxable income in excess of $10,000,000.

Unlike individual tax rates (which are graduated), corporations lose some or all of the benefit of the lower tax brackets as their incomes rise. This is accomplished by two tax *surcharges* imposed at different corporate income levels. The first surcharge is the lesser of 5% of corporate earnings in excess of $100,000 or $11,750. If the corporation's taxable income is $335,000 or more, the full surcharge will be levied against it, resulting in the corporation's entire taxable income being taxed at a 34% rate, thereby eliminating the graduated aspect of corporate tax rates.

The second surcharge is the lesser of 3% or $100,000 that is imposed on corporate taxable income in excess of $15,000,000. The net effect of this surcharge is to totally eliminate the graduated nature of corporate tax rates and cause a flat 35% rate for corporations with taxable income of $18,333,333 or more. Personal service corporations are subject to a flat 35% rate regardless of their income levels.

Chapter 9
Tax Credits

The ultimate tax benefit from the taxpayer's perspective is the *tax credit*. Deductions, at best, reduce a taxpayer's taxable income and thereby reduce his or her tax liability by the amount of the deduction times the rate the income would have been taxed if it not been excluded from taxation. Further, in the worst cases, it is possible that a taxpayer's deductions will not reduce a taxpayer's tax liability at all. On the other hand, tax credits may be used to offset a taxpayer's actual *tax liability* dollar for dollar. They can even generate a refund.

EXAMPLE: Beth and her husband filed a joint return in which they itemized deductions. Their itemized deductions would have been virtually equal to the standard deduction available to them, except Beth made a $2,000 contribution to a qualified charitable organization just before the end of the year. Had she not made the contribution, that contribution would have been part of her taxable income and taxed at a 25% rate. Therefore, the contribution reduced her tax liability by $500.

The couple has one minor child and is entitled to take a full Child Tax Credit of $1,000 as a result. This $1,000 tax credit will be fully subtracted from their income tax liability. The net result is, although the child tax credit was only half as large as the charitable deduction, it resulted in twice the tax savings.

In past years, tax credits for businesses for investments in equipment and other income producing items were widely used as a source of economic stimulus, while tax credits for individuals were somewhat rare. More recently, that situation has changed with elimination of the traditional investment tax credits for businesses and the creation of several tax credits for individuals.

Some credits are *refundable credits*, which means that they are regarded as if they were tax payments. If they exceed the taxpayer's tax liability, the difference will be refunded to him or her. Still other tax credits are *nonrefundable credits*. Any excess credit beyond the tax liability of the party claiming the credit will not be refunded. In some cases, the excess credits may be carried to other years, while in others they are simply lost.

GENERAL BUSINESS CREDIT

The *General Business Credit* is actually a group of business-oriented credits. Most of the tax credits available to businesses today are relatively specialized and are unlikely to be of benefit to the typical small business. Among the most specialized credits are the:

- *Enhanced Oil Recovery Credit* for certain costs incurred by companies involved in oil recovery;
- *Indian Employment Credit* for part of the wages paid by companies to employees who are members of an Indian tribe and who perform substantially all of their employment services within an Indian reservation while living on or near the reservation;
- *New York Liberty Zone Business Employee Credit* for employers who provide jobs to employees in a targeted area known as the Liberty Zone;
- *Orphan Drug Credit* for those incurring expenses to develop drugs that are used to treat only rare diseases and conditions (known as *orphan drugs*);
- *Renewable Electricity Production Credit* for those who sell electricity that was produced from qualified resources at a qualified facility;

◆ *Credit for Employee Social Security and Medicare Taxes* paid on certain *employee tips* that applies to the part of Social Security and Medicare payments made by restaurant owners on the tip income of employees that exceeds the federal minimum wage; and,

◆ *Alcohol Fuels Credit* available to sellers of ethanol and methanol for use as a fuel.

Businesses are still eligible to take an *investment credit* that is made up of three different types of credits that generally do not apply to most small businesses. The components of the business credit are:

◆ *Energy Credit* for expenditures on geothermal or solar energy property;

◆ *Reforestation Credit* for expenditures by producers of timber to reforest land; and,

◆ *Rehabilitation Credit* for expenditures for qualified rehabilitation of either certified historic structures or structures placed in service before 1936.

There are several other tax credits that small businesses are more likely to be able to take advantage of, although most small businesses are still unlikely to benefit from them in any given year. Among them is the *Disabled Access Credit* for expenditures by eligible small businesses to provide access to those who have disabilities. The expenditure must be made in an effort to comply with the *Americans with Disabilities Act of 1990*.

The *Empowerment Zone Employment Credit* entitles qualified employers to a credit of 20% of the first $15,000 that they pay to each employee in wages per calendar year, especially if the business is located in a designated empowerment zone, enterprise community, renewal community, or other distressed community, and the employee lives in the same designated zone or community. The designation of areas as such zones or communities is made by the Secretary of Housing and Urban Development (HUD) for urban areas and by the Secretary of the United States Department of Agriculture for rural areas. IRS Publication 954 provides general information concerning what areas have been designated as zones or communities that qualify for the credit, as well as information concerning the types of businesses that qualify for the credit and other particulars that affect eligibility.

Taxpayers who either construct a new building to provide housing for low-income tenants or acquire an existing building for that purpose may be eligible for the *Low Income Housing Credit*. A credit totaling 70% of the qualified basis over a ten year period is available on new construction. A credit totaling 30% of the qualified basis over a ten year period is available on existing buildings. The credit is calculated on *Form 8586* and the instructions for that form provide specific details regarding the credit.

There is a credit available for small business *pension start-up costs* that is available to qualified businesses that start a defined benefit or defined contribution plan, a SIMPLE plan, or simplified employee pension. However, it is of little impact since it is limited to 50% of the first $1,000 of the qualified start-up costs.

The credit for *employer-provided child care facilities and services* offers employers an opportunity to take up to $150,000 in such credits each year. Employers are entitled to a credit of 25% of the qualified expense paid for employee child care per year and 10% of the qualified expense of child care resource and referral services paid on behalf of employees each year. The credit is calculated on *Form 8882*. The instructions for that form provide details concerning eligibility for the credit.

Some credits available to businesses have recently expired or are set to expire soon. The *Research Credit* that provides businesses with credit of 20% of expenditures for research and experimental activities to the extent that they exceed the company's base amount will not apply to such expenditures made after June 30, 2004. The *Welfare-to-Work Credit* provides a credit for part of the wages paid to long-term family assistance recipients. The *Work Opportunity Credit* gives employers a credit for part of the wages that they pay to employees hired from a targeted group of people with either histories of high unemployment or special employment needs. (These credits will not apply to wages paid after December 31, 2003.)

All of the credits described above are components of the *General Business Credit* provided for in the Code Sec. 38. With the exception of the *Low Income Housing Credit*, all of the General Business Credits are combined on *Form 3800*. This form then directs the taxpayer to enter the total on the appropriate line of the appropriate return depending on the taxpayer's type of business organization. Those who have only one current year of business credit that is not from a passive activity and who have no carryback or carryover credits are not required to be a corporation or other type of formal business organization in order to qualify for the General Business Credit. Individuals who meet the criteria for taking any of the various components of the General Business Credit are entitled to take it, as well.

The General Business Credit is a *nonrefundable credit* that (with limitation) can be used to *fully offset* a party's regular tax liability, but cannot exceed it. Taxpayers are permitted to use the General Business Credit to offset the first $25,000 of their regular tax liability that is, their regular tax liability less their nonrefundable personal credits and their miscellaneous nonrefundable credits. However, the General Business Credit cannot be used to offset income tax that is considered *unoffsettable, tentative minimum tax*. The tentative minimum tax is derived in the calculation of *Alternative Minimum Tax*. (For an explanation of how the tentative minimum tax is calculated, see Chapter 8.) The part of a taxpayer's income tax that is considered unoffsettable is 25% of the part of his or her regular tax liability that exceeds $25,000.

The *New York Liberty Zone Business Employee Credit* component of the General Business Credit can be used to offset 100% of a party's tentative minimum tax. The *Empowerment Zone Employment Credit* can be used to offset up to 25% of a party's *tentative minimum tax*. None of the other components of the General Business Credit may be used to offset any part of the tentative minimum tax.

In essence, for most taxpayers, their General Business Credit may be used to fully offset their entire regular tax liability with the exception of the larger of their tentative minimum tax or their unoffsettable income tax. Any unused General Business Credit must first be carried back one year and used to offset eligible tax liability. Any remaining, unused balance can be carried forward for up to twenty years and used to offset future eligible tax liabilities.

EXAMPLE: Bellard, a self-employed marketing consultant, had a regular income tax liability of $29,000. Due to having built some rental property for low-income tenants and establishing a day-care for his employees, he is entitled to a $30,000 General Business Credit. Since Bellard had no tax preference items for the year, his AMT exemption fully offset his alternative minimum taxable income and left him with no tentative minimum tax.

The first $25,000 of his regular income tax liability can be offset by the General Business Credit, but 25% of his regular tax liability in excess of the first $25,000 in tax liability, cannot be offset by the credit. Therefore, Bellard cannot use his General Business Credit to offset 25% of $4,000 ($29,000 - $25,000), a total of $1,000, of his income tax liability. The result will be that he can use $28,000 of his $30,000 General Business Credit as an offset against his $29,000 tax liability, leaving him with $1,000 liability that he must pay.

Had Bellard had some tax preference items that resulted in a tentative minimum tax of $5,000, he would not have been allowed to use his General Business Credit to offset his tax liability below that amount. In that case, he would have been allowed to use only $24,000 ($29,000 - $5,000) of his General Business Credit. Bellard's unused General Business Credit, in either situation would be available for him to carryback one year and apply to eligible tax payments and generate a refund. If it is not fully used by the carryback, he can carry the unused portion forward for up to twenty years.

PERSONAL CREDITS

There are a number of personal credits that have little or no impact on small businesses or the owners and operators of small businesses. These credits include the *Household and Dependent Care Credit*, credit for the *Elderly and Permanently and Totally Disabled*, the credit for *Adoption Expenses*, the *Home Mortgage Interest Credit*, and the *Adjusted Expense Credit*.

However, there are several personal tax credits that may prove beneficial to small businesses or those employed by (or otherwise associated with) a small business.

Education Tax Credits

The *Hope Scholarship Credit* and the *Lifetime Learning Credit* are generally referred to together as *Education Tax Credits*. They were established by the Code Sec. 25A. Both credits apply to *qualified tuition* and *related expenses*, such as lab fees or activity fees, that are paid to an eligible educational institution for enrollment of the taxpayer, his or her spouse, or a dependent for whom the taxpayer is allowed to claim as a deduction. The costs of books, supplies, and other materials are not eligible for either credit unless payment for them must be made directly to the eligible educational institution. Payments for room and board or other personal living expenses are not eligible for the credit, even if they are made directly to the school in which the eligible party is enrolled. Eligible educational institutions are those whose students are eligible for federal student aid. No unused portion of either credit may be carried to another year.

The *Hope Credit* for 2003 is 100% of the first $1,000 of qualified expenses and 50% of the next $1,000 of such expenses, for a total of $1,500. The amounts to which the credit rates will be applied are subject to adjustments for inflation after 2003. The Hope Credit is available only to eligible parties for the first two years of a post secondary degree program or certificate program. The party must be enrolled at least as a half time student and can continue to take the credit until he or she completes two years of the work (regardless of how many years it actually takes to do so). If a taxpayer is allowed a deduction for education expenses, he or she is not allowed to take a Hope Credit in connection with those expenses. An advantage of the Hope Credit is that it is available to a taxpayer for as many eligible parties as he or she is entitled to claim as a dependent.

The *Lifetime Learning Credit* is limited to 20% of the first $10,000 of qualified expenditures incurred on behalf of the taxpayer and dependents per year. The Lifetime Learning Credit is available for eligible expenditures for even a single course and has no limit on the number of years it can be taken. However, if a student is eligible for the Hope Credit, he or she cannot also take the Lifetime Learning Credit. For 2004 and beyond, the credit cannot be used to reduce a party's tax liability below his or her *tentative minimum tax.* (see Chapter 8.)

Both the Hope Credit and Lifetime Learning Credit are *phased out* at certain levels of modified adjusted gross income. For purposes of both of these credits, modified adjusted gross income is merely the taxpayer's adjusted gross income, with any permitted exclusions of foreign earned income, foreign housing, income of residents of American Samoa, or income from Puerto Rico being added back to it. Therefore, for all but a very few taxpayers, their modified adjusted gross income is equal to their adjusted gross income for purposes of calculating eligibility to take either the Hope Credit or the Lifetime Learning Credit. The income levels for the phase out are altered annually to reflect inflation. For those whose modified adjusted gross incomes fall within the phase-out range of income, their credit phase out is prorated. *Form 8863* must be used to claim each of the credits and it contains a section for calculating the proration of the phase out.

EXAMPLE: Trudy and Roy filed a joint return showing a modified adjusted gross income of $92,500 in 2003. They spent $2,000 on qualified education expenses on behalf of their dependent son, Roy Jr., for whom they were entitled to take a Hope Credit. Were they entitled to the full Hope Credit, they could take 100% of the first $1,000 of expenditures as a credit and 50% of the next $1,000 for a total of $1,500. However, since their modified adjusted gross income of $92,500 exceeded the maximum of $83,000 allowed without a phase out by $9,500, this figure must be divided by the full range of the phase out ($83,000 to $103,000) of $20,000 leaving a 47.5% phase out. Trudy and Roy would have been entitled to 52.5% of their $1,500 credit for a total Hope Credit of $787.50.

RETIREMENT SAVINGS CONTRIBUTIONS

A credit is available for elective deferrals and IRA contributions, known as the *Credit for Retirement Savings Contributions*, by virtue of the Code Sec. 25B. A credit of up to 50% of the first $2,000 of a qualified party's qualified retirement savings contribution is allowed. A qualified party is someone who is at least eighteen years of age; who is not claimed as a dependent on someone else's tax return; and, who was not a full-time student during five or more months during the calendar year for which the credit is sought. A contribution to an IRA of any type provided for in the the Code, to a qualified retirement plan, to a simplified employee pension, a 401(k) plan, or any contribution to a plan or annuity of a tax exempt organization, school, or government entity will be considered to be a qualified retirement savings contribution.

The Credit for Retirement Contributions was designed to encourage relatively moderate income earners to make contributions to some type of retirement program beyond Social Security. As a result, the percentage of the credit is reduced from 50% to 20% for married taxpayers filing joint returns who have adjusted gross income in excess of $30,000, but not over $32,500. It is reduced to 10%, if their adjusted gross income exceeds $32,500, but is not over $50,000, (past which they are no longer eligible for the credit). A taxpayer who files as head of household must reduce his or her credit to 20% when adjusted gross income exceeds $22,500, but is not over $24,375. The taxpayer must further reduce the credit to 10%, if his or her adjusted gross income exceeds $24,375, but is not in excess of the $37,500 level at which the credit is lost. For everyone else, the reductions in the percentage of the credit and loss of the credit occur at income levels that are exactly one half of the levels for married couples filing jointly.

The credit for retirement contributions does not affect a taxpayer's right to exclude such contributions from adjusted gross income. In fact, those deductions must be taken first, along with credits for household and dependent care, the elderly and disabled, education, qualified home mortgage interest, the Child Credit, and the Foreign Tax Credit, before the Credit for Retirement Contributions can be used to offset regular tax liability, as well as AMT. However, any unused portion cannot be carried to another year. This credit is set to expire after 2006, but is refundable in 2004 and thereafter.

OTHER NONREFUNDABLE CREDITS

These are other nonrefundable credits that are available to individuals, corporations, and other taxable entities, and include:

◆ *Credit for Producing Fuel from a Nonconventional Source* that was enacted to encourage production of fuel from sources other than petroleum;

◆ *Puerto Rico Economic Activity Credit* that was enacted to encourage business activity in Puerto Rico; and,

◆ *Credit to Holder's of Qualified Zone Academy Bonds* that was enacted to encourage expenditures to improve certain targeted public schools.

Although the benefits from these credits can be substantial, they are simply not applicable to most small businesses. However there are two such nonrefundable credits that are at least a little more likely to apply to the typical small business.

Qualified Electric Vehicle Credit

A credit equal to 10% of the cost of a qualified electric vehicle (up to a maximum of $4,000) is allowed by the Code Sec. 30 for such vehicles purchased and put in service prior to January 1, 2004. The credit will be reduced by 25% for such vehicles bought and placed in service in 2004, with reductions of 50% and 75% of the original credit to follow in 2005 and 2006, respectively. After 2006, the credit is set to expire. (However, in the interest of conservation, it would not be surprising to see Congress renew this credit.)

In order to qualify for the credit, a vehicle must be powered primarily by an electric motor that is powered by a portable source, have at least four wheels, be used primarily on public streets, and must have been acquired new by the taxpayer for his or her use, rather than for resale. Hybrid vehicles that use both gasoline powered motors and electric motors do not qualify for the credit, but may qualify for a deduction allowance for purchase of a *clean fuel vehicle* as provided for in the Code Sec. 179A.

No credit is allowed for the purchase of a qualified electric vehicle to the extent that the cost is expensed under the Code Sec. 179. Furthermore, to the extent that a credit is taken, the taxpayer must correspondingly reduce his or her basis in the vehicle. The credit may be used to offset a taxpayer's regular tax for the year to the extent that it exceeds his or her tentative tax, but cannot be carried to other years if it is not fully used.

Foreign Tax Credit

Since the U.S. takes the position that all income earned by U.S. taxpayers is subject to U.S. taxation regardless of where it is earned, and most other countries levy taxes on income generated within their borders, this creates the potential for taxation of the same income by two separate countries. The *Foreign Tax Credit* was enacted to avoid this result.

The Foreign Tax Credit allows a taxpayer to take the lesser of the tax on income or profits paid to the foreign government or the tax due the U.S. government on the same income or profits. Income in the form of wages is eligible for the credit, as well as interest, dividends, and royalty income. Taxpayers may elect to take a *deduction* for the foreign taxes that they paid, rather than the credit. However, it is rarely to the taxpayer's advantage to do so unless he or she is unable to utilize the credit. The credit may be used to offset regular income taxes and a recalculated version may even be used to offset AMT. Unused Foreign Tax Credits may be carried back two years and may then be carried forward five years.

No Foreign Tax Credit will be allowed for taxes paid to countries that the U.S. Secretary of State has identified as *supporting terrorist activities*. Among those countries are Cuba, Libya, North Korea, Syria, Sudan, and Iran. Also, no credit will be allowed for tax payments made to foreign governments to the degree that the payments are actually disguised payments for goods or services.

EXAMPLE: In an effort to entice him to locate his computer manufacturing company in Ireland, the Irish government offered to tax Henry's U.S. company at exactly the same rate as the U.S. government would, but would then, at no charge, provide the company with plant facilities and utilities equal in value to the taxes that it levied. Henry would not be allowed to take a U.S. tax credit for his company for the Irish *tax* that it paid since the payments were actually for plant facilities and utilities, rather than bona fide taxes.

REFUNDABLE CREDITS

The most coveted of all tax credits are those that are *fully refundable*. Such credits are regarded as if they were cash payments made by the taxpayer and, in fact, several of the refundable credits result from just such payments. Refundable credits may be used to offset any type of a taxpayer's tax liability, including AMT. A *refund* may be claimed for any unused portion of such credits, even if the taxpayer had no tax liability at all.

Taxes Withheld on Wages

The refundable credit that most taxpayers are familiar with is the credit for taxes withheld from a taxpayer's wages by an employer. Since taxes that are withheld from wages represent merely an estimate of the worker's anticipated tax liability, it is only appropriate that any excess withholdings be returned to the taxpayer, and the Code Sec. 31 requires just that. Rather than claiming a credit for *excess tax withholdings* in the section of *Form 1040* where most credits are claimed, taxpayers enter the total of federal income tax withheld from their earnings in the area of *Form 1040* designated for *payments*, along with certain other payments and credits, and the total is netted against the party's total tax to yield the refundable balance.

Although the most common source of tax withholdings from a person's income is money withheld on earnings by an employer, the credit provided in Sec. 31 also applies to withholdings of taxes from unemployment benefits, gambling winnings, various types of retirement income, and investment income such as dividends and interest. Taxpayers will be given credit for taxes withheld even if the party withholding them fails to pay them to the U.S. Treasury.

Excess Social Security and Railroad Retirment Tax Withheld

The Social Security system in the U.S. was created by the *Federal Insurance Contribution Act* (FICA). In order to fund the program, the FICA mandates the collection of taxes on a certain initial amount of each worker's earnings. Employers must pay a matching share of these taxes commonly referred to as Social Security taxes. Railroad workers are covered by the *Railroad Retirement Tax Act* (RRTA), rather than Social

Security. Part of RRTA taxes are considered to be the equivalent of Social Security and are levied on the same amount of income and at the same rate as Social Security.

If a person works for more than one employer, since each employer is to withhold Social Security taxes from each employee's wages as if the worker had no other job, it is possible for a taxpayer to have had more of the *Old Age and Survivors Disability Income* (Social Security) portion of FICA taxes (and its RRTA equivalent) withheld from his or her combined wages than should be. In such cases, the Code Sec. 31 provides that a credit shall be available to the taxpayer for the excess withholdings. The excess Social Security and RRTA payments are entered in the *payments* section of *Form 1040* and are used first to offset the taxpayer's total tax liability with any balance being a refundable overpayment. If a single employer withholds too much in Social Security taxes from an employee's earnings, the employee must seek a refund of the overpayment directly from the employer. An employee will be given credit for FICA taxes withheld from earnings even, if the employer failed to pay them to the U.S. Treasury as required.

Estimated Tax Payments and Overpayments from Prior Years

Since self-employed individuals do not have an employer to withhold taxes from their earnings, they are expected to make *quarterly estimated tax payments* of a sufficient amount to equal at least 90% of their tax liability for the year. The estimated payments, which are sent in with a *Form 1040 ES*, are due April 15th, June 15th, September 15th, and January 15th. If the due date falls on a weekend or holiday, payment is due on the next business day. If the payment is sent by U.S. mail, it is considered to have been made on the date that the payment is postmarked.

If a taxpayer has a refund due on his or her tax return, he or she may stipulate in the refund section of *Form 1040* that all or part of the refund is to be applied to his or her next year's estimated tax liability. Taxpayers who file a request for an automatic extension of the deadline for filing their income tax returns are expected to estimate and fully pay any remaining tax liability for the year. Payments that accompany such extension requests are another source of estimated tax payments.

Taxpayers are allowed to take a credit for their estimated tax payments made in each of these ways. The credit is taken by entering the amount of the payment on the appropriate line in the *payments* section of *Form 1040*.

Taxes Withheld on Nonresident Aliens and Foreign Corporations

Parties who make payments of U.S. sourced income to foreign persons who are not considered to be residents of the U.S., a group commonly referred to as *nonresident aliens*, must withhold taxes in respect to that income. Likewise, payments to foreign corporations that are organized under the laws of a foreign country or a U.S. possession, are also subject to the withholding of U.S. taxes. Section 33 of the Code permits such parties to take a credit against their U.S. tax liabilities for the amounts withheld and to collect a refund for amounts withheld in excess of their tax liabilities. Individual, nonresident aliens must claim their credit for taxes withheld of *Form 1040 NR* and foreign corporations must use *Form 1120 NR* to claim their credit.

Fuel Tax Credit

Most fuel for vehicles, equipment, and aircraft are subject to *excise taxes* that are incorporated in their sale price. However, some users of these fuels are exempt from the excise tax. Therefore, if such users have paid the excise tax in the price of their fuel, the Code Sec. 34 permits them to claim a credit for those excise taxes paid. The primary parties who qualify for such credits are farmers, those who use the fuels in off-the-road vehicles and equipment or in noncommercial aircrafts, and those who use substances that are taxed as fuel for a purpose other than as a fuel, such as using it as an ingredient in a manufacturing process. The maximum credit available to qualified parties is an amount equal to the amount of excise tax paid by them on the fuels in question, although some qualified parties face limitations that reduce their credits to less than the amount of excise tax that they paid.

Health Insurance Costs of Eligible Individuals

Only a very limited group of taxpayers are eligible for this credit. Included among them are those receiving *trade readjustment* because they were displaced from their jobs due to competition from imports and those who are age 55 or older and receiving benefits from the Pension Benefit Guaranty Corporation under provisions of Title IV of ERISA.

Those who qualify for it are allowed to take a credit equal to 65% of the premiums that they pay for a qualified health insurance plan for themselves, their spouses, and their dependents. In the situation of divorced parents, a dependent child will be deemed to be the dependent of the custodial parent, regardless of which party is entitled to take an exemption deduction for the child.

Qualified health insurance plans include individual health insurance, group plans, and governmentally administered programs. Coverage obtained through a spouse's employer or from a former employer under COBRA also qualify. However, no credit will be allowed for otherwise qualified insurance premium payments if the taxpayer either takes an itemized deduction for them as a medical expense or takes a deduction for health insurance expenses of a self-employed individual.

Earned Income Credit

The *Earned Income Credit* is essentially a form of welfare payment that rewards low-income earners for remaining in the workforce and earning what they can. The credit is determined by applying a specified percentage to a party's earned income up to a certain maximum amount. Once the larger of a taxpayer's earned income or adjusted gross income reaches a certain level, a phasing out of the credit begins and continues until it is eventually fully phased out at sufficiently high levels of income. The percentage of the credit allowed and the range of income over which it is available are determined on the basis of whether the taxpayer has no qualifying children, one qualifying child, or more than one qualifying child.

To be considered as a qualifying child, the person must be either under the age of nineteen at the end of the calendar year, a student under the age of twenty-four at the end of the calendar year, or permanently and totally disabled at any time during the calendar year. The child must also have resided with the taxpayer in his or her principal residence, located in the U.S., for over half of the taxable year. Furthermore, the eligible child must be:

- the taxpayer's child;
- the taxpayer's stepchild;
- a descendant of his or her child or stepchild;
- the taxpayer's sibling;
- the taxpayer's step-sibling;
- a descendant of his or her sibling or step-sibling, as long as the taxpayer cares for that descendant as if the child were his or her own; or,
- a foster child that was placed with taxpayer by a placement agency and is cared for by the taxpayer as if the child were his or her own.

Taxpayers claiming a party as their qualifying child for purposes of establishing eligibility for the Earned Income Credit must provide each qualifying child's name, age, and Social Security number on their tax returns.

There are a number of factors that will render a party ineligible to claim the Earned Income Credit. A taxpayer who is claimed as a qualifying child on another taxpayer's tax return cannot claim the Earned Income Credit for him or herself, even with a qualifying child of his or her own. A party generally cannot claim another party as a qualifying child if that child is married, unless he or she can also claim an exemption deduction for the child. If a taxpayer has income from interest, dividends, tax exempt interest, net rent and royalty income, net capital gain income, or net passive activity income (all of which are considered *disqualified income* for purposes of calculating the Earned Income Credit) and the total from all of these sources exceeds $2,600, he or she will be ineligible for the Earned Income Credit.

In order to be eligible for the Earned Income Credit, a taxpayer or spouse, if a joint return is filed by a married couple, must be at least twenty-five years of age, but cannot be sixty-five years of age or older. Also, married couples must file joint returns in order to qualify for the Earned Income Credit. They must have resided in the U.S. for over half of the year. A party who was a nonresident alien for any part of the year cannot claim Earned Income Credit for that year unless married to a U.S. citizen or resident and agrees to make his or her entire income subject to U.S. taxation.

Rather than require taxpayers to calculate their Earned Income Credits, the IRS supplies them with a worksheet for calculating their earned income and an Earned Income Credit Table which shows the credit available for various levels of earned income in $50 increments for each filing status. Once the credit is determined, the amount is entered on the designated line in the *Payments* section of *Form 1040*.

A taxpayer with at least one qualifying child who expects to qualify for the Earned Income Credit may fill out a *Form W-5*, give the lower portion to his or her employer, and the employer must then pay the employee part of the anticipated credit in installments with his or her regular paycheck. Any such advance payment must be included on the employee's W-2 at the end of the year and must then be reported on *Form 1040* in the *other taxes* section as if it were a tax obligation of the taxpayer. Even when a taxpayer has received advance payments toward an anticipated Earned Income Credit, he or she will still show the full amount of his or her credit on *Form 1040*. The amount will eventually be netted against the advance payments received and reported in the *other taxes* section, thereby leaving only the net difference to offset tax liability or generate a refund. A Schedule EIC must also be attached to the return.

Child Tax Credit

A credit may be available to taxpayers for each qualifying child that they have. A qualifying child is one that is under the age of seventeen at the end of the year, a citizen or resident of the U.S., and is claimed as a dependent on the tax return of the party claiming a *Child Tax Credit* for the child. Also, the child must be:

- ♦ the taxpayer's child or stepchild;
- ♦ the taxpayer's sibling or step-sibling;
- ♦ his or her descendant;
- ♦ an adopted child or grandchild, or;

◆ a foster child that was placed in the taxpayer's home by a placement agency and that the taxpayer cared for as if the child were the taxpayer's own child.

Legislation was enacted to gradually increase the maximum credit per qualifying child from $500 in 2000 to $1,000 in 2010. However, the *Jobs and Growth Tax Relief Reconciliation Act* of 2003 (JGTRRA) temporarily sped up the process and raised the maximum credit per child to $1,000 for 2003 and 2004. After that time, the credit amounts revert back to the scheduled gradual increases provided for in prior legislation. As a result, the credit per qualified child will be $700 in 2005 through 2008, $800 in 2009, and $1,000 thereafter.

The Child Tax Credit is reduced by $50 for every $1,000 that an otherwise qualified taxpayer's modified adjusted gross income exceeds what is referred to as the *threshold amount*. Modified adjusted gross income for purposes of the Child Tax Credit is the taxpayers adjusted gross income plus any earnings from Puerto Rico or American Samoa that are excluded from adjusted gross income by special provisions in the Code. Therefore, since very few taxpayers have such exclusions, the modified adjusted gross income for most taxpayers for purposes of calculating the phase out of the Child Tax Credit is simply their adjusted gross income.

EXAMPLE: Joe and Denise have one qualifying child for purposes of the Child Tax Credit. Their combined adjusted gross income on their joint return, which is also their modified adjusted gross income for purposes of the credit, was $124,000 for 2003. Since they must reduce their Child Tax Credit by $50 for every $1,000 of their modified adjusted gross income in excess of $110,000, they will be required to reduce their $1,000 Child Tax Credit by $700 (14 x $50). This will leave them with a net Child Tax Credit of $300 for 2003.

Part of the Child Tax Credit is refundable. If any of a taxpayer's Child Tax Credit remains unused after applying it to the total of his or her regular tax liability plus any alternative minimum tax liability, less foreign tax credit and personal nonrefundable credits other than the credits for adoption expenses, elective deferrals, and IRA contributions, the unused balance can be used to generate a refund up to an amount equal to 10% of an amount determined by subtracting $10,500 from the taxpayer's earned income. The $10,500 base that must be subtracted from the taxpayer's earned income provided for in Sec. 24, was the figure for 2003. It is subject to increase due to inflation. The figure for each new year is calculated and published in a Revenue Procedure from the IRS.

The 10% rate that is applied to the portion of the taxpayer's earned income in excess of his or her base income for purposes of calculating his or her refundable child credit is scheduled to increase to 15% for 2005 and thereafter. The unused Child Tax Credit may be applied against his or her FICA taxes or one-half of any self-employment taxes to generate a refund of those taxes. This applies only if those taxes exceed the Earned Income Credit for the year.

EXAMPLE: Ozzie and Harriet have two qualifying children for Child Tax Credit purposes. Their earned income for 2003 was $35,000. Their regular income tax liability was $1,654, of which $960 was offset by the Child and Dependent Care Expenses Credit, leaving a regular income tax of $694. They had no Alternative Minimum Tax. Of the $2,000 in Child Tax Credit to which they are entitled (two children x $1,000), they can use only $694 to offset regular tax liability. However, they can use the remaining $1,306 ($2,000 - $694) of the Child Tax Credit to offset an amount equal to their earned income ($35,000) less $10,500, for a balance of $24,500, which times 10% is $2,450. Since the $2,450 exceeds the $1,306 unused balance of their Child Tax Credit, the couple will be permitted a refund of the $1,306 as well as an offset of the $694 of net regular tax. Their Child Tax Credit will be a fully refundable credit for them for the year.

ORDER OF APPLICATION OF TAX CREDITS

Since some credits may be carried forward and some may not, the order in which tax credits must be applied is important to taxpayers with multiple credits. The order is as follows.

Nonrefundable

1. The *Hope and Lifetime Learning Credit*, credit for *Elderly and Permanently and Totally Disabled*, and the *Household and Dependent Care Credit*. These credits must be taken first, but in no particular order since any unused portion of any of these three credits cannot be carried to other years.
2. The *Home Mortgage Interest Credit*. Any unused portion of it may be carried forward for up to three years.
3. The *Adjusted Expense Credit*. Any unused portion may be carried forward for up to five years.

Refundable

4. The *Foreign Tax Credit*. This may be carried back two years and forward for five years.
5. The *Nonconventional Source Fuels Credit*.
6. The *Qualified Electric Vehicle Credit*.
7. The *General Business Credit*. This credit may be carried back one year or forward for up to twenty years.
8. All remaining refundable credits, in any order.

Chapter 10

Tax Considerations in Entity Selection

The major entity choices for a business are sole proprietorship, partnership, corporation, limited liability company, and limited liability partnership. Among the less frequently used forms of organization are joint venture and the limited partnership. Each type of entity has its own requirements, as well as its own advantages and shortcomings. Following is a closer look at each type of organization.

SOLE PROPRIETORSHIPS

The very name of the sole proprietorship reveals one of its most important characteristics—there can be only one owner. If there is more than one owner of the business, it simply cannot be a sole proprietorship.

Formation of Sole Proprietorships

Many small businesses are proprietorships simply by default. When someone is the sole owner of a business and no formal business entity sanctioned by a governmental entity is formed, then that business is a sole proprietorship. This ease of formation is generally regarded as a major advantage of this form of organizational structure. A person will have started a sole proprietorship simply by doing business, provided that person is the sole owner of the business.

There is no minimum amount of business that must be done to qualify as a sole proprietorship, nor is there a requirement of acknowledgment of existence by any governmental entity. Many jurisdictions do require all businesses to purchase a business license, but this is generally designed to alert state and local governmental units to the existence of the business for the purpose of levying taxes on the business. Failure to purchase such a license may result in penalties such as fines, but will not alter the fact that the business in operation was a sole proprietorship.

Advantages

A significant advantage to the sole proprietorship entity is the way in which it is taxed. At the federal level, there is no requirement that a sole proprietorship file a separate tax return. The profit or loss from a sole proprietorship is calculated on Schedule C of *Form 1040*. The results are shown on the individual owner's tax return. The Schedule C, which is a profit and loss statement, will show whether the proprietor made a profit or a loss from the business and how much. It is far easier to fill out a Schedule C for an individual's *Form 1040,* than it is to do an entire tax return for one of the other types of entities available.

Sole proprietors generally use the *cash method of accounting* so they do not have to pay taxes on goods sold or services rendered until they actually receive payment for them. By contrast, the *accrual method of accounting* requires that, once a seller of goods or services is owed money from a sale, he or she must treat it as if the money had already been received when calculating income tax liability. This can result in the bewildering situation of having taxable profits according to the profit and loss statement, but no actual cash income with which to pay the taxes on those profits. Using the cash method of accounting will enable proprietors to avoid having to pay taxes on their accounts receivable before the money is collected. (see Chapter 1.)

There are instances where a proprietor's accounting income will be greater than his or her available income. This is due to the fact that even when profits are reinvested in the business to increase inventory or buy new equipment, those profits are still taxable. Expenditures for inventory offer no deduction at all to offset the profits used for that purpose. Expenditures for equipment must often be deducted in increments over the life of the asset.

A major tax advantage for sole proprietorships is the way in which their profits and losses are treated for tax purposes. Since there is no formal separate business entity, all the proprietor's profits are simply regarded as a component of his or her total personal income and taxed as such. Likewise, losses from any active business enterprise that the proprietor engages in are also regarded as just another component of his or her various sources of personal income. It may be used to offset other income or even a spouse's income, if filing a joint return. There are limitations on using losses from *passive activities* or *hobbies* to offset other income. (see Chapter 6.)

Disadvantages

The least appealing aspect of a sole proprietorship lies in the fact that all of the proprietor's income will be considered to be *earned income*, rather than *investment income*. As a result, all of the proprietor's income will be subject to *self-employment tax*. Neither personal itemized deductions nor the standard deduction are subtracted from self-employment income before calculating the self-employment tax and no allowance is made for exemptions. However, there are some specific adjustments available that reduce the self-employment tax burden. Therefore, although the stated self-employment tax is 15.3%, the effective rate of taxation on income up to the amount that is fully subjected to self-employment tax is actually about 12%. (For a detailed analysis of how to calculate the effective rate of self-employment tax, see Chapter 8.)

Taxpayers who earn a modest income from a self-employment activity are the hardest hit by self-employment taxes. For example, a taxpayer who files a joint return with his spouse and has two children that he could claim as dependents, would pay virtually no income tax if his sole income were $21,000 from self-employment, but would have a self-employment tax liability of nearly $3,000.

PARTNERSHIPS

Partnerships are a form of business entity that are often entered into unintentionally and even unknowingly. The *Uniform Partnership Act* (which has been adopted in practically every state) defines a partnership as *an association of two or more persons to carry on as co-owners of a business for a profit*. Most states consider the term *persons* to include other types of business entities, such as corporations, as well.

EXAMPLE: Courtney's neighbor saw her painting her own house and asked her if she would consider hiring herself out to paint. Courtney told her neighbor that she would paint her house for $2,500 and then contacted Suzy, a friend that she knew to be a good painter and asked if she would help her paint houses for payment. She suggested that they would split all profits evenly between them. Each supplied some ladders and other equipment and, starting with Courtney's neighbor's house, began to paint houses for profit. They will more than likely be deemed to have formed a partnership.

Formation of Partnerships

There is no requirement that partnership agreements be written in order to be valid, unless the partnership's underlying business activities are required to be in writing to be valid. This is the case when the partnership was formed to buy and sell real property, but there are few other such situations.

Partners are at risk of losing everything they personally own to satisfy judgments against them arising from some problem in the partnership. Whenever a partner is acting in the scope of the partnership business, all of the other partners will be bound to any contracts made by one partner, will be liable for any partner's negligence, and may also be liable for intentional misdeeds of other partners. Since employees of a partnership are considered to actually be employees of the partners, each individual partner will be *personally vicariously liable* for the misdeeds and omissions of those employees.

In the event that a person or other entity were to suffer an injury at the hands of a partner or an employee of a partnership, each of the partners would have *joint and several liability* for the judgment. This means that the plaintiff could collect any amount of the judgment from any one or combination of the partners, even up to 100% of the judgment from only one partner.

Creditors' rights to recover from partners are different. Partners have only *joint liability* to creditors on partnership debts, so creditors attempting to recover unpaid debts of the partnership can get judgments against a partner only for his or her share of the debt.

Investigation and Start-up Costs

Few people start or acquire partnerships without investigating the feasibility of the venture. The investigations usually involve costs such as travel expenses and fees to experts such as accountants, attorneys, appraisers, and marketing consultants. Once the decision is made to form or acquire the partnership, businessmen often incur start-up costs, such as the cost of training employees, fees to consultants, and the costs of promoting the business prior to beginning to do business. The question then arises as to whether either the newly formed or acquired business, or the individual partners, or neither of them, will be permitted to take a tax deduction for the investigation expenses and startup costs.

In determining the deductibility of investigation costs and start-up costs associated with a newly forming partnership, the law distinguishes between taxpayers who are already in the same business or one similar to the one he or she is investigating or starting up, and taxpayers who are not. Those who are already in the same or a similar business are authorized by the Code Sec. 162 to fully deduct both investigation expenses and start-up expenses for the year in which they are incurred, regardless of whether or not they ever actually get the business open.

On the other hand, those who are not already in the same or similar business cannot take a deduction for either investigation expenses or start-up expenses. However, the Code Sec. 195 permits those who are new to a given type of business to amortize both their investigation expenses and their start-up expenses over a period of not less than sixty months, provided that they actually begin to operate a new enterprise in that trade or business. The deduction may start for the first month that the business begins to operate.

If, rather than starting a new partnership, a taxpayer who is not already engaged in the same or similar trade or business contemplates the purchase of an existing partnership, he or she will not be permitted to take a deduction for either investigation expenses or start-up expenses.

Further, if he or she actually buys the partnership, he or she will be permitted to amortize only investigation expenses over a minimum of sixty months.

Any expenses incurred after the investigation that has led to the decision to purchase the partnership are no longer considered to be *investigation expenses* and must be added to the basis in his or her partnership share, a concept known as *capitalizing* the expenditure. A party who is already in the same or similar trade or business as the one acquired will be entitled to deduct both investigation and acquisition expenses incurred in connection with the newly acquired partnership, again relying on Sec. 162.

Transferring Appreciated Property for a Partnership Interest

Taxpayers who wish to acquire an ownership interest in a partnership may do so in exchange for appreciated property. The Code. Sec. 721 provides that they will not have to recognize any gain or loss on the transaction, unless any of the following three exceptions applies:

- if the partnership is an *investment company*, which is an organization that holds more than 80% of its assets as cash or some form of investment such as stocks or other securities;
- if the partnership assumes debt on property transferred in exchange for a partnership interest, and that debt exceeds the party's basis in that property plus his or her share of the debt on that property as a partner; or,
- if, rather than transferring property in exchange for a partnership interest, a taxpayer exchanges services for the interest, he or she will have to recognize the fair market value of the partnership interest received as taxable payment for those services.

EXAMPLE: Some of Rick's friends started a home maintenance business. They have not created a formal business entity, so their company is a partnership. Since Rick is a skilled carpenter, they want him to participate in the business and will make him a partner to get him. Rick owns a van in which he has an adjusted basis of $12,000, but owes $20,000 on. Rick will become a partner if the partners will give him a 10% interest in exchange for his van and have the partnership fully and exclusively assume the $20,000 indebtedness on it. If this occurs, Rick will have to recognize income of $6,000 due to relief from indebtedness, which is the difference in his basis in the van and the debt ($20,000 - $12,000 = $8,000) less his $2,000 share of the indebtedness on the van due to his being a 10% partner (.10 x $20,000).

In the absence of these exceptions, the only tax consequences of a transfer of appreciated property for partnership interest are that the transferor's basis in the newly acquired partnership interest will be limited to his or her adjusted basis in the property transferred. The partnership's basis in the acquired property will be equal to the transferor's adjusted basis in that property.

There are corresponding provisions pertaining to corporations that permit nonrecognition of gain when appreciated property is transferred in exchange for stock, but the rules for partnerships are much more favorable. In order for such transfers to corporations in exchange for stock to qualify for nonrecognition of gains and losses, the person or group making such a transfer must control 80% or more of the corporation after the exchange. There is no such requirement in exchange for a partnership interest. Therefore, unlike corporations, partnerships have the opportunity to acquire assets from owners who have experienced appreciation in them in exchange for a noncontrolling interest in the partnership without causing the transferor to have to recognize a gain on the transaction.

Advantages

The ease of formation may be viewed as an advantage of the partnership form of entity but, once the disadvantages are considered, along with the fact that partnerships are sometimes unintentionally formed, ease of formation may actually be a disadvantage.

There is no question that the primary advantage of the partnership form of business entity is its favorable tax treatment. There is no federal taxation at the partnership level. A partnership return must be filed on *Form 1065*, but it is merely an *informational return* that shows each partner's profit or loss from the partnership and how that profit or loss was calculated. The partnership then sends a *Form K-1* to each partner and to the IRS, showing each partner's share of the partnership's income or loss. Each partner then reports his or her share of partnership income on his or her individual tax return.

This approach, known as a *pass through* of partnership profits and losses (since they pass through the partnership entity to the individual partners) allows partners to use their entire partnership losses to offset other taxable income that they (or their spouses when filing a joint return) may have. At the same time, unlike C corporations that must pay taxes on their earnings only to have dividend distributions of those earnings taxed again in the hands of their shareholders, partnership profits are taxed only once in the hands of the partners.

Disadvantages

Whether or not a general partner works for the partnership, any distribution received from the partnership will be considered *self-employment income*. Sometimes general partners will take a periodic *draw* from the partnership, which they may regard as *wages* or *salary*, but for federal tax purposes, it is still self-employment income. Therefore, distributions from a partnership to a general partner, whether labeled as some form of earnings or a type of investment income, will be subject to self-employment tax to the same extent as the earnings of a sole proprietor.

Partners have repeatedly challenged this aspect of U.S. tax law in court and have always lost. Even partners who have attempted to divide their share of partnership earnings between the equivalent of salary and the equivalent of investment income have met with absolutely no success at all. The *Self-employment Contribution Act* makes it abundantly clear that every general partner's *distributive share* of partnership income is subject to self-employment tax. The Act also provides that a general partner's distributive share of losses from a partnership may be netted against self-employment income from other sources, including, but not limited to, other partnerships.

EXAMPLE: Leroy has a 30% ownership share in a partnership, but does not work for the partnership in any capacity. Leroy is a self-employed, sole proprietor in the operation of a charm school. The partnership he was involved in lost $100,000 for the year and his distributive share of that loss was $30,000. His self-employment income that year from the charm school was $55,000. He will be allowed to net his partnership loss against his charm school self-employment income leaving only $25,000 of his self-employment income subject to self-employment tax.

Another potential tax-related disadvantage to a partnership stems from the very provision that is generally touted as its greatest advantage. The fact that partnership income is automatically passed through the partnership entity and allocated to the partners denies them the option to allow any part of partnership income to be kept by the partnership as *retained earnings* and taxed at the partnership level. If this were an option, taxpayers whose individual income tax rates have reached the maximum 35% level would probably find it appealing to leave some partnership profits in their partnership to meet its capital needs.

Another potential drawback to the passing through of partnership profits to partners is the creation of *phantom income*. This arises when partnerships generate accounting profits that are deemed to be distributed to the partners, but that are not actually distributed as cash. To the degree that partnership income takes the form of increased accounts receivable for a partnership on the accrual method of accounting or it is used to acquire inventory, buy out a partner, or acquire assets, there will be no cash available for distribution. However, each partner will be required to pay both income taxes and self-employment taxes on his or her share of that partnership income.

EXAMPLE: Bubba, Spike, and Bruce were partners in a sporting goods store. Bubba and Spike actually operated the store and Bruce was merely an investor with no day-to-day involvement in the store's operation. The store made a profit of $90,000 for the year, but just before the year's end, a salesman persuaded

Bubba and Spike to add a line of mechanical squirrel decoys and other hunting gear aimed at avid squirrel hunters. In order to get a special introductory price, the products had to be paid for right away.

In January, Bruce got his *K-1* from the partnership showing that his distributive share of its profits was $30,000 for the year, but $75,000 of the partnership's profits was used to pay for the squirrel decoys and other gear. The remaining profit is being used to operate the business. Bruce will have to pay self-employment taxes and income taxes on his $30,000 share of partnership income, despite not having received any of it.

There are many tax disadvantages to partnerships. They are also fraught with so much risk, that the partnership form of business entity is simply not a good choice. There are alternatives that offer the tax advantages of a partnership without most of the disadvantages and with much less potential for personal liability on the part of the owners.

JOINT VENTURES

There is a noteworthy variation on the partnership form of organization. When two or more persons enter into a *single, specific endeavor* in hopes of realizing a profit and they do not create a formal organization, then they are generally regarded as *joint venturers*. What distinguishes the joint venture from the partnership is the fact that there is to be no ongoing relationship beyond a single activity. For instance, a group that decided to buy, renovate, and sell a single building would likely be considered joint venturers, unless they organize and operate as some other entity.

Income from a joint venture is self-employment income that is passed through the entity and taxed in the same manner as income from a partnership. In fact, profits and losses from joint ventures are reported on the same *Form 1065* that partnerships use to file their returns.

LIMITED PARTNERSHIPS

In past years, limited partnerships enjoyed some popularity. Limited partnerships are created by filing a *Limited Partnership Certificate* with the state in which the company is to be *domiciled* (legally resides).

Formation of Limited Partnerships

The certificate must contain the information required under the provisions of that state's limited partnership laws. Among the usual requirements that must appear in the Limited Partnership Certificate are:

- the name of the firm, which usually must include the actual words *limited partnership*;
- the purpose of the business;
- the location of the business;
- the names, addresses, and capital contributions of all general partners and all limited partners;
- provisions for the allocation of profits and losses; and,
- under what terms additional limited partners may be subsequently added to the company.

There must be at least one general partner in every limited partnership. The general partners will have the authority to operate the business and will have unlimited liability on matters arising within the scope of the business. There must also be at least one limited partner in a limited partnership. Limited partners have no right to participate in the management of the business, but each limited partner's liability from business matters will be limited to his or her investment, but not less than the amount indicated in the Limited Partnership Certificate as that limited partner's capital contribution.

Typically, limited partners are allowed to give advice to general partners concerning management of the company and are allowed to vote on major issues such as dissolution or removal of a general partner. However, if a limited partner becomes involved in the operation of the limited partnership or if a limited partner's name appears in the company name, then that limited partner will be subjected to unlimited liability.

Advantages

Limited partnerships have been used primarily where parties desired to be taxed as partners, but wanted limited liability. The most common application has been in the *tax sheltered* investments such as rental real estate. The profit or loss generated by the limited partnership passes through the partnership entity directly to the partners in proportion to each partner's ownership share. In recent years, revisions in the Internal Revenue Code have greatly limited favorable tax treatment for the more popular former tax shelter investments, thereby curtailing the *paper losses* that limited partners formerly used to offset income from other sources. However, since limited partnership distributions to limited partners are viewed for tax purposes as *investment income* rather than self-employment income, limited partners will generally *not* have to pay self-employment tax on the distributions they receive from the limited partnership. This could only occur to the extent that the distribution is actually a guaranteed payment for services rendered to the limited partnership.

Disadvantages

When a limited partnership generates profits that the limited partners must report and pay taxes on, the general partner may have the discretion to withhold distributions of those profits, thereby resulting in the limited partners incurring tax liability, but not receiving any funds with which to pay the taxes. This fact, coupled with the requirement that there must be at least one partner willing to take on the *unlimited liability* that goes with being a general partner have made the limited partnership form of organization a poor choice for most businesses.

LIMITED LIABILITY PARTNERSHIPS

Some groups, particularly professionals such as accountants or physicians, may favor the partnership concept of organization. Some state licensing bodies simply will not permit groups to practice in some other form of organization, while other groups are simply drawn to partnerships out of a sense of tradition. The *limited liability partnership* (LLP) offers a viable alternative to the general partnership.

Formation of Limited Liability Partnerships

Creation of a limited liability partnership requires *registration* with a state agency, usually the secretary of state, by filing an application. The application must contain;

- the name of the partnership, which must contain either *limited liability partnership*, *L.L.P.*, or *LLP;*
- its address;
- the name and address of a registered agent to receive service of process, which is legal notice that a party is being sued on behalf of the partnership; and,
- a brief description of the nature of the partnership's business.

Existing general partnerships can convert to LLPs by merely filing the appropriate application, but will achieve limited liability only prospectively rather than retroactively. State LLP laws have largely taken the form of mere amendments to existing general partnership law, whereby the partners' liability arising from the partnership business is reduced. As a result, when a general partnership converts to an LLP, it is generally not viewed as a change of entity, so there is no need to get the consent of creditors or other business associates in order to make the change. Further, the federal employment identification numbers and state sales tax numbers of the general partnership can be used by the LLP.

Advantages

The primary advantage of the LLP organizational structure is that it is taxed in the same favorable way as a general partnership, but with less potential exposure to liability from the business for the partners. The potential liability of partners in an LLP varies from state to state. Every state's LLP laws protect partners from vicarious liability for the *tortious acts* (wrongful conduct) of their fellow partners and of agents or employees of the company, as long as they were not involved in the supervision of the offending party.

Partners in limited liability partnerships, however, are still subject to unlimited personal liability for their own wrongful conduct and the wrongful conduct committed in the scope of partnership business by those they supervise. Additionally, partners in an LLP are free to participate in management of the LLP without having to surrender limited liability for having done so. There is no requirement that any partner in an LLP must be a general partner.

Disadvantages

Since LLP law is generally an extension of general partnership law, with the exception of limitations on liability, the LLP still has some of the major disadvantages that general partnerships have. Foremost among them is the fact that all of the earnings of each partner in the limited liability partnership are considered to be self-employment income that is fully subject to self-employment taxes. The fact that some of the payments may be made as if they were a salary and some in the form of an annual or other periodic distribution will not prevent any of the payments from the LLP from being considered to be self-employment income that is subject to self-employment taxes.

Additionally, the same events that cause dissolution of a general partnership, such as death of a partner, will also cause dissolution of the LLP. The remaining partners after the death of a partner in an LLP are liable to the heirs of the deceased partner to the extent of the value of the deceased's partnership interest. Also, partners in limited liability partnerships, as in general partnerships, are still expected to devote their undivided employment efforts to partnership business. They must direct to the partnership any business opportunities even remotely related to partnership business.

FAMILY PARTNERSHIPS

Family businesses, including *family partnerships*, have been common in the U.S. long before the imposition of federal income taxes. Grooming family members to assume ownership of the family business has generally been a good way to see to it that family members have good jobs, the business has trustworthy employees, and there is an orderly transfer of ownership from one generation to the next. However, in recent years, tax issues have been the major motivation for many parties in creating some form of family partnership.

Transferring Income

A major tax-based motivation for creating family partnerships is to transfer taxable income from parties who are being taxed in high marginal brackets to those being taxed in lower marginal brackets. To the degree that such a transfer is merely an *assignment of income* from the high income earner to the lower income earner, the IRS will attribute the income to the higher income earner and he or she will be taxed on it. However, to the degree that a party is a *bona fide partner*, the degree of partnership income attributed to his or her partnership interest will be taxable to him or her.

In order for a party to be a bona fide partner in a family partnership, he or she must be the actual owner of a partnership interest. There is likely to be little dispute with the IRS over this issue when a taxpayer *purchases* his or her partnership share for its fair market value. However, acquisition of an interest in a family partnership by *gift* may draw close scrutiny from the IRS. Those who have acquired their interest in a family partnership by gift can still pass the test for being a bona fide owner of their interest provided that they have actual control of the their partnership interests.

In making the determination of whether a partner has actual control, Treasury Regulation Sec. 1.704(e)(2) provides considerable guidance. The Regulation states that if a partner has obtained his or her family partnership interest by gift but the donor has retained certain controls associated with that interest, the donee will not be considered to be the bona fide owner of that interest. The controls that the Regulation labels as being of *particular significance* are:

- ◆ control of distribution of income;
- ◆ the right to further transfer a partnership interest;
- ◆ control of essential assets; and,
- ◆ retention of management powers inconsistent with normal partnership structure.

Among the other major factors for determining the legitimacy of the transfer of a family partnership interest by gift are whether there are indirect controls over the donee's interest, such as:

- control of trust distributions that could be used to influence the donee;
- whether the donee actually participates in management of the partnership;
- whether the donee's distributive share of partnership income is actually distributed to the donee for his or her sole benefit without restrictions on its use; and,
- whether the party is actually treated as a partner and held out as such to the public and business associates of the partnership.

However, the Regulation does take into consideration and make allowances for donees who are minors, trustees, or limited partners. For purposes of determining whether a partnership is a family partnership, the term *family* is defined by Sec. 704(e) as including a spouse, lineal descendant, and ancestors.

Even if it is determined that a partner has sufficient control over his or her partnership interest to be considered a bona fide partner, Sec. 704 establishes two other factors that will determine whether a partner's distributive share of partnership income will be attributed to someone else. One of those factors is whether sufficient partnership income was allocated to partners as compensation to them for services rendered to the partnership. Any distribution of partnership income that does not reflect such compensation is subject to being recharacterized by the IRS to properly attribute adequate compensation to partners who rendered service to the partnership.

EXAMPLE: Paul and his sons, Paul Jr. and Art, are partners in a dry cleaning business. Paul managed the business and performed services for the business, which had a compensable value of $72,000 based on the prevailing average salary rate for the type of job in that geographic area. The partnership had net income of $150,000. Although they are bona fide partners, neither Paul Jr. nor Art actively worked in the partnership. Paul's distributive share of partnership income must include the $72,000 that represents reasonable compensation for his services to the partnership and then one third of the remaining $78,000 for a total of $98,000. Both Paul Jr. and Art will be entitled to one third of the $78,000 left after allocation of payment for services to Paul, leaving them with a distributive share of partnership income of $26,000 each for the year.

If no allocation of partnership income were made to Paul for his service to the partnership and the partnership's $150,000 income were split evenly between the three partners, the effect would be to permit Paul to assign a significant portion of his income to his sons for tax purposes. By requiring distributions of income to a partner to reflect reasonable compensation for his earnings, Sec. 704 prevents such prohibited assignments of income.

A further consideration established by Sec. 704 begins with a determination of whether the partnership is one where *capital is a material income producing factor*. Partnerships that manufacture and/or sell goods and must invest in equipment and inventory will be considered to be among those in which capital is a material income producing factor, whereas partnerships that provide services will not be. Once the determination is made, Sec. 704 then provides that distributive earnings of bona fide partners of partnerships in which capital is a material income producing factor will, after allocation is made to partners for service rendered to the partnership, be considered as the legitimate recipients of their distributive shares of partnership income. On the other hand, if capital is not a material income producing factor for the partnership, even a bona fide partner's share of distributive partnership income is subject to being reattributed, for tax purposes, to partners who are active in the partnership unless the partners to whom the income was originally attributed also render services to the partnership.

Discounts

Another popular use of family partnerships as a tax planning tool involves transferring assets that are owned either individually or by a married couple, to a partnership and then giving *minority interests* in the partnership to family members. The tax advantage comes from being allowed to assign a *discounted value* to the partnership interest given away because it is a minority ownership interest. In such plans, it will be absolutely necessary to obtain an appraisal from a qualified appraiser that reflects the value of the partnership interest after allowance for the minority interest discount. The IRS recognizes the validity of such discounts, provided they are reasonable. A discount of 20% is not likely to be questioned, but discounts much greater than that are likely to be closely scrutinized and challenged.

EXAMPLE: Audi owned a shopping center with a fair market value of $1,000,000. She transferred it to a partnership and gave each of her two sons, Alex and Alan, a 10% interest in the partnership. For purposes of calculating gift tax on the transfers, she got an appraisal that reflected a 22% minority interest discount in the partnership share that she gave to each son. Therefore her gift to each son would be valued at $78,000 for gift tax purposes, despite the fact that the sole asset of the partnership was a shopping center with a fair market value of $1,000,000.

CORPORATIONS

The most well established entity that limits liability for its owners is a *corporation*. The corporate form of business entity is permitted even when all of the stock will be owned by one person or entity. This enables sole proprietors to opt for a corporate existence and gives existing business entities the option of incorporating subsidiary companies that they will wholly own.

Formation of Corporations

The laws of the state in which a corporation is created will govern its creation and existence. However, since most of the states in the United States pattern their corporate laws after the *Uniform Corporations Act*, there will not be a lot of disparity between the various laws. Formation involves obtaining a *charter*, known as *Articles of Incorporation* in some states, from the office of the Secretary of State or its equivalent in the state in which the organizers wish to be chartered. The charter application must contain:

- the name of the corporation, which must include either *Company*, *Corporation*, *Incorporated*, or *Inc.* in it;
- the principal business address of the company and the name of an agent to receive service of process at that address on behalf of the corporation;
- the names and addresses of each incorporator;
- a disclosure of how many shares of stock the corporation will be authorized to issue; and,
- whether or not the corporation will be *for profit*.

Investigation and Start-up Costs

Conducting investigations into the feasibility and advisability of starting a new corporation or acquiring an existing one is a standard practice among most *promoters* (which is the term used to refer to anyone starting up a corporation). The cost of such investigations often include travel expenses and fees to accountants, attorneys, appraisers, and other professionals can be costly. If the promoters decide to move forward with starting or acquiring a corporation, they commonly incur start-up costs in the form of additional professional fees, the costs of formation of the corporation, and costs associated with advertising and promoting the corporation prior to its actually commencing operation. Understanding the deductibility or other tax treatment of these investigations and start-up expenses is valuable to promoters, since they may be able to minimize nondeductible expenses. They may even convert them to deductible expenses by controlling the time at which the expenses are incurred.

Just as in the case of parties who are investigating and starting up partnerships, a promoter of a corporation who is already in the same or similar business is entitled by the Code Sec. 162 to fully deduct both investigation or start-up expenses in the year in which they were incurred. Such parties are allowed to take a tax deduction for investigation expenses even if they decide not to start or acquire a corporation upon conclusion of their investigation. However, those who are not already in the same or a similar business cannot take a deduction for either investigation or start-up expenses, although the Code Sec. 248

does permit the corporation that is newly formed or acquired to amortize certain investigation and start-up expenses over a period of not less than sixty months. If parties who are not already in the same trade or business conduct an investigation and decide against the venture, they will not be allowed any type of tax write off for the costs of their investigation.

Among the expenses that are eligible for amortization in situations where a corporation cannot flatly deduct pre-incorporation expenses, are incorporation fees and the cost of professional fees paid to attorneys, accountants, and other experts for setting up a new corporation. Also, when a party conducting an investigation to determine whether or not to buy an existing corporation incurs expenses that he or she cannot deduct because he or she is not already in the same or similar trade or business, the Code Sec. 195 permits the costs of the investigation to be amortized up to the point when he or she decides to actually purchase the company. Expenses incurred in completing the purchase of a corporation must be *capitalized* and added to the party's basis in the corporation. The costs associated with issuance and sale of stock in a newly formed corporation or the cost of transferring assets must also be capitalized.

Transferring Appreciated Property in Exchange for Stock

Taxpayers who acquire stock in a corporation in exchange for property they own that has appreciated may avoid recognition of that appreciation if they meet the requirements of the Code Sec. 351. By far the most stringent requirement of Sec. 351 is that immediately following the transfer, the person or persons who made the transfer must control at least 80% of the combined voting power of all classes of stock of the corporation. This provision effectively limits the nonrecognition provisions of Sec. 351 to situations involving initial start-up or acquisition of a corporation. Also, transfers of appreciated property to an *investment company* (one that holds more than 80% of its assets as cash or some form of investment) are ineligible for nonrecognition of gain under Sec. 351.

Even when all the requirements of Sec. 351 are met, a taxpayer must still recognize gain in the form of *debt relief* when the property transferred to the corporation for stock is encumbered with debt in excess of his or her basis in the property. At that time, the corporation becomes responsible for the indebtedness. Also, parties who render services for a corporation in exchange for stock as compensation for those services must recognize the fair market value of the shares as part of their gross income.

EXAMPLE: Stan, Willie, Mickey, and Hank started a corporation and retained 100% ownership among them. Stan transferred land in which he had a basis of $200,000 to the corporation for $600,000 worth of stock. This reflects the fair market value of the land which Stan owned free of debt. Willie transferred equipment worth $300,000 to the company in exchange for $200,000 worth of stock, plus the company assumed $100,000 in debt that Willie owed on the equipment. Willie had depreciated the equipment such that his adjusted basis in it at the time of the exchange was $50,000. Mickey paid $150,000 in cash for $150,000 worth of stock in the corporation. Hank performed services in organizing the corporation in exchange for $50,000 worth of stock. The corporation was not an investment company.

Stan will not be required to recognize gain on the land he transferred to the company since the group that organized the corporation controlled over 80% of it after the exchanges. Since the corporation assumed $100,000 in debt owed by Willie and his adjusted basis in the property that he transferred was only $50,000, he must recognize the excess of the debt over adjusted basis ($100,000 - $50,000), the sum of $50,000, as income. Since Mickey purchased his shares for cash, there will be no tax consequences from his acquisition. Because Hank obtained his corporate share in exchange for services, he must fully recognize the $50,000 value of those shares as ordinary income.

Nonrecognition of gain on appreciated property exchanged for stock in a corporation does not come without a price. The taxpayer who exchanges such property for stock will be required to carry over the low basis from the property given up to the stock acquired. At the same time, the corporation will have to use the transferor's basis as its basis in the property that it receives.

In the example, Stan's basis in his stock will be the $200,000 basis that he had in his land rather than the $600,000 fair market value of the stock received. Willie will have a zero basis in his stock since his $50,000 basis in the equipment that he transferred was totally offset by corporate assumption of his debt. Mickey's basis in his stock will be the $150,000 cash price that he paid for it. Hank will have a $50,000 basis in his stock, since he fully recognized its fair market value of $50,000 as ordinary income.

Because they are sanctioned by the state through the grant of a charter, corporations are recognized as *artificial legal beings* with an identity separate from the identities of their shareholders. As separate legal entities, they must file a tax return of their own. Small corporations have a choice as to whether they will be taxed under subchapter C or subchapter S of the Internal Revenue Code.

C Corporations

In the absence of an election to the contrary by the stockholders of eligible corporations, subchapter C of the Internal Revenue Code governs taxation of corporations. This is the source of the term *C corporation.* After deducting all of its business expenses, the corporation must pay a tax on its *net income.* There are no such things as a standard deduction or exemptions for corporations. The rate of taxation for corporations is set in the Code Sec. 11(b).

Most corporations must pay a 15% tax on their first $50,000 of taxable income, a 25% tax on all taxable income over $50,000 up to $75,000, a 34% tax on all taxable income over $75,000 up to $10,000,000 and a 35% tax on all taxable income in excess of $10,000,000. A surtax of 5%, up to a maximum of $11,750, is levied on corporate taxable income in excess of $100,000 which phases out the benefits of the lower 15% and 25% tax brackets and results in an effective tax rate of 34% on taxable income in excess of $335,000.

Corporations with taxable income in excess of $15,000,000 must pay a 3% surtax up to a total of $100,000, which eliminates the effect of the 34% tax bracket once the corporation's income reaches $18,333,333. Personal service corporations are taxed at a flat 35% without any graduation in rates.

Disadvantages

Distributions made by C corporations to their shareholders are generally *dividends*. In determining their tax liability, corporations are *not* allowed to take a deduction for the dividends they pay. The result is that the cash dividends that a corporation pays will come from the company's *after-tax income*. However, the shareholders who receive the dividends will still be required to include them as income in calculating their personal tax liabilities. The maximum tax rate for individuals is only 15% on dividends. This *double taxation* is a major criticism of C corporations.

Companies may *accumulate* some earnings, rather than pay them out as dividends, but the Code Sec. 531 provides for the imposition of an *accumulated earnings tax* equal to the highest marginal tax rate for individuals when earnings have been allowed to accumulate beyond the reasonable needs of the business. The Internal Revenue Code Sec. 536 allows most corporations to accumulate earnings of $250,000 without any question as to whether this amount exceeds the company's reasonable needs. However, in order to avoid the accumulated earnings tax on amounts in excess of that, the corporation must be prepared to demonstrate a genuine need. Section 537 of the Internal Revenue Code provides some guidance to corporations for showing reasonable needs for accumulating earnings beyond $250,000.

Many new C corporations do not have sufficent earnings to either accumulate or pay out in dividends. In those C corporations, losses generated by the company can be used only to offset past or future profits. Since there are no past profits for newly formed corporations, the C corporation's loss would not be available to offer any relief from taxation until the company became profitable. The individual shareholders could not deduct any part of the C corporation's loss, since there is no such thing as a negative dividend. If the C corporation that has suffered losses never makes profits sufficient to offset those losses, the tax benefits of the losses may be lost. If a C corporation's losses cause it to become insolvent and its stock to become worthless, then the shareholders may take a capital loss in the amount of each of their respective investments.

Some relief from this disadvantage may be found if the stock in question had been issued by the corporation directly to a shareholder who held it until it became worthless or otherwise disposed of it at a loss and

the conditions of the Code Sec. 1244 were met. In that case, the shareholder could take up to $50,000 ($100,000 for a married couple filing
jointly) as ordinary loss. The requirements of the Code Sec. 1244 are that
the corporation was a *small business* and that it derived over 50% of its
aggregate gross receipts from sources other than royalties, rents, dividends, interest, annuities, or sale or exchange of securities. For purposes
of the Code Sec. 1244, a *small business* is defined as one that has not
received over $1,000,000 totally in exchange for all the stock it issued or
as a contribution to capital or as paid in surplus.

The advantage of being able to treat losses as ordinary losses is that
they can be used to offset any other income. If losses are capital losses,
they must be used to offset capital gains first, even though some or all of
the capital gains may have been long-term and otherwise eligible for special favorable tax treatment. There is no limit as to how much capital
gain may be offset by capital loss, but only $3,000 of ordinary income of
individuals may be offset by capital loss in a given year. This amount is
reduced to $1,500 for married taxpayers who file separately. Any unused
loss may be carried forward until it is fully used.

Advantages

Although the tax treatment of C corporations is generally viewed as a
major disadvantage, it can actually be beneficial in some situations. In
smaller corporations, the stockholders of the company are usually also on
the board of directors. It is the board of directors that makes the decision
of whether or not to declare a dividend. Declaration of dividends is solely
within the board's discretion. There is no law requiring declaration of
dividends, although the accumulated earnings tax clearly provides incentives for directors to pay dividends rather than pay that tax.

However, it may be advantageous for shareholders who have reached
the higher individual tax brackets to forego dividend distributions and
allow taxation to occur at the corporate level at only 15% on up to
$50,000 in profits per year. This may be a better choice if the company
can do so without incurring accumulated earnings tax. It is a sound business practice for businesses to accumulate reserves for emergencies or
future expansion. It is also better to let the corporation retain a net of
85% of its pre-tax earnings. The corporation can do this rather than pay-

ing dividends to shareholders in marginal tax brackets of up to 35% and then having them reinvest only what they have left after taxes.

Having a corporation accumulate some earnings enables the company to avoid having to turn to shareholders for more capital in times of emergency. Since shareholders may not have chosen to accumulate past distributions, they may not have funds readily available to meet the corporation's needs. The result may even be the creation of an atmosphere of crisis from a situation that the company could easily have handled had it had sufficient accumulated earnings to meet its needs.

If the company is being sold, the shareholders should be able to sell their shares of stock in the company at a price that reflects the fact that the corporation has some accumulated earnings. In that situation, the shareholders would realize a direct benefit from the corporation's accumulated earnings, but in the form of a *capital gain*, rather than a distribution.

If a shareholder has held his or her shares for over one year prior to selling them, the Code Sec. 1222 defines any gains from such a sale as *long-term capital gain*. The Code Section 1(h) provides for a maximum tax rate of 15% on long-term capital gains in this situation—the same as the tax rate on dividends. If the sale proceeds do not qualify as long-term capital gains, it would be better to pay the accumulated earnings out as dividends and reduce the sale price.

For shareholders who have owned their shares for over five years, the Code Sec. 1202 may allow them to completely exclude 50% of their gain from the sale of those shares from taxation. In order to qualify for the 50% exclusion, the stock must be *qualified business stock*. (See Chapter 2 for more detailed information about qualified business stock.)

A further requirement of the Code Sec. 1202 is that the corporation be an *active business*, except for a special rule waiving the requirement for specialized small business investment companies (see Chapter 2 for more information about an active business). The corporation must also be an *eligible* corporation. This means that it must be a domestic corporation and not one of the few types of companies listed in Sec. 1202(e)(4).

Although the Code specifically states that these provisions are for *small business stock*, the companies involved can actually have assets of up to $50,000,000 and still qualify. In addition, shareholders may use the

50% exclusion on at least $10,000,000 of eligible gains from the sale of qualified small business stock. These provisions have historically made the C corporation an especially attractive choice for promoters who were planning on starting a company in hopes of eventually selling it once it is well established.

Most really small C corporations do not have a significant problem with double taxation. Corporations cannot take a tax deduction for the dividends they pay, but they can take a deduction for the wages and salaries that they pay. If the owners of the corporation are also all employees of the company, they can merely adjust salaries and bonuses sufficiently to leave little or no profit in the corporation when that would yield a lower tax liability.

However, paying a *salary* to someone who does not actually work in the corporation is inappropriate and would likely result in the IRS recharacterizing the payment as a dividend if detected in an audit. Also, the wages and salaries of those who work in the corporation should be reasonable in light of the work that they do, but in small companies where the owners fill the key positions it is certainly reasonable to conclude that any success enjoyed by the company is the result of the owners' efforts, and that they should be compensated accordingly.

On the other hand, some dividends are not subject to FICA taxes or self-employment tax. These dividends are taxed at a maximum 15% rate. As a result, it may be beneficial for some small corporations to sufficiently reduce salaries to allow the company to earn up to $50,000; pay the 15% corporate income tax rate on it; and, pay the balance out as a dividend to owners in the higher tax brackets.

S Corporations

There is another option for small corporations. The shareholders of small corporations may choose to be taxed under subchapter S of the Internal Revenue Code. If they do, they are known as *S corporations*. As with C corporations, the shareholders of S corporations enjoy true limited liability from both the *tortious conduct* of their fellow owners and company employees and the contractual obligations of the company.

The legal existence of an S corporation is unaffected by the death of any shareholder. Shareholders are free to transfer their shares without restrictions other than those that may have been imposed by the share-holders themselves, such as the right of first refusal by the corporation before shares may be transferred.

Formation of S Corporations

The reason that C corporations and S corporations share similar charac-teristics is that they both originate from a corporate charter. The charters for S corporations are the same as those for C corporations. After a cor-porate charter is granted, the corporation will be a C corporation unless the shareholders of an eligible corporation choose to be an S corporation. (See the section on Corporations, p.180, for more information on matter affecting corporations in general.)

If such a choice is made, all that the shareholders are doing is choos-ing to be taxed under subchapter S of the Internal Revenue Code. Becoming an S corporation will not result in any change in the structure of the corporation, nor will its charter have to be changed in any way. Selection of S corporation status merely means that the corporation will be taxed as if it were a partnership.

The *election* to be an S corporation, provided for in the Code Sec. 1362, may be made by the shareholders of a newly formed eligible corporation or by the shareholders of an existing qualified C corporation. There can be only one class of stock in a corporation in order for it to be eligible to make a subchapter S election. Differences in voting rights among the shares in that one class are permitted without affecting the shareholders' eligibility to make such an election.

There are a few corporations that, by virtue of the Code Sec. 1361(b)(2), are ineligible to become subchapter S corporations, even if they would otherwise qualify. In order to qualify for the S corporation election, the corporation must be a domestic corporation with no more than seventy-five shareholders, none of whom is a nonresident alien. There is a special provision in the Code Sec. 1361(c)(1) that allows the stock holdings of a husband and wife in a given corporation to be treated as if the stock were held by one shareholder.

The election by the shareholders of a newly formed corporation must be made within two months and fifteen days of the earliest event of:

♦ the date the corporation first had shareholders;

◆ the date the corporation first had assets; or,

◆ the date the corporation first began doing business.

The election by the shareholders of an existing C corporation to become an S corporation may be made at any time during the preceding tax year and on or before the fifteenth day of the third month of the taxable year in which the S corporation status is to begin. S corporations are generally required to be on a calendar taxable year; however, the Code Sec. 1378 does permit them to use an alternative accounting period if the company can show a satisfactory *business purpose* for doing so.

The valid S corporation election is made on *Form 2553*. It requires the company's address, employee identification number, specification as to the year in which the election is to be effective, and a brief consent statement that must be executed by every shareholder by the time the form is submitted. In addition to the signatures on the consent statements, the overall form must bear the signature of an officer of the company.

In cases when the subchapter S election is made after the deadline, the Code Sec. 1362(b)(5) gives government officials the authority to treat the election as having been made in a timely manner if it is determined that there was *reasonable cause* for the failure to make a timely election. The statute even permits a determination that a timely filing was made when there was no filing at all upon proper showing of reasonable cause for the failure to file.

Once a subchapter S election is made, it will be effective for the year it initially goes into effect and each subsequent year until it is terminated. Subchapter S status will terminate by law if the corporation ceases to qualify as a small corporation by virtue of having too many shareholders or if the corporation has passive investment income (such as rents, interest, dividends, and capital gains from sale of securities) that consist of more than 25% of its gross receipts for three consecutive years in which it has accumulated earnings and profits.

Subchapter S status may also be voluntarily relinquished through revocation by the corporation, as long as a majority of the shareholders consent to the revocation. If subchapter S status of a corporation is terminated, the company will retain its status as a corporation, but will be taxed as a C corporation. Further, the shareholders cannot elect to return to subchapter S status for five years, even though the company may otherwise be eligible.

There may be tax consequences to a corporation's loss of subchapter S status. If the S corporation holds appreciated assets, surrendering subchapter S status may result in capital gains tax on that appreciation.

Advantages

Clearly, the decision to elect S corporation status over C corporation status is strictly a taxation issue. However, it is not always clear as to which choice will be better for a given business. S corporations are often referred to as *pass through* entities, similar to partnerships. This is due to the fact that, for purposes of taxation, the income of both S corporations and partnerships pass through the business entity and is generally taxed only at the ownership level. The essence of a subchapter S election by the shareholders of a corporation is that the corporation will be taxed as if it were a partnership, while still enjoying the advantages of incorporation.

S corporations must file a federal tax return, but it is merely an *informational return* that shows how the profits and losses of the corporation were derived and how much was allocated to each owner. The S corporation is not expected to actually pay taxes. By contrast, the C corporation must file a return and pay taxes on its taxable income and its distributions, other than salaries to shareholders, that are subject to taxation as dividends. This elimination of *double taxation* has been a major factor in the popularity of S corporations.

Another consideration for choosing S corporation status is to avoid a challenge by the IRS. Shareholders who are also employees of small C corporations, upon realizing that their corporations are about to finish a tax year with a profit, will often simply pay out sufficient salary bonuses to themselves to give their corporations enough salary expense deduction to eliminate the profit. If these bonuses bear little or no reasonable relationship to the efforts expended by the shareholders on behalf of the corporation, the IRS may challenge the appropriateness of considering these *bonuses* as a form of salary.

If the IRS is successful, a corporation's salary deduction for the bonus payments will be disallowed, resulting in taxable income to the corporation in the amount of the lost deductions. The payments to the shareholders will be recharacterized as dividends and taxed as such to the recipients. There will also be interest on the newly computed corporate tax liability as well as additional penalties. There is no such *reasonableness of compensation* test for distributions to shareholders in an S corporation. All the corporation's profits are automatically allocated to the shareholders on the basis of each shareholder's ownership interest or as otherwise provided by agreement among the shareholders for *guaranteed payments beyond distributions* to some shareholders.

Guaranteed payments beyond distributions result in some shareholders receiving greater than their pro rata share of company profits based solely on ownership. Such guaranteed payments are usually for shareholders who make a disproportionate contribution to the company. Situations where shareholders who work for the corporation receive guaranteed payments and those who do not work for the company receive no such payments would be typical. Generally, the IRS will respect the corporation's allocation of guaranteed payments.

However, the Code Sec. 482 does allow the IRS to reapportion income allocations among related taxpayers in order to *prevent evasion of taxes*. Such a reallocation is most likely to occur when corporate income is allocated as a guaranteed payment. At this time, such income (and the incidence of its taxation) is shifted away from taxpayers who are in high tax brackets to related taxpayers in low tax brackets.

In order to avoid the consequences of the Code Sec. 482, the company making guaranteed payments should be able to demonstrate justification for the payments. This justification will usually be work performed or other contributions to the company. For example, if a father and son were to form an S corporation as equal owners, but only the son actually worked in the company, it would be easy to justify guaranteed payments to the son. The father's income from the corporation would consist only of distributions of corporate profits if any were earned.

A major advantage of becoming an S corporation arises when the company suffers a *net operating loss*. If an S corporation suffers an operating loss, it is passed through the corporate entity to the shareholders, who may use it to offset ordinary income on their next individual tax returns. Losses of the S corporation are *immediately* available to shareholders for a write off. The importance of this immediate tax relief can better be appreciated when viewed in the context of the typical new small business scenario.

Usually, newly formed small businesses suffer operating losses in the beginning as they struggle to develop a customer base. Small businesses also usually start out undercapitalized. With only a short history of existence and no profits to show for that limited period of operation, the newly formed small corporation will not be likely to find readily available sources of credit from commercial lenders. It will generally be up to the shareholders to help the corporation meet its needs by making loans to the company.

When a shareholder has income from sources other than the corporation (or has a spouse with income and files a joint tax return) the tax savings realized by being able to offset this other taxable income with losses from the S corporation may be a source of funds from which loans to the corporation may be made. If, as an alternative, the decision is made to attempt to attract additional investors to the corporation to meet its capital needs, it will be less difficult if they are able to immediately use their share of any further losses to offset taxable income from other sources.

FICA

The passing of losses through an S corporation to the shareholders is a major reason such corporations are said to be taxed as if they were partnerships. However, there is actually a distinct difference in one aspect of the taxation of S corporation shareholders and partners of a partnership that makes the S corporation even more attractive. This difference lies in the way distributions from S corporations and partnerships are subjected to FICA taxes.

The distributions by partnerships to the partners are considered self-employment income under the provisions of the Code Sec. 1402(a). In addition to regular income taxes, the recipients of self-employment income must pay full, self-employment tax on a designated amount of income ($87,000 in 2003) and the Medicare hospital insurance portion of self-employment tax on income in excess of that amount.

The full rate of taxation on self-employment income is 15.3 %. The nominal rate of the Medicare hospital insurance portion of self-employment tax is 2.9%. The Internal Revenue Code permits certain adjustments in the amount of self-employment income to which the tax rate is applied, so that the effective rate of self-employment tax is, for most taxpayers, a little over 12.3% on the fully taxable amount. It is about 2% on the Medicare hospital insurance portion.

NOTE: *When a partner works in a partnership and is paid some periodic draw or salary, even those payments are taxable as self-employment income to that partner.*

By contrast, payments by S corporations to shareholders are distinctly divided into two categories. Payments for work that shareholders do for the company are referred to as *wages* or *salaries*. All of the wages and salaries paid by a corporation to its employees are subject to Social Security and Medicare tax under the *Federal Insurance Contributions Act* (FICA). Tax rates are the same as the nominal self-employment tax rates, but one half is paid by the employer and one half is paid by the employee.

There are no adjustments to an employee's income before applying the tax rate. There is no deduction allowed for taxpayers from total income for any portion of the FICA tax liability. The corporation may deduct its FICA payments as a business expense. The combined employer and employee shares of FICA taxes that are levied on wages drawn by a shareholder who is an employee of an S corporation are obviously not less than the self-employment tax that a partner would pay on money received as a distribution from the partnership. The tax savings for the shareholders of an S corporation come from the fact that distributions other than salary actually escape FICA taxation altogether.

Distributions of earnings of a shareholder who does not work in the S corporation are totally excluded from FICA taxation. If these same distributions were made by a partnership to a partner, even one that is not active in the business of a general partnership, they would be subject to self-employment tax on the partner's individual tax return.

Rather than being merely investors, the shareholders in most small corporations are also employees of the company they own. It would be beneficial for the shareholders who are employed by the S corporation to take all of their income as distributions, rather than any salary and avoid FICA taxes altogether. However, this is not an option.

By law, the shareholder/employee of an S corporation must be paid a reasonable salary for work performed. This salary will be subject to FICA tax. Any payments available to such a shareholder in excess of a reasonable salary can and should be made in the form of a distribution, rather than as added salary. It is these distributions that are not subject to either FICA taxes or self-employment tax.

EXAMPLE: In 2003, Shaka operated a day care center as a proprietorship and realized a self-employment income of $100,000 for the year. His net, self-employment tax was $13,466.15. If he could establish that a fair market rate of salary for someone serving in his capacity as manager of the day care were $30,000 a year, he could incorporate, make a timely subchapter S election and have the corporation hire him as its manager at a $30,000 annual salary. The result would be that the combined FICA taxes would be $4,590.00 on the $30,000 salary. The employee would pay $2,295 of this tax, for which he would receive no tax deduction. The corporation would also pay $2,295 of the tax, but would be allowed to deduct it as a business expense.

Had the taxpayer received the $2,295 that was paid by the employer on his behalf, he would have had to pay income tax on that money at his highest marginal rate. Therefore, since the employer's share of FICA tax paid on behalf of the employee is made on a before-tax basis rather than after tax (as is the employee's share), the total FICA tax burden to the owner/employee of the S corporation has the same net effect as self-employment tax would on the same sum. The balance of the day care's earnings would be allocated to the shareholder/employee as a distribution subject to income tax, but without any FICA tax or self-employment tax levied on it. Using the S corporation entity, rather than a proprietorship, would have saved the company's owner almost $8,900 in self-employment taxes for 2003.

Disadvantages

One of the most highly touted advantages of the S corporation, that of being taxed as a partnership, can actually be a *disadvantage*. The calculation of profits of corporations is done on the basis of accepted accounting principles that do not leave corporations much flexibility in the treatment of expenses and income in arriving at profits. Also, many corporations must adopt the *accrual method of accounting*, which means that, once the money is owed to a corporation for accounting purposes, it is treated the same as if it were cash that had been received by the company. As a result, it is common for corporations to show profits on their books that do not show up as balances in the companies' bank accounts. These profits will usually take the form of increases in accounts receivable, but may also develop as additions to inventory. The result is a *phantom income* that is fully taxable but which, due to its *illiquidity*, offers no source of funds from which to pay the taxes on it.

When a new corporation is formed and bills customers for the goods and services that it provides (rather than making cash sales), it is quite possible that the corporation's accounts receivable will generate a phantom income problem for its first year of operation. This is due to the fact that the corporation started with no accounts receivable, so any accounts receivable balance generated by the end of the year will constitute an increase. The problem will usually subside in subsequent years since newly generated accounts receivable merely replace those that were already recognized.

EXAMPLE: A newly formed corporation on the accrual method of accounting closed out its first year of operation with profits in the form of accounts receivable of $100,000. The entire amount must be recognized as income to the corporation in that first year. If, at the end of the second year of operation, the company had $120,000 in accounts receivable due to additional uncollected profits, it would only have to recognize the $20,000 addition as income in year two, since $100,000 of it had already been recognized in year one. But, if the corporation has sizable increases in its profits in future years that also generate sizeable growth in its accounts receivable, it will experience corresponding increases in phantom income.

The problem of having taxable income that takes the form of accounts receivable is especially acute in an S corporation because all of the corporation's income is passed through the company to the shareholders. The result is taxable income, but no cash distributions with which to pay the tax liability.

Businesses that do not generate significant accounts receivable as well as those who have gotten past their start-up years and stabilized their accounts receivable levels are still not immune to the phantom income problem. It is not uncommon for operators of small businesses to mistakenly believe that as long as they do not actually take money out of the corporation, but reinvest the company's income, it will not be taxed. For the most part, this is simply not true. Increasing the company's inventory under the belief that such expenditures are an expense that the corporation may deduct from taxable income is a relatively common misguided attempt to reduce taxes. Under provisions of the Internal Revenue Code, any increase in inventory is actually a form of income to a taxpayer.

Still others reinvest profits in equipment, only to later discover that it cannot be *expensed* (fully deducted at once in the year it was purchased) but must be depreciated over a number of years. The money spent on the equipment must be recognized in full as income in the year it was received, but only part of the expenditure can be used that year as an offsetting deduction. Again, the result is taxable income which does not generate a cash distribution with which to pay the tax because it was used to buy inventory or spent on equipment. Even when the business operators fully understand the consequences of adding to inventory or acquiring depreciable equipment, they may simply have no other choice if they intend to stay in business or meet their targets for growth.

Often shareholders who are faced with having to pay taxes on S corporation distributions, but who have not received actual cash will have taxable income from other sources as well, or will file a joint return with a spouse who has taxable income. The shareholder's phantom income will be added to other taxable income, resulting in its being taxed at the taxpayer's highest marginal tax rate. Had the corporation been a C corporation, the shareholders would have been able to adjust their salaries so that part, if not all, of what was phantom income to S corporation shareholders would be taxed at the corporate level. With the first $50,000 of C corporation income being taxed at only 15%, this allows the corporation to develop an accounts receivable. It can also reinvest at least some of its profits in inventory or equipment without losing a great deal of those earnings to income taxes.

Such retention of profits is regarded as accumulated earnings, even though they are not retained as cash. It is not practical for a business to have total accumulated earnings in excess of $250,000, in most cases, so this opportunity to reduce taxes will probably be available only to new corporations in the early years of their existence. However, the early years are those in which most corporations are in the greatest need of capital. Tax reduction is a source of that capital that neither adds to debt nor dilutes ownership equity.

PROFESSIONAL CORPORATIONS

For many years, professionals such as doctors, attorneys, and accountants were not permitted to practice their professions through corporate entities. The reason for this prohibition was the fear that professionals could escape liability for their negligence in performing their duties due to the limited liability enjoyed by corporations. The theory was that not only would injured parties be denied the recoveries that they deserved, but also that the professionals would be more careless since they would not be held accountable for their negligence.

However, when revisions in the tax laws gave corporations certain tax advantages compared to unincorporated entities with regard to pension funds, the professionals began to clamor for some relief. The laws were changed and now *professional corporations,* known as PCs, are permitted in virtually every state, even though the tax laws that prompted their creation have long since been changed.

Professional practitioners are still liable for their negligence in either performing their profession or supervising others for the professional corporation. Many states still provide for imputing the negligence in the professional practice of each shareholder to every other shareholder. In states where shareholders of a professional corporation are not liable for the negligent practice of their fellow shareholders, it is obvious that this limitation on liability is a major advantage to forming a PC. But, since professionals who practice together without forming a professional corporation are likely to be considered partners, even when the negligent malpractice of one shareholder is imputed to the other shareholders, there are still advantages to operating as a PC.

While professional corporations are still basically corporations with most of the same advantages and disadvantages of nonprofessional corporations, there is one major advantage that is exclusive to professional corporations. Professional corporations are allowed to use the *cash method of accounting* instead of the accrual method. This permits the professional corporation's shareholders to make a subchapter S election without facing the problem of having income in the form of accounts receivable and no cash with which to pay the tax.

However, the *right* to use the cash method of accounting is predicated on professional corporations being service providers. If the PC also sells goods, it may also be required to use the accrual method of accounting. Some sale of goods by professional corporations is permitted, but if the company's revenues from sale of goods is 15% or more, the IRS is likely to challenge the company's right to use the cash method of accounting.

LIMITED LIABILITY COMPANIES

In 1977, the legislature of Wyoming enacted legislation that created a new form of business organization known as the *limited liability company* or simply LLC. Other states have followed suit and limited liability companies may be established in each of the fifty states of the U.S. Unlike corporate laws and partnership laws (which are based on model acts, making them relatively uniform nationwide), LLC laws can vary from state to state.

Formation of LLCs

Despite variations in state laws pertaining to LLCs, there are certain common characteristics of most. Limited liability companies are all sanctioned by the specific state in which they are formed. In order to become sanctioned, the organizers must file a form with the appropriate state department (usually the Secretary of State or its equivalent) of the state in which they are organizing. The form to be filed, most commonly referred to as *Articles of Organization*, generally must contain:

- ◆ the name and address of the company, which must contain the words *limited liability company* or the abbreviation *LLC* or *L.L.C.*;
- ◆ the name of the agent who is to receive service of process for the company at its principal business address; and,
- ◆ the duration of the existence of the company.

The articles of organization must also usually contain information pertaining to the owners of the company.

Almost every state in the U.S. permits an LLC to be formed and owned by as little as one person. Typically an Articles of Organization must include:

- ◆ the number of owners, who are referred to as *members*;
- ◆ the names and addresses of the members;
- ◆ an indication of whether the LLC will be *member-managed* or *board-managed* (manager-managed);
- ◆ whether or not members have preemptive rights; and,
- ◆ whether or not the company has the right to expel a member.

Some states also require relatively extensive financial disclosures when forming an LLC.

Advantages

In many respects, the limited liability company may be viewed as a new and improved version of the old limited partnership. The option of taxation as a partnership is available, but all of the owners are free to participate in the management of the company. No one is required to be the equivalent of a general partner with unlimited liability.

Initially, there was an issue as to how limited liability companies would be taxed. Those forming LLCs had to be careful to organize each company so that it did not have too much resemblance to a corporation, or it would be taxed as a corporation, despite the lack of issuance of a corporate charter to the company. However, in 1996, the Internal Revenue

Service issued a regulation that established the *check the box* approach to the taxation of limited liability companies.

What the regulation provides is that the determination of how an LLC will be taxed will be made on the basis of the company's choice indicated on its tax return. This provision relieves the organizers of a company from the burden of meeting a deadline to file a form to elect tax treatment as a partnership, as must be done with an S corporation, as well as permitting them to put off the decision until the time that the tax return actually must be prepared. This gives the organizers an opportunity to make the decision on the basis of the company's actual performance for its first taxable year of operation.

Disadvantages

In situations where LLCs chose to be taxed as partnerships, there was a question as to whether the distributions of profits to members were to be regarded as self-employment income to the recipients for tax purposes. This is a very important issue since, as previously discussed, self-employment income is subject to self-employment tax, which may yield relatively burdensome levels of tax liability, whereas investment income is not subject to self-employment tax.

The issue is unresolved leaving it up to the individual taxpayer to decide. If he or she chooses to designate only part of his or her LLC income as self-employment income and pay self-employment taxes on it, he or she runs the risk of being challenged in an IRS audit for designating the balance as investment income and excluding it from self-employment tax calculations.

FAMILY LIMITED LIABILITY COMPANIES

As with partnerships, *family limited liability companies* have become a popular device for legitimately transferring the realization and taxation of income from one taxpayer to another and for transferring assets at discounted values for gift and estate tax purposes. The very same restrictions and requirements that govern family partnerships also apply to the family LLCs. (See the discussion of Family Partnerships on p.176.)

Chapter 11

Retirement Plans

Usually, one of the major sacrifices made by those who start their own businesses is the loss of a retirement program. Some large corporations' pension plans are among the most attractive aspects of employment, but small companies, particularly in their earliest years of development, can rarely afford any type of retirement benefit. As a result, it will be necessary for most owners of small businesses to provide for their own retirement funds.

INDIVIDUAL RETIREMENT ARRANGEMENTS

One of the most fundamental approaches available to those seeking to establish a retirement fund on their own is the *Individual Retirement Arrangement* (IRA). Under the provisions of the *Economic Growth and Tax Relief Reconciliation Act of 2001* (EGTRRA 2001), a taxpayer who is under 70½ years of age and is not covered by a retirement plan maintained by an employer is allowed to deposit the lesser of his or her adjusted gross income or $3,000 in an IRA. He or she can then deduct the deposit from total income in arriving at taxable income for tax years 2003 and 2004.

The $3,000 limit is scheduled to increase to $4,000 for 2005 through 2007 and further increase to $5,000 for 2008 with annual adjustments for inflation in $500 increments in subsequent years. Taxpayers over fifty years of age are allowed an extra $500 in the limit for 2003 through 2005 and an extra $1,000 thereafter.

Even if a party is an active participant in an employer-sponsored retirement plan, he or she is still eligible to take a deduction for the full allowable IRA contribution if his or her adjusted gross income for the year 2003 was no more than $40,000 and he or she was single, an unmarried head of household, or a widower. Adjusted gross income above $40,000 results in reductions in the deduction allowed for IRA contributions until it becomes zero at adjusted gross income levels of $50,000 or more. Increases in the adjusted gross income level that a party may have before deductions for an IRA contribution will be reduced, are scheduled on a yearly basis until 2005, at which time, it will be $50,000.

A married taxpayer filing a joint return in 2003 is permitted to have up to $60,000 in combined adjusted gross income and still take the deduction for a full allowable IRA contribution, despite actively participating in a retirement plan provided by an employer. Eligibility for the deduction is phased out between $60,000 and $70,000 of combined adjusted gross income. Increases in the level of combined adjusted gross income that a taxpayer may have and still take a deduction for IRA contributions, despite being covered by a retirement plan provided by an employer, are scheduled until 2007, when it will reach $80,000.

Whether or not a taxpayer is eligible to make a deductible contribution to his or her own IRA, the party's spouse may make a deductible contribution of up to $3,000 to his or her own IRA, even if the spouse had no income, as long as he or she is not covered by an employer retirement plan and the couple's combined adjusted gross income does not exceed $150,000 (at which level there is a phasing out of the deduction, which becomes zero at $160,000). These provisions enable a married couple to exclude as much as $6,000 per year from their taxable income. A deductible IRA contribution reduces the participant's amount of income upon which federal income taxes are imposed for the year in which the deposit is credited, as well as deferring federal taxation on the earnings generated by cumulative IRA deposits.

When IRA deposits and earnings are withdrawn, they are subject to federal income taxation. However, there is no doubt that those who have chosen to take advantage of the IRA option will have a much larger total value in their accounts than they would have if they paid federal income taxes on those same funds, invested what was left, and then paid annual federal income taxes on the earnings as well. Moreover, there is also a significant likelihood that when a taxpayer withdraws funds from an IRA he or she will be retired and in a lower federal income tax bracket than when the IRA deposits were made, or when they generated earnings.

As with other tax provisions, there are drawbacks to investing in an IRA. If an IRA participant withdraws funds from the account before he or she is 59½ years of age, a 10% penalty on the withdrawal must be paid. The amount withdrawn must be included as taxable income for the year in which it was received. However, no early withdrawal penalty will be imposed if the withdrawal is for:

- ◆ payment of the cost of higher education for the participant, spouse, a child of the participant, or grandchild of the participant;
- ◆ qualified first-time home purchases;
- ◆ payment of medical bills that exceed 7.5% of the taxpayer's adjusted gross income;
- ◆ payment of health insurance premiums during long-term unemployment; and,
- ◆ the death or disability of the participant.

Even when a premature withdrawal is penalty-free, the recipient still must include the funds received in his or her taxable income for the year in which they were obtained. Once a participant attains the age of 70½, he or she must also withdraw funds from the IRA at a rate that will exhaust it by the end of his or her life expectancy, or such an amount will be imputed by the IRS as withdrawn and be subject to federal income taxation each year.

ROTH IRAS

Provisions for an alternative to the traditional IRA have also been enacted. A taxpayer of any age may choose to make deposits in a *Roth IRA*, regardless of whether he or she is covered under an employer sponsored-retirement plan as long as his or her income does not exceed the statutory limits for eligibility.

For the years 2003 and 2004, married taxpayers who file a joint tax return may annually deposit the lesser of $3,000 each or their combined marginal adjusted gross income for the year (even if only one of them had income) unless their combined income exceeds $150,000. Eligibility for participation in a Roth IRA is phased out between $150,000 and $160,000 of combined modified adjusted gross income for a married couple filing jointly. Limitations on eligibility to participate in a Roth IRA also begin at the $150,000 level of modified adjusted gross income for qualifying widows and widowers. Single taxpayers and those filing as head of household will begin to lose eligibility when their modified adjusted gross incomes exceed $95,000. They will lose eligibility altogether at $110,000. Maximum amounts allowed for Roth IRA contributions are scheduled to increase to $4,000 for 2005 through 2007 and further increase to $5,000 for 2008 with annual adjustments for inflation in $500 increments in subsequent years.

Contributions to Roth IRA's are not tax deductible; however, if the participant waits at least five years from the beginning of the year in which the first deposit in the account was made, known as the *five year holding period*, before withdrawing any funds from the account, and is at least $59\frac{1}{2}$ years of age, he or she will be exempt from having to pay taxes on any of the earnings on it. Return of the principal is tax free since it is money that was previously taxed. If a participant dies before expiration of the five year holding period, his or her heirs must hold the account for a sufficient time to complete the period in order to avoid paying taxes on the earnings it has generated.

If a Roth IRA participant withdraws funds from the account prior to completion of the five year holding period, income tax must be paid on the part of the distribution that consists of earnings. Further, if the participant is under $59\frac{1}{2}$ years of age at the time of the withdrawal, he or she will also be subject to a 10% penalty for early withdrawal, unless the withdrawal was due to one of the reasons for which such penalties are waived for a standard IRA.

NOTE: *There is no mandatory age for withdrawal from a Roth IRA, as there is for a standard IRA.*

Taxpayers are not allowed separate eligibility for both the standard and the Roth IRA. However, they are allowed to divide their IRA eligibility between the two. Married taxpayers who file their tax returns as *married filing separately* face severe limitations on eligibility to make deposits in a standard IRA or a Roth IRA. A phase out of eligibility for a standard IRA begins with the first dollar of adjusted gross income, just as it does with the first dollar of modified adjusted gross income for the Roth IRA, with no eligibility remaining for either once the relevant income measure reaches $10,000.

SIMPLIFIED EMPLOYEE PENSION PLANS

Upon reaching stability and profitability in their small businesses, owners may find themselves in sufficiently high tax brackets to warrant concern over their income tax liabilities. The amount eligible for tax deductions for deposits in the standard IRA is relatively small and offers little tax relief. Therefore, establishment of a *Simplified Employee Pension Plan* (SEP) may be a viable source of tax relief. Virtually all types of business entities, including sole proprietors, are eligible to establish a SEP.

All that is required to start a SEP is completion of a SEP employer agreement. A signed copy of which must then be given to each employee, along with disclosures concerning details of the plan. This is followed by establishment of a separate, individual SEP-IRA by each eligible employee, into which the employer may then make contributions. Qualified SEP contributions are a deductible expense to the employer that makes them, but are not taxable income to the employee in whose account the contribution was deposited until the money is withdrawn.

As with a standard IRA, earnings generated by the account are not taxed until they are withdrawn. A 10% penalty is imposed on withdrawals before age $59\frac{1}{2}$ (unless they were for a reason for which withdrawals may be made from the standard IRA without penalty). It is mandatory that a program of withdrawal be implemented when the owner of the account reaches $70\frac{1}{2}$ years of age.

The most striking advantage of the SEP is the potentially large amount that an employer may be eligible to put in each employee's SEP-IRA each year. The maximum contribution that the employer may place in each worker's SEP-IRA per year is 25% of his or her compensation, subject to a specific dollar limitation. The dollar limitation is adjusted annually for changes in cost-of-living, but there is a $40,000 cap set in the current legislation.

The percentage calculation must be done in such a way that the contribution equals the appropriate percentage of the employee's earnings after deduction of the contribution. The *Economic Growth and Tax Relief Reconciliation Act of 2001* (EGTRRA 2001) favored taxpayers who had attained fifty years of age by the end of the year by allowing them to make an extra $2,000 in tax deferred contributions to their SEP-IRAs in 2003, an extra $3,000 in 2004, an extra $4,000 in 2005 and an extra $5,000 for 2006 and subsequent years.

These added amounts of eligibility, known as *catch up contributions*, are to be adjusted for inflation in $500 increments after the year 2006. Publication 590 is available from the IRS to help employers calculate their eligible contributions; however, most brokerage houses and financial institutions will gladly assist employers in establishing and administering their SEPs at no charge in hopes of being chosen by their employees to administer their SEP-IRAs.

Historically, owner/employees of small businesses who wanted to be able to put money in pension funds for themselves and defer taxes on it until retirement got around rules that required inclusion of all employees in the company's pension fund by either *leasing* their nonowner employees from another company, or establishing a second company that they worked for, then subcontracted their services to their original company. Under the SEP rules, all eligible employees of the employer, including leased employees and those of affiliated companies, must be included in the plan. An employee *must* be included in the employer's SEP if he or she:

- ◆ is at least twenty-one years of age;
- ◆ has worked for the employer at least three of the past five years;
- ◆ is not a nonresident alien;
- ◆ is not a member of a collective bargaining unit; and,
- ◆ earned at least $450 during the year (for the year 2002, subject to cost of living adjustments in future years).

Employers are free to establish less stringent requirements for eligibility, such as eliminating the minimum age requirement or reducing the required number of years of employment. They cannot impose more burdensome requirements.

Contributions to each employee's SEP-IRA *must* be proportionate to his or her compensation, up to the level for maximum contribution. Once contributions are made into an employee's SEP-IRA, they are considered *immediately vested*, which entitles the employee to retain the entire account upon voluntary or involuntary termination of employment. Therefore, a SEP is best suited for small businesses in which the owners are also employees of the business and there are few, if any, nonowner employees.

In such a case, adoption of a SEP simply results in a significant amount of money that would have otherwise been paid out to the owners as taxable distributions or wages and salaries being placed in tax deferred IRAs for them. The SEP offers the owners a way to reduce their income tax burden. The tax savings becoming available to earn tax deferred returns, all of which helps them fulfill their needs for a pension fund. Moreover, each employee is free to control how the money in his or her own SEP-IRA is invested, rather than every participant having to make the same investment.

SIMPLE IRAS

Employers who have several employees who are not owners of the company may not be willing to make the relatively large contributions to their employee's retirement plans required by a SEP. The *SIMPLE IRA* may be the preferable choice for them. For 2003, EGTRRA permits company employees, whether they are owners or not, to put up to $8,000 of their own money into a SIMPLE IRA and defer taxation on that money. The employer may choose between depositing an amount equal to 2% of annual earnings on behalf of each qualified employee or merely matching employee contributions up to an amount equal to 3% of the employee's earnings. By choosing the 3% matching approach, the employer may end up making little, if any, contribution to nonowner SIMPLE IRAs, since employees with relatively modest incomes are not likely to be able to afford to significantly fund a SIMPLE IRA from their earnings and there will be nothing for the employer to match.

In 2004, EGTRRA raises the deferral limit to $9,000 with subsequent increases to $10,000 in 2005, after which the deferral limit will be adjusted for inflation in $500 increments. For participants over fifty years of age by the end of the year, the Act raises the deferral limit by an extra $1,000 for 2003, an extra $1,500 for 2004, an extra $2,000 for 2005 and an extra $2,500 for all subsequent years. In 2007 and beyond, the *catch up contribution limits* will be adjusted for inflation in increments of $500.

Any type of business entity may establish a SIMPLE IRA retirement plan as long as it does not have over 100 qualified employees. As long as an employee has earned at least $5,000 in any two prior years and expects to earn $5,000 or more in the current year, he or she is qualified to participate in the company's SIMPLE IRA. The maximum amount that a participant may defer taxation on by making deposits in a SIMPLE IRA is large enough that it will probably exceed the amount that most small business owners and their employees will want to put aside for retirement.

401(k) PLANS

Business owners who place high priority on accumulating tax deferred income for retirement may find the *401(k)* plan to be their best choice. In 2003 employees may make *pre-tax contributions* of up to $12,000 to a 401(k) plan, thereby deferring federal income taxes on their earnings until the funds are withdrawn. A participant may put up to 100% of annual earnings in such a plan, up to the maximum limit, but cannot put more money into the plan than he or she earns that year.

Also, the earnings must be generated from actual employment, thereby preventing a business owner from giving a spouse or child a salary for purposes of qualifying the recipient for the company's 401(k) plan. Under the provisions of EGTRRA, the annual limit on employee contributions increases by $1,000 per year until 2006, when it reaches $15,000.

Taxpayers who are at least fifty years of age by the end of the year are allowed additional *catch up contributions* of $2,000 in 2003. The catch up contribution limit is also increased by $1,000 per year until 2006 when it reaches $5,000. Therefore, in 2006 a 401(k) plan participant could make a deferred contribution of up to $20,000 to his or her plan, provided he or she was at least fifty years old by the end of the year and had earnings of at least $20,000. Both the regular annual limit for 401(k) plan contributions and the catch up annual limits will be adjusted for inflation in $500 increments after 2006.

Although they are not required to do so, employers may also make contributions on behalf of employees into their 401(k) plans. The limit on such contributions is 25% of the employee's compensation, but the combined contributions of the employer and employee cannot exceed $40,000 annually.

There are some significant requirements that a 401(k) plan must meet in order to qualify the contributions for the deferral. In order to be eligible to establish a 401(k) plan, a company must have at least ten qualified employees. Companies may require workers to be at least twenty-one years of age and work for the company over 1,000 hours per year in order to participate in the plan. Employers may relax these requirements to the point that every employee qualifies for participation.

Another obstacle to establishing a 401(k) plan of any significance is the fact that such plans must pass the *discrimination test*. The object of the test is to prevent *highly compensated employees* from being the only ones who significantly benefit from a company's 401(k) plan. By definition, a highly compensated employee (HCE) is:

- an individual whose annual compensation is $85,000 or more;
- an individual who owns more than 5% of the company; or,
- a lineal descendant or spouse of such an owner regardless of earnings.

Essentially, highly compensated employees are not to make contributions into 401(k) plans or have company contributions made for them that exceed the level of contributions made by or for employees who are not highly compensated employees by more than 20%. For example, if the average contribution of nonhighly compensated employees is 3%, highly compensated employees would be limited to a maximum 5% contribution. The discrimination test is applied separately to both the employee salary deferral and the employer contributions, and may be based on either the past year or the current year. Newly formed businesses may assume a 3% participation rate for the prior year even though they were not in business that year.

The discrimination test, by its nature, creates still another requirement that must be met in order to establish a qualified 401(k) plan. Since the discrimination test entails a comparison of contribution and deferral rates of highly compensated employees to such rates of employees who are not highly compensated, there must be at least one plan participant who is not highly compensated.

There is an alternative version of the 401(k) plan, the *Safe Harbor 401(k)*, which requires no minimum number of employees for the company to be eligible to start a plan, although there still must be at least one participant who is not highly compensated. The primary advantage of the Safe Harbor 401(k) is that it eliminates discrimination testing and replaces it with the option of the company either making a contribution of 3% of pay to every employee's account or making a matching contribution of up to 4% of pay for employees who choose to make contributions. If a company meets one of the safe harbor requirements, highly compensated employees may then make deferred contributions to the full extent allowed by statute, regardless of how much the other employees choose to contribute.

In general, 401(k) plans offer business owners a significant opportunity to defer income taxes on their earnings and may also help them retain employees. However, such plans require substantially more expertise to establish and administer than some of the alternatives. In order to establish and maintain a 401(k) plan, it is imperative that a company engage the services of a CPA or attorney with the necessary expertise to work in concert with a financial planner or brokerage company to create and implement a qualified plan.

OTHER RETIREMENT PLANS

There are still other retirement plan options available to businesses, such as *profit sharing plans* and *defined benefit plans*. The rules and regulations governing the establishment and administration of such plans are relatively complex and require the services of experts. However, those whose businesses are highly profitable and who feel the need to establish a retirement program designed to build up assets rapidly may find such programs appealing, and should seek the advice of qualified consultants to see if such plans can best meet their needs.

Chapter 12
Withholding Taxes

One of the more intimidating aspects of starting a small business is having to comply with tax laws regarding employees. Among the requirements that employers must meet are:

- withholding taxes from their employee's wages;
- paying the amount withheld from wages to the U.S. Treasury;
- filing the Employer's Quarterly Federal Tax Return; and,
- filing the Federal Unemployment Tax Return.

Withholding taxes from employee checks, paying it to the U.S. Treasury in a timely fashion, and filing quarterly returns may seem burdensome to small business owners, especially because they are held to the same basic requirements as large corporations. However, once an employer understands what his or her duties are and establishes a routine for compliance, the requirements should not prove to be unreasonably difficult. Moreover, the penalties for noncompliance are so onerous that business owners simply cannot afford to ignore the requirements.

WITHHOLDING EMPLOYEE TAXES

Business entities that hire employees are required, under the provisions of the Code Sec. 3402, to withhold federal taxes from their workers' earnings. Income taxes, as well as Social Security taxes and Medicare taxes, must be deducted and withheld from each employee's earnings. The employer must pay a matching amount of both Social Security taxes and Medicare taxes for all employees.

Employers do not have to trouble themselves with deducting and withholding federal taxes from the compensation of nonemployees, nor are they required to pay any Social Security taxes or Medicare taxes in their behalf. As a result, there is considerable incentive for employers to treat employees as if they were nonemployees. A common approach is for the employer to label employees as *independent contractors*. However, the IRS will make its own determination as to whether a worker is an independent contractor or an employee and impose appropriate sanctions when there has been a misclassification.

Distinguishing Between Employees and Independent Contractors

Whether a party refers to someone as an *employee* or an *independent contractor* does not determine the worker's actual status. The issue of whether or not a taxpayer's workers are employees or independent contractors has frequently been raised by the IRS, resulting in a substantial amount of litigation. The Treasury Department issues *Regulations* that supplement the Internal Revenue Code by offering guidance in interpreting the various sections of the tax law. Section 31.3401(c)-1 of the Income Tax Regulations sets forth *twenty factors* that are considered in determining whether a worker is an employee or an independent contractor. The *Regulation,* which was formulated to help resolve tax disputes, is largely a summary of case decisions on the issue and provides an extensive (although not exhaustive) list of the major factors used in determining whether a particular worker is an independent contractor under common law principles.

Probably the most important determinant in ascertaining whether someone is an independent contractor or an employee is the extent of the *right of control* that the party for whom work is being performed has over the worker. If a worker is subject to someone's control as to how to perform the assigned work, he or she is likely to be considered an employee. If the right to control the worker is limited to dictating the result of his or her efforts, the worker is likely to be an independent contractor. What must be considered is the right of control—whether or not that right is actually exercised is immaterial.

The first eleven factors of the twenty set forth in Sec. 31.3401(c)-1 of the *Regulations* are concerned with who has the right to control a worker's performance. These factors include:

1. the type of instructions given to a worker (the more detailed the instructions given regarding how to perform the assignment, the more likely the worker will be considered an employee);
2. the employer setting the hours of work by the worker;
3. the employer requiring that the worker work full time;
4. the order or sequence of the work being set by the employer;
5. requiring that the services to be provided by the worker be rendered personally by him or her;
6. integrating the worker into the employer's business operation;
7. establishing an ongoing relationship between the parties;
8. requiring the worker to perform on the employer's premises even though some of the work could be done elsewhere; and,
9. requiring regular oral or written reports from the worker.

Another factor indicating an employee status is if a worker is *provided training* by the party who engaged him or her. Training is typically provided to employees more than independent contractors, and is also a way to further control how the worker performs the job. If a worker has *assistants, another factor* to consider is who hires, supervises, and pays those assistants. If a worker has the right to choose and control his or her own assistants, and must pay them him or herself, this would be typical of an independent contractor and indicative of having a high degree of control of his or her own performance.

Three of the factors set out in the *Regulation* for determining independent contractor status deal with some aspect of the worker's *remuneration*. Payment of a worker by the hour, week, or month is typical of an employee, rather than of an independent contractor. Employees are usually *paid a uniform amount at regular intervals,* whereas the independent contractor is usually paid upon completion of an entire contract, or at certain stages of its completion. If a worker can actually incur a loss from the job that he or she has agreed to perform, and will realize earnings only in the form of a *profit if successful* in keeping costs below the price at which he or she agreed to perform that job, this is forceful evidence that the worker is an independent contractor.

Another factor to be considered pertaining to compensation is whether or not a worker must *pay business and travel expenses* without being directly reimbursed for them by the party on whose behalf he or she incurred them. Independent contractors typically estimate the anticipated business and travel expenses that will be connected with a given job and allow for them in the price they quote for their work. Employees generally supply their employers with proof of their actual business and travel expenses and are directly reimbursed for those specific items.

Somewhat related to the compensation issue is the question of who bears the cost of the various necessities that a worker must have in order to do the job. Two factors among the twenty in the *Regulation* address this question. The first of the two factors is to determine whether the *tools and materials necessary* to render performance are furnished by the worker (which indicates independent contractor status) or by the employer (which is strong evidence that the worker is an employee). The second of these two factors is whether or not the *worker must personally invest* in anything else needed to perform the job. If a worker must personally pay for needed equipment for the job or has to furnish, staff, and pay rent for an office, this is evidence that he or she is an independent contractor.

Independent contractors typically work for a number of clients, whereas employees usually work for a single employer during the course of employment, even though they may render services for a number of customers on their employer's behalf. This characteristic is addressed in two of the *Regulation's* twenty factors. The actual number of businesses that a worker is working for at a given time is considered in determining whether he or she is an independent contractor. The worker's availability to render services to the public in general is considered as well. The greater the number of parties that a worker is actually employed by and the greater his or her availability to the public, the more likely he or she is to be considered an independent contractor.

The final two factors of *Regulation* Sec. 31-3401(c)-1 address the method whereby the relationship between the worker and employer may be terminated. If either the worker or the employer may terminate their relationship without cause at any time, this is almost certainly an employment relationship that is being governed by the *employment at-will doctrine*. Independent contractors labor under a contractual arrangement and usually cannot be terminated as long as they are making reasonable progress toward completion of their contracts. If an independent contractor quits before completion of the contract without justification for having done so, he or she will likely be in breach of the contract and will face the possibility of a suit for damages.

Even if a worker may otherwise qualify as an independent contractor, the parties can agree to regard the worker as an employee. If an employer wishes to have the workers regarded as independent contractors, there should be written contracts with the workers, expressing that intent, and a structure to the relationship that meets the tests for independent contractor status set forth in the Regulation. It is then imperative that the employer send a *Form 1099* to each independent contractor, detailing payments to the worker as a nonemployee.

Employers who are unsure about whether a worker is an employee or an independent contractor may request a determination from the IRS. The request to have the IRS make the determination as to whether a worker is an independent contractor is made on *Form SS-8*, which is available at any IRS office. The form can also be obtained by calling 800-829-1040 or contacting the website at **www.irs.gov.**

Form SS-8 is essentially a three page questionnaire that asks the employer questions about the relationship with the worker or workers for whom the determination is to be made, as well as questions concerning the nature of the employer's business. The answers to these questions are then used by the IRS to apply the twenty factors set forth in the *Regulation* and make a determination as to the worker's status. Once such a determination is made, it will apply to other workers who labor under similar conditions and arrangements. The IRS does not charge for this service.

Penalties

If it is determined that an employer has treated an employee as a non-employee and failed to deduct and withhold the appropriate federal taxes, Sec. 3509 of the Code provides that the employer may be liable for the taxes that should have been withheld. Due to the severity of the penalty, it is probably wise for taxpayers with any doubt about how to classify a worker to request a determination from the IRS as to whether he or she is an employee or an independent contractor. However, if such a request is made and the IRS rules that a worker is an employee, the employer will then have no choice but to follow the IRS ruling. Also, it must be remembered that a ruling as to one employee applies to all other employees who are similarly situated and the employer will be expected to act accordingly.

Minors Working for Parents

There is a special provision that exempts children under eighteen years of age from Social Security and Medicare taxes when they work in the trade or business of a sole proprietor who is one of their parents, or a partnership consisting of both parents and no one else. This exception does not apply when the entity for which a minor works is a corporation or a limited liability company, even if it is owned entirely by one or both of the child's parents.

AMOUNT TO WITHHOLD

The amount of federal income tax, Social Security tax, and Medicare tax that an employer must withhold from an employee's earnings will depend on:

- ◆ the tax rates in effect at the time;
- ◆ the employee's taxable earnings;
- ◆ the employee's marital status; and,
- ◆ the number of withholding allowances that the employee has.

The IRS has developed charts that factor in the prevailing tax rates. There is a separate chart for each marital status and an individual column showing the tax liability on the worker's earnings at each level of withholding allowances, up to a total of ten. These charts are published by the IRS in Publication 15—a booklet known as *Circular E, Employer's Tax Guide*. It contains a considerable amount of information to help employers comply with their duties to deduct, withhold, and pay federal taxes on behalf of their employees. It is available at no charge from the IRS. The IRS also periodically conducts classes to instruct employers on how to comply with their duty to withhold and pay these taxes. These classes are conducted at IRS offices that serve the public and are offered free of charge.

The employer must require an employee to fill out a W-4 to establish marital status and the number of withholding allowances of the employee. Otherwise, in the absence of a W-4, the employer must withhold taxes as if the employee were single and without any withholding allowances.

Tax protestors have historically evaded taxes on their wages by filling out W-4 forms showing a large number of withholding allowances or claiming exemption from taxation. Therefore, although employers are not usually required to send their employees' W-4 forms to the IRS, they are required to do so in the instances when an employee claims ten or more withholding allowances or claims exemption from taxation and is expected to earn at least $200 per week. In such cases, the employer must send the W-4 forms in question to the IRS no later than the next quarter of the year following the quarter of the year in which the employer received the forms.

In order to be able to earn money from employment in the U.S., a worker must have a Social Security number. Employers are required to obtain each of their employee's Social Security number and to verify its accuracy. Verification may be obtained by calling 800-772-6270. If it is discovered that an employee has used a false Social Security number and the employer had not taken steps to verify it, the employer may be penalized.

PAYMENT OF WITHHOLDING TAXES

Once an employer deducts and withholds the appropriate taxes from employees' earnings, these earnings must then be paid, along with the employer's portion of Social Security tax and Medicare tax, to the U.S.

Treasury. In order to be able to make such payments, the employer must obtain an *employer identification number* (EIN). Application for such a number is made on *Form SS-4*, which may be obtained at an IRS office or requested by telephone. Once the form is completed, it must be faxed to the appropriate IRS service center with a cover sheet containing instructions for faxing back the number. It will take about ten days to get an EIN, but an employer can request it over the telephone. The specific details concerning the use of an EIN are available in the IRS Publication 1635.

Employers must *deposit* their share of Social Security tax and Medicare taxes, their employees' shares of those taxes, and the federal income tax withheld from their workers' wages in an authorized financial institution or Federal Reserve Bank. These withholdings are collectively known as *payroll taxes*. The deposit must be made in an authorized depository institution in order for the payment to be considered made at the time it was deposited. Most banks of significant size are authorized institutions for the deposit of such taxes. However, it would be advisable to verify that fact before opening the company account, since authorized institutions are not required to take tax deposits in the form of checks drawn on other financial institutions, and, even if they do, credit will not be given for such deposits until sufficient time has passed for such a check to go through the check clearing process. The simplest and most reliable way for an employer to handle the payment of withholding taxes is to write a check to the institution where the employer has an account, and, if sufficient funds are available to cover the check, an immediate credit for having made the payment will be given.

Most small businesses must deposit the payroll taxes by the 15th day of the month following the month in which they accrued. If the due date falls on a weekend or a holiday, the deposit will be due on the next business day. An employer may pay the payroll taxes quarterly if the liability for the quarter is less than $1,000. Otherwise, all businesses start out on a monthly deposit schedule and will remain on it until they have been in business for a length of time sufficient to have operated for a full fiscal year running from July 1 to June 30. At that time, each business will apply the *lookback rule* to see if its total deposits for payroll taxes exceeded $50,000. If they did, the employer will then have to deposit payroll taxes on a semiweekly schedule.

If payroll taxes deposited from July 1 to June 30 of the prior lookback period did not exceed $50,000, the employer will continue with monthly deposits. When semiweekly deposits are required, the employer must deposit payroll taxes withheld on Wednesday, Thursday and/or Friday by the next Wednesday, and must deposit payroll taxes withheld on Saturday, Sunday, Monday and/or Tuesday by the following Friday. If such payments by a semiweekly depositor fall on a bank holiday, they are then due on the next banking day.

Once an employer reaches the level of over $200,000 for all federal taxes for a year, payment deposits *must* be made electronically. Enrollment in the Electronic Federal Tax Payment System may be accomplished by calling 800-555-4477 or 800-945-8400. If the total federal taxes for the relevant previous year do not exceed $200,000, they can be paid electronically or not.

Deposits that are not made electronically must be accompanied by a *Federal Tax Deposit coupon*. The IRS will send an employer a book of the coupons a few weeks after assigning the business an employer identification number. The IRS will automatically send additional books periodically to replace the coupons as they are used up. The coupons are preprinted with the taxpayer's name, address, and EIN. A misapplication of a deposit is likely if a taxpayer makes a deposit using another entity's coupon.

Penalties

Employers who fail to make their payroll tax deposits in a timely and proper manner due to willful neglect will be subject to a penalty. Deposits that are made one to five days late will be subject to a 2% penalty. Deposits that are six to fifteen days late carry a 5% penalty. A 10% penalty will be imposed on deposits that are:

- sixteen or more days late;
- made within ten days of the date that the IRS first sends notice asking for payment of past due payroll taxes;
- made other than to an authorized financial institution; or,
- deposits that were required to be made electronically but were not deposited in this way.

If a taxpayer fails to make payment of delinquent payroll taxes within ten days after the date of the first notice from the IRS demanding their immediate payment, the penalty is 15%. There are also provisions for a *trust fund recovery penalty*, which is the most severe penalty. The part of an employer's payroll taxes made up of withholdings from the employees' earnings are what comprise the *trust fund* portion. The part of an employer's payroll tax liability that is comprised of his or her matching share of Social Security tax and Medicare tax is not included in the trust fund portion.

If a business or individual employer withholds payroll taxes from employees' earnings and willfully fails to pay them over to the U.S. Treasury as required, a penalty of 100% of the delinquent trust portion of the payroll tax may be imposed. The justification for such a severe penalty is that the trust fund portion of payroll taxes is made up of funds that were the employees', in the form of a part of their earnings, and then became the U.S. Treasury's funds, by virtue of law, subject to the employees' claims for refunds in the event of overpayment.

Therefore, although payroll taxes are deposited from an employer's account or funds, the employer is deemed to be a mere *custodian* of those funds. Failure to properly pay them is viewed as a breach of fiduciary duty, rather than a failure to pay its own tax liability. In fact, an employee who has had payroll taxes deducted from earnings will be given credit by the IRS for having paid those taxes, even though his or her employer has failed to properly deposit them. The employee can actually get a refund, when it is appropriate, on the basis of withheld, but unpaid, payroll taxes.

Despite the fact that the potential penalty is so severe, many small businesses find themselves in trouble for failure to properly deposit their payroll taxes. This is probably due to the fact that in theory an employer merely allocates funds from a pool made up of employees' earnings, but in reality there is no such pool. Employers calculate their employees' earnings, determine the appropriate amount of withholdings, and write each employee a check. The employers generally pay all of their other business expenses from the same account that they pay their employees. Once all the bills have been paid, there simply may not be enough money left to make the payroll tax deposit. Faced with the prospects of resignations from employees who are not paid, evictions by unpaid landlords, discontinuance of service by unpaid utility and telephone companies, and interruption of the supply of materials and inventory from unpaid suppliers, employers often view the consequences of failure to make payroll tax payments as being less imminent and, therefore, preferable when there simply is not enough money to go around.

However, although the event may be a while in coming, the IRS has the authority to seize an employer's assets and liquidate them to satisfy a delinquent payroll tax liability and the penalty and interest on it. Furthermore, rather than being limited only to the business entity as a source for recovery of delinquent payroll taxes, penalties, and interest, the IRS may seek recovery of them from the individual owner, officer, or employee of that entity who was responsible for collecting and paying those taxes but knew that it was not being done.

Individuals therefore may be *personally liable* for a business entity's failure to pay its payroll taxes. Penalties of up to 100% of the tax may be assessed, interest will accumulate on the unpaid balance, and neither businesses nor responsible individuals may discharge such liabilities by filing bankruptcy. Bankruptcy law simply excludes the right to discharge any liability arising from delinquency in the payment of the trust portion of payroll taxes.

If a company does get into financial trouble, payroll tax payments should be the last payment put off, rather than the first. Virtually all of a company's other obligations may be discharged in bankruptcy. Personal liability will result only if the business entity chosen is characterized by unlimited liability or an individual has agreed to be personally liable. The company that defaults on a loan will be able to discharge that obligation in bankruptcy, even if the proceeds of the loan were used to meet various commitments.

If an employer is in the position of being unable to pay all of the payroll tax liability, yet can pay some of it, the employer should clearly indicate on the check that it the partial payment is *for the trust portion of payroll taxes*. A cover letter to that effect should also accompany the payment. The IRS must observe the dictates of the taxpayer in applying credit for the payments. To the degree that an employer can pay the trust portion of the payroll tax obligation and confine the delinquency to the employer's *matching share* of Social Security taxes and Medicare tax, the employer:

- ◆ will incur no 100% penalty;
- ◆ will be able to discharge the liability in bankruptcy after three years from the time it first came due; and,
- ◆ will be able to avoid personal liability for the tax if organized as a business entity with limited liability.

FILING APPROPRIATE RETURNS

Although employers may meet their duty to pay the payroll taxes that they have withheld from their employees' earnings, as well as their matching shares of FICA taxes, their duty to file returns in connection with their payrolls does not end there. There are two quarterly returns related to payroll that employers must also file.

Employer's Quarterly Federal Tax Return

In addition to their duty to make payroll tax deposits, employers who deduct and withhold taxes from employees' wages must also file a *Form 941, Employers Quarterly Federal Tax Return*. It is due on the 15th day of the month following the last month of the quarter. Payments are not generally made along with *Form 941*; however, employers who accumulate less than $1,000 in payroll taxes for the quarter may forego monthly deposits and pay the taxes with their quarterly return. If an employer discovers a shortfall in monthly payroll tax deposits for a quarter, that shortfall may be paid along with *Form 941*. No penalty will be assessed if the shortfall does not exceed the greater of $100 or 2% of the payroll tax liability for the quarter. When filing *Form 941*, employers should use the preprinted forms supplied by the IRS in order to ensure proper credit. The forms should be automatically sent by the IRS, but in the event they are not, taxpayers may obtain a blank form from the IRS to file timely, and then request preprinted forms by telephone or at an IRS office.

Federal Unemployment Tax Returns

In addition to payroll taxes, employers must also pay *Federal Unemployment Tax*. Both state and federal unemployment taxes are levied, but employers are given credit against their federal liability for most, if not all, of the state unemployment taxes they pay. This usually results in a net federal rate of less than 1% for unemployment tax. Furthermore, the tax is applied to only a small specified amount of each employee's earnings. This results in small federal unemployment tax liability for most small businesses.

Since the tax liability is generally modest, businesses are required to deposit federal unemployment taxes only quarterly. Moreover, if the liability for a quarter is $100 or less, no payment is required and the liability may be carried forward to the next quarter. Federal unemployment taxes are reported on *Form 940*, which is due on the last day of the month following the last month of the quarter. If the total federal unemployment tax liability of an employer does not exceed $100 for the entire year, the employer has the option of paying the tax with the last *Form 940* of the year.

ESTIMATED TAX PAYMENTS

Sole proprietors, partners in the various forms of partnership, and members of limited liability companies that choose to be taxed as partnerships are all considered to be self-employed. Despite the fact that such parties may receive money from the company on a regular or irregular basis, such payments are not subject to withholding of payroll taxes. Rather, self-employed taxpayers are required to make estimated tax payments on a quarterly basis to cover their federal tax liability. That liability consists of income taxes, which are calculated at the same rate as those who are employed by others, and self-employment tax, which supplants the Social Security tax and Medicare tax that are shared equally by employers and employees.

Although estimated tax payments are said to be payable quarterly, they are actually due on April 15th, June 15th, September 15th, January 15th, or the next business day when the due date falls on a weekend or holiday. Payments are to be made by mail to the IRS Service Center designated for the taxpayer's geographic area, and must be accompanied by a *Form 1040 ES* voucher in order to ensure proper credit for the payment. The vouchers and an instruction booklet are available at IRS offices that assist the public or they may be requested by telephone. Once a taxpayer sends in a *1040 ES*, the IRS will generally send preprinted vouchers and instructions at the beginning of each new year.

Penalties

Self-employed taxpayers who do not make adequate and timely estimated tax payments will be subject to penalties and interest on their deficiencies. An individual who pays estimated tax payments will be considered to have paid an adequate amount if the combination of payroll taxes from any employment he or she may have held and the estimated tax payments on the self-employment earnings total 90% of his or her tax liability for the year. The remaining unpaid balance can be paid with his or her tax return, without penalty. As long as a taxpayer's total tax payments for a year equal at least as much as his or her previous year's tax liability, penalties for underpayment will be waived, even if the total payments fall short of 90% of the total tax liability.

Since the estimated taxes that are paid come from the taxpayer's own funds and not from monies withheld from the earnings of others (as does the trust portion of payroll taxes) the penalty for nonpayment of estimated taxes is not nearly as severe as that for nonpayment of the trust portion of payroll taxes. The penalty is actually a form of interest on the delinquent estimated payments, calculated at the federal short-term rate, plus 3%.

Glossary

A

accounts receivable. Monies owed to a party for goods or services that were provided, but were not paid for at the time that they were provided.

accrual method of accounting. A system of income reporting that recognizes the right to receive it, rather than when it is actually received. Expenses are recognized when they are incurred, rather than when they are actually paid.

adjusted gross income. A taxpayer's gross income less various deductions that are provided for by law such as educator expenses, student loan interest, and alimony payments. The deductions are shown on the lower fourth of the front of *Form 1040* and adjusted gross income is the last figure at the bottom of *Form 1040.*

B

basis. The value assigned to property in the hands of a taxpayer upon which depreciation and gain or loss from sale or deemed sale are calculated. The starting point for calculating a taxpayer's basis in his or her property is usually its original cost plus capital improvements less depreciation and insurance proceeds received for losses that are not repaired or replaced.

bonus. Compensation over and above a party's base salary or wages. Such payments are often based on performance, but are also sometimes used by small business owners as a method for reducing profits that will be realized by their companies.

C

capital gain. Income that a taxpayer realizes when a capital asset is sold or exchanged for more than the taxpayer's basis in the asset.

capital loss. The difference between the value that a taxpayer receives in the sale or exchange of a capital asset and the taxpayer's basis in that asset when the sale or exchange occurs at a value that is less than the taxpayer's basis in the asset.

cash method of accounting. A system of income reporting that does not recognize income until receipts from a sale are actually received. Expenses incurred in connection with such sales are not recognized until they are actually paid.

commission. Compensation paid to a party for services rendered that is generally calculated on the basis of the party's performance. This commonly occurs in the form of a percentage of either the gross sale price or profit generated from the sale of a good or service.

cost of doing business. A term used to refer to the price incurred as a consequence of carrying on a given business enterprise. Although it usually refers to the price in money, it may also include the sacrifice of alternative choices that must be made when one enterprise is chosen over others.

D

deduction. A tax term used to refer to an amount of money that may be subtracted from a taxpayer's gross income in arriving at the party's taxable income.

deficit. A shortage in the amount of money that is required for some purpose.

dependency exemption. The right to take a prescribed amount of money as a tax deduction for purposes of arriving at taxable income due to having provided support for a party who is considered to be the taxpayer's dependent as provided by tax law.

dependent. A party for whom a taxpayer is entitled to take a dependency exemption, generally due to having provided more than half of the person's support for the tax year. The person may be deemed to be a taxpayer's dependent by agreement between divorced parents or among multiple parties who provide support for a person.

direct expense. Costs that are readily traceable to a particular activity or business venture.

direct tax. A levy specifically imposed on a given source of revenue or income.

dividends. Distributions of property or money made by corporations out of earnings and profits to their shareholders.

E

earned income. A taxpayer's total income from 1. wages, salaries and tips; 2. net earnings from self-employment; or, 3. gross income received as a *statutory employee*.

Earned Income Credit. A type of welfare payment for those taxpayers whose earned incomes are beneath certain statutorily prescribed amounts. The purpose of the credit is to keep moderate income earners working since they must have earned income in order to qualify for the credit.

employee. One who labors under the direction and control of another in exchange for wages, salary, and/or other compensation.

excise tax. A levy imposed by a governmental entity upon the sale or use of a good or service or upon the right to engage in certain occupations or activities.

exemptions. Allowances that entitle a taxpayer to exclude some statutorily prescribed amount of income from taxation. The allowances are generally based on the number of parties that the taxpayer provides support to including the taxpayer.

F

fair market value. The amount of money at which property or services would change hands in an arms length transaction between unrelated parties.

federal income tax. A levy imposed by the federal government on earnings.

Federal Insurance Contributions Act (FICA) Tax. The combination of *Old Age Security and Disability Income* (OASDI) taxes and *Medicare* taxes that are assessed on the earnings of employees in the U.S. These must be withheld from workers' earnings by their employers and paid to the U.S. Treasury along with a matching share paid by the employer.

filing status. One of five categories of individual taxpayers (single, married filing jointly, married filing separately, head of household, and qualifying widow or widower) that determine the level of income at which a taxpayer will be required and at what rate.

financial records. Written records which pertain to a party's money matters.

flat tax. A levy by a governmental entity on income or revenue whereby a single rate of taxation is applied on the entire amount that is subject to the levy.

form W-4 (Employee's Withholding Allowance Certificate). A federal tax form that employers must require their employees to complete indicating their number of dependents and basis for other withholding allowances thereby enabling the employer to determine how much income tax to withhold from each employee's earnings.

fringe benefits. Nonmonetary compensation provided to employees in addition to wages or salary. Among the most common fringe benefits are health insurance, life insurance, and pension plans.

G

gasoline excise tax. A levy by a governmental unit on gasoline used as fuel. The tax is usually imposed upon a party in the distribution chain and the tax is then added to the price of the gasoline as part of the sale price paid by the consumer, rather than as a direct tax paid by the consumer.

gross income. A party's total income from all sources before any allowances for exemptions or deductions from adjusted gross income.

H

head of household filing status. 1. A taxpayer who is single and who provides a home and over half of the support for over half of the year to his or her child or to any relative (other than a cousin). 2. A taxpayer who is married, but has lived apart from his or her spouse for the last six months of the tax year and who has provided over half of the cost of maintaining a home for himself or herself and a dependent child for whom the party is entitled to claim a deduction as an exemption.

I

income taxes. A levy imposed by a governmental entity upon what it defines as the *income*. Generally, such entities define income to include wages, salaries, profits, gains from the sale of assets, and returns from investments.

independent contractor. One who performs work for others but retains the right of control over how the work will be performed.

indirect expense. Costs that are not specifically related to a given transaction or venture, but which must be incurred to support the activity.

indirect tax. A levy by a governmental entity upon a good, service, or privilege that is imposed upon a party in the chain of distribution but which is then passed on to the consumer as a part of the price of what is sold.

inflation. A general increase in prices throughout a particular economy.

interest. A form of income that is payment by one party to another for the use of money.

interest income. Money received as compensation for the right to use ones money.

Internal Revenue Service (IRS). An agency within the U.S. Treasury Department that is charged with administration of the U.S. Internal Revenue Code.

investment income. Revenue generated as a result of ownership of assets that promise such payments as a reward for ownership. The most common types of investment income include interest and dividends.

K

key-man insurance. Life insurance and/or disability insurance taken out by an employer on employees who are of critical importance to the employer. The benefits of the policy accrue to the employer in order to provide the employer with funds to help offset the disruption caused by the death or disability of such an employee.

L

luxury tax. A levy imposed on the sale and/or purchase of goods or services that are considered frivolous. The tax may be imposed on the full sale price or merely on the part of the price that exceeds a certain exempt amount. The tax is often imposed to discourage consumption of a good or service.

M

married filing joint filing status. A category for filing a tax return that is available to married couples as long as they were married on the last day of the tax year and both elect such status. The filing status will determine whether or not the parties must file a return and their rates of taxation if they do file.

married filing separate filing status. A category for filing a tax return that is available to married couples. If either party of a married couple residing together chooses to file separately then both must. The status will determine if the parties must file a return and their rates of taxation if they do file.

Medicare tax. The portion of *Federal Insurance Contributions Act* (FICA) tax that is used to provide medical care primarily to the elderly. Unlike the Social Security part of FICA taxes, there is no limit to the amount of a party's income to which the Medicare part of FICA taxes applies.

modified adjusted gross income. A taxpayer's income remaining after certain additions are made to his or her adjusted gross income. Such adjustments will be prescribed for purposes of calculating a particular credit, deduction, or tax liability and they will be provided for in the instructions for making such calculations.

N

net operating loss (NOL). The degree to which a business operation's expenses exceed its business income for the tax year.

P

payroll taxes. Income taxes and *Federal Insurance Contributions Act* (FICA) tax withheld from the earnings of employees by their employers as well as the matching share of FICA taxes that are paid by employers.

personal exemption. A statutorily provided allowance that a taxpayer is permitted to exclude from taxation. Personal exemptions are usually available to taxpayers for the parties for whom they provide support including themselves.

personal identification number (PIN). A series of numbers, letters, or characters selected by a party that must be entered in able to access certain information or an account or in order to conduct certain business transactions.

phantom income. An amount of money that a party is deemed to have earned according to standard accounting practices, but which the party has not yet actually received.

progressive tax. A levy imposed upon income, revenue, or spending that is structured such that as the amount of money that is being taxed increases, the rate at which it is being taxed is increased at certain intervals.

property taxes. A levy imposed upon the realty or personal property that is owned, leased, or used by parties.

proportional tax. *See flat tax.*

Q

qualifying child. A party who, by virtue of his or her age, relationship, income, and dependency, enables another party to qualify for certain tax advantages such as a dependency exemption, child credit, or earned income credit.

qualifying person. A party, other than a taxpayer's child, who, due to their relationship with or dependency upon a taxpayer, enables the taxpayer to be eligible for certain tax advantages.

qualifying widow(er) filing status. A category for filing a tax return available to a surviving spouse that permits him or her to use the married filing jointly rates for the year of the deceased spouse's death and even the next two years if the surviving spouse has provided over half support for a qualifying child.

R

refund. Money paid to a taxpayer by a taxing authority due to overpayment of the party's tax obligation.

regressive tax. A levy imposed upon the income, revenue, or spending that is structured such that as the taxpayer's taxable base increases, the rate of tax levied on that base decreases.

rents. Payments made to the owner of rights in realty or personal property for the right to use that property.

resources. Assets of virtually any kind, including, but not limited to, money as well as the ability to meet future needs.

revenue. Income received.

S

salary. Payment to an employee as compensation for his or her employment that is often calculated without regard to hours spent on the job or actual work performed during the payment period but, rather, is calculated at a fixed rate.

sales tax. A levy imposed on the sale of goods and/or services. Such taxes are usually calculated as a fixed percentage of the amount of the sale and are generally paid directly by the buyer.

Section 1244 stock. Stock issued by a U.S. corporation whose capital and paid-in surplus at its inception did not exceed $1 million; has not derived over 50% of its gross receipts of the past 5 years from passive income sources; and, whose stock is owned by either an individual or partnership to whom it was issued at its inception.

self-employment tax. A levy imposed upon those who earn income through self-employment as a replacement for the *Federal Insurance Contributions Act* (FICA) tax that is paid by employees and their employers.

single filing status. A category for filing a tax return available to those who are unmarried on the last day of the tax year.

Social Security tax. The portion of *Federal Insurance Contributions Act* (FICA) tax that is used to finance retirement benefits for the aged, disability benefits for the disabled, and survivors benefits for dependent children of deceased taxpayers. (It is also referred to as *Old Age Security and Disability Income* (OASDI) tax.)

standard deduction. An amount set by Congress that taxpayers may exclude from taxation without having to offer any proof as to the amount of expenditures to support the deduction. (The standard deduction is a simplified alternative to itemizing deductions.)

T

tax code. A compilation of laws by a governmental entity that mandate the payment of levies to that entity by those over whom it has jurisdiction.

tax credit. An allowance that can be used to offset tax liability on a dollar-for-dollar basis.

tax credits. The sum total of each tax credit that a taxpayer is allowed to take. Some tax credits are permitted to generate tax refunds (refundable credits) whereas others can be used only to the extent that they offset tax liability (nonrefundable credits). Some can be carried to other years and some cannot.

tax liability. The amount of money that a party owes as the result of the levy of some tax upon him or her.

tax shelters. Activities that are designed to produce tax deductions and credits that may be used to offset regular taxable income.

taxable interest income. The portion of money received for allowing another party to use ones money that is subject to taxation.

taxes. Mandatory levies imposed by a governmental entity upon those over which it has jurisdiction.

tax-exempt interest income. That portion of funds received for allowing another party to use ones money that is not subject to taxation.

telefile. A paperless method of filing a tax return by telephone.

tentative minimum tax. An intermediate figure arrived at in the process of calculating a taxpayer's alternative minimum tax. It consists of his or her alternative minimum tax before deducting the party's federal tax liability, less foreign tax credits and taxes paid on lump sum distributions from qualified plans.

tip income. Payment given to a party for personal services that were rendered. Typical of such payments are those made to waiters and waitresses.

W

wages. Payments made to an employee as compensation for his or her employment. Such payments are generally made on the basis of the number of hours that the employee has spent on the job during the pay period.

withholding. Money held out of an employee's compensation by his or her employer that are to be paid to the U.S. Treasury by the employer in order to enable the employee to meet his or her obligation to pay income taxes and the *Federal Insurance Contributions Act* (FICA) tax.

Index

About the Author

James O. Parker has repeatedly encountered clients who were somewhat bewildered by our country's tax laws, having been a practicing attorney for almost twenty-five years. Calling upon his twenty-seven years as a educator at Christian Brothers University in Memphis Tennessee, and being a small business owner himself for over forty years, Parker takes the mystery out of the tax code.

A former U.S. Marine and community advocate, Parker possesses both a Masters of Arts in Economics from the University of Memphis and an LLM from Emory University in Atlanta, Georgia.

A frequent speaker on tax topics, as well as business succession planning and small business development, Parker continues to advise others on the importance of tax planning.

Mr. Parker lives with his wife, Linda, in Memphis, Tennessee.

Your #1 Source for Real World Legal Information...

Sphinx® Publishing
An Imprint of Sourcebooks, Inc.®

• Written by lawyers   • Simple English explanation of the law
• Forms and instructions included

THE ENTREPRENEUR'S LEGAL GUIDE

This book provides information to build a framework on which a new business can succeed. Get your new venture financed, find the right location, and price your goods to sell.

340 pages; $26.95;
ISBN 1-57248-235-4

THE ENTREPRENEUR'S INTERNET HANDBOOK

Learn how to create a legal and attractive business website. Everything you need to know to sell your product online and have success on the Internet.

192 pages; $21.95;
ISBN 1-57248-251-6

What our customers say about our books:

"It couldn't be more clear for the layperson." —R.D.

"I want you to know I really appreciate your book. It has saved me a lot of time and money." —L.T.

"Your real estate contracts book has saved me nearly $12,000.00 in closing costs over the past year." —A.B.

"...many of the legal questions that I have had over the years were answered clearly and concisely through your plain English interpretation of the law." —C.E.H.

"If there weren't people out there like you I'd be lost. You have the best books of this type out there." —S.B.

"...your forms and directions are easy to follow." —C.V.M.

Sphinx Publishing's Legal Survival Guides are directly available from Sourcebooks, Inc., or from your local bookstores.

For credit card orders call 1–800–432-7444,
write P.O. Box 4410, Naperville, IL 60567-4410, or fax 630-961-2168

SPHINX® PUBLISHING'S STATE TITLES
Up-to-Date for Your State

California Titles

CA Power of Attorney Handbook (2E)	$18.95
How to File for Divorce in CA (4E)	$26.95
How to Probate & Settle an Estate in CA	$26.95
How to Start a Business in CA (2E)	$21.95
How to Win in Small Claims Court in CA (2E)	$18.95
The Landlord's Legal Guide in CA	$24.95
Make Your Own CA Will	$18.95
Tenants' Rights in CA	$21.95

Florida Titles

Child Custody, Visitation and Support in FL	$26.95
How to File for Divorce in FL (7E)	$26.95
How to Form a Corporation in FL (6E)	$24.95
How to Form a Limited Liability Co. in FL (2E)	$24.95
How to Form a Partnership in FL	$22.95
How to Make a FL Will (6E)	$16.95
How to Probate and Settle an Estate in FL (5E)	$26.95
How to Start a Business in FL (7E)	$21.95
How to Win in Small Claims Court in FL (7E)	$18.95
Land Trusts in Florida (6E)	$29.95
Landlords' Rights and Duties in FL (9E)	$22.95

Georgia Titles

How to File for Divorce in GA (5E)	$21.95
How to Make a GA Will (4E)	$21.95
How to Start a Business in Georgia (3E)	$21.95

Illinois Titles

Child Custody, Visitation and Support in IL	$24.95
How to File for Divorce in IL (3E)	$24.95
How to Make an IL Will (3E)	$16.95
How to Start a Business in IL (3E)	$21.95
The Landlord's Legal Guide in IL	$24.95

Maryland, virginia and the district of columbia

How to File for Divorce in MD, VA and DC	$28.95
How to Start a Business in MD, VA or DC	$21.95

Massachusetts Titles

How to Form a Corporation in MA	$24.95
How to Make a MA Will (2E)	$16.95
How to Start a Business in MA (3E)	$21.95
The Landlord's Legal Guide in MA	$24.95

Michigan Titles

How to File for Divorce in MI (3E)	$24.95
How to Make a MI Will (3E)	$16.95
How to Start a Business in MI (3E)	$18.95

Minnesota Titles

How to File for Divorce in MN	$21.95
How to Form a Corporation in MN	$24.95
How to Make a MN Will (2E)	$16.95

New Jersey Titles

How to File for Divorce in NJ ... $24.95

New York Titles

Child Custody, Visitation and Support in NY ... $26.95
File for Divorce in NY ... $26.95
How to Form a Corporation in NY (2E) ... $24.95
How to Make a NY Will (2E) ... $16.95
How to Start a Business in NY (2E) ... $18.95
How to Win in Small Claims Court in NY (2E) ... $18.95
Landlords' Legal Guide in NY ... $24.95
New York Power of Attorney Handbook ... $19.95
Tenants' Rights in NY ... $21.95

North Carolina Titles

How to File for Divorce in NC (3E) ... $22.95
How to Make a NC Will (3E) ... $16.95
How to Start a Business in NC (3E) ... $18.95
Landlords' Rights & Duties in NC ... $21.95

Ohio Titles

How to File for Divorce in OH (2E) ... $24.95
How to Form a Corporation in OH ... $24.95
How to Make an OH Will ... $16.95

Pennsylvania Titles

Child Custody, Visitation and Support in PA ... $26.95
How to File for Divorce in PA (3E) ... $26.95
How to Form a Croporation in PA ... $24.95
How to Make a PA Will (2E) ... $16.95
How to Start a Business in PA (3E) ... $21.95
The Landlord's Legal Guide in PA ... $24.95

Texas Titles

Child Custody, Visitation and Support in TX ... $22.95
How to File for Divorce in TX (3E) ... $24.95
How to Form a Corporation in TX (2E) ... $24.95
How to Make a TX Will (3E) ... $16.95
How to Probate and Settle an Estate in TX (3E) ... $26.95
How to Start a Business in TX (3E) ... $18.95
How to Win in Small Claims Court in TX (2E) ... $16.95
The Landlord's Legal Guide in TX ... $24.95

SPHINX® PUBLISHING'S NATIONAL TITLES
Valid in All 50 States

LEGAL SURVIVAL IN BUSINESS

The Complete Book of Corporate Forms	$24.95
The Complete Patent Book	$26.95
Employees' Rights	$18.95
Employer's Rights	$24.95
The Entrepreneur's Internet Handbook	$21.95
The Entrepreneur's Legal Guide	$26.95
How to Form a Limited Liability Company (2E)	$24.95
How to Form a Nonprofit Corporation (2E)	$24.95
How to Form Your Own Corporation (4E)	$26.95
How to Form Your Own Partnership (2E)	$24.95
How to Register Your Own Copyright (4E)	$24.95
How to Register Your Own Trademark (3E)	$21.95
Incorporate in Delaware from Any State	$24.95
Incorporate in Nevada from Any State	$24.95
Most Valuable Business Legal Forms You'll Ever Need (3E)	$21.95
Profit from Intellectual Property	$28.95
Protect Your Patent	$24.95
The Small Business Owner's Guide to Bankruptcy	$21.95
Tax Smarts for Small Business	$21.95

LEGAL SURVIVAL IN COURT

Attorney Responsibilities & Client Rights	$19.95
Crime Victim's Guide to Justice (2E)	$21.95
Grandparents' Rights (3E)	$24.95
Help Your Lawyer Win Your Case (2E)	$14.95
Jurors' Rights (2E)	$12.95
Legal Research Made Easy (3E)	$21.95
Winning Your Personal Injury Claim (2E)	$24.95
Your Rights When You Owe Too Much	$16.95

LEGAL SURVIVAL IN REAL ESTATE

The Complete Kit to Selling Your Own Home	$18.95
Essential Guide to Real Estate Contracts (2E)	$18.95
Essential Guide to Real Estate Leases	$18.95
Homeowner's Rights	$19.95
How to Buy a Condominium or Townhome (2E)	$19.95
How to Buy Your First Home	$18.95
Working with Your Homeowners Association	$19.95

LEGAL SURVIVAL IN SPANISH

Cómo Hacer su Propio Testamento	$16.95
Cómo Restablecer su propio Crédito y Renegociar sus Deudas	$21.95
Cómo Solicitar su Propio Divorcio	$24.95
Guía de Inmigración a Estados Unidos (3E)	$24.95
Guía de Justicia para Víctimas del Crimen	$21.95
Guía Esencial para los Contratos de Arrendamiento de Bienes Raices	$22.95
Inmigración a los EE. UU. Paso a Paso	$22.95
Manual de Beneficios para el Seguro Social	$18.95
El Seguro Social Preguntas y Respuestas	$14.95

LEGAL SURVIVAL IN PERSONAL AFFAIRS

101 Complaint Letters That Get Results	$18.95
The 529 College Savings Plan (2E)	$18.95
The Antique and Art Collector's Legal Guide	$24.95
The Complete Legal Guide to Senior Care	$21.95
Credit Smart	$18.95
Family Limited Partnership	$26.95
Gay & Lesbian Rights	$26.95
How to File Your Own Bankruptcy (5E)	$21.95
How to File Your Own Divorce (5E)	$26.95
How to Make Your Own Simple Will (3E)	$18.95
How to Write Your Own Living Will (3E)	$18.95
How to Write Your Own Premarital Agreement (3E)	$24.95
Living Trusts and Other Ways to Avoid Probate (3E)	$24.95
Mastering the MBE	$16.95
Most Valuable Personal Legal Forms You'll Ever Need (2E)	$26.95
Neighbor v. Neighbor (2E)	$16.95
The Nanny and Domestic Help Legal Kit	$22.95
The Power of Attorney Handbook (4E)	$19.95
Repair Your Own Credit and Deal with Debt (2E)	$18.95
Sexual Harassment:Your Guide to Legal Action	$18.95
The Social Security Benefits Handbook (3E)	$18.95
Social Security Q&A	$12.95
Teen Rights	$22.95
Traveler's Rights	$21.95
Unmarried Parents' Rights (2E)	$19.95
U.S. Immigration and Citizenship Q&A	$16.95
U.S. Immigration Step by Step	$21.95
U.S.A. Immigration Guide (4E)	$24.95
The Visitation Handbook	$18.95
The Wills, Estate Planning and Trusts Legal Kit	&26.95
Win Your Unemployment Compensation Claim (2E)	$21.95
Your Right to Child Custody, Visitation and Support (2E)	$24.95

SPHINX® PUBLISHING ORDER FORM

BILL TO:			SHIP TO:		
Phone #		Terms	F.O.B. Chicago, IL		Ship Date

Charge my: ☐ VISA ☐ MasterCard ☐ American Express   ☐ **Money Order or Personal Check**

Credit Card Number   Expiration Date

Qty	ISBN	Title	Retail	Qty	ISBN	Title	Retail
		SPHINX PUBLISHING NATIONAL TITLES		_____	1-57248-230-3	Incorporate in Delaware from Any State	$26.95
_____	1-57248-363-6	101 Complaint Letters That Get Results	$18.95	_____	1-57248-158-7	Incorporate in Nevada from Any State	$24.95
_____	1-57248-361-X	The 529 College Savings Plan (2E)	$18.95	_____	1-57248-250-8	Inmigración a los EE.UU. Paso a Paso	$22.95
_____	1-57248-349-0	The Antique and Art Collector's Legal Guide	$24.95	_____	1-57071-333-2	Jurors' Rights (2E)	$12.95
_____	1-57248-347-4	Attroney Responsibilities & Client Rights	$19.95	_____	1-57248-223-0	Legal Research Made Easy (3E)	$21.95
_____	1-57248-148-X	Cómo Hacer su Propio Testamento	$16.95	_____	1-57248-165-X	Living Trusts and Other Ways to	$24.95
_____	1-57248-226-5	Cómo Restablecer su propio Crédito y	$21.95			Avoid Probate (3E)	
		Renegociar sus Deudas		_____	1-57248-186-2	Manual de Beneficios para el Seguro Social	$18.95
_____	1-57248-147-1	Cómo Solicitar su Propio Divorcio	$24.95	_____	1-57248-220-6	Mastering the MBE	$16.95
_____	1-57248-166-8	The Complete Book of Corporate Forms	$24.95	_____	1-57248-167-6	Most Val. Business Legal Forms	$21.95
_____	1-57248-353-9	The Complete Kit to Sellng Your Own Home	$18.95			You'll Ever Need (3E)	
_____	1-57248-229-X	The Complete Legal Guide to Senior Care	$21.95	_____	1-57248-360-1	Most Val. Personal Legal Forms	$26.95
_____	1-57248-201-X	The Complete Patent Book	$26.95			You'll Ever Need (2E)	
_____	1-57248-369-5	Credit Smart	$18.95	_____	1-57248-098-X	The Nanny and Domestic Help Legal Kit	$22.95
_____	1-57248-163-3	Crime Victim's Guide to Justice (2E)	$21.95	_____	1-57248-089-0	Neighbor v. Neighbor (2E)	$16.95
_____	1-57248-367-9	Employees' Rights	$18.95	_____	1-57248-169-2	The Power of Attorney Handbook (4E)	$19.95
_____	1-57248-365-2	Employer's Rights	$24.95	_____	1-57248-332-6	Profit from Intellectual Property	$28.95
_____	1-57248-251-6	The Entrepreneur's Internet Handbook	$21.95	_____	1-57248-329-6	Protect Your Patent	$24.95
_____	1-57248-235-4	The Entrepreneur's Legal Guide	$26.95	_____	1-57248-344-X	Repair Your Own Credit and Deal with Debt (2E)	$18.95
_____	1-57248-346-6	Essential Guide to Real Estate Contracts (2E)	$18.95	_____	1-57248-350-4	El Seguro Social Preguntas y Respuestas	$14.95
_____	1-57248-160-9	Essential Guide to Real Estate Leases	$18.95	_____	1-57248-217-6	Sexual Harassment: Your Guide to Legal Action	$18.95
_____	1-57248-254-0	Family Limited Partnership	$26.95	_____	1-57248-219-2	The Small Business Owner's Guide to Bankruptcy	$21.95
_____	1-57248-331-8	Gay & Lesbian Rights	$26.95	_____	1-57248-168-4	The Social Security Benefits Handbook (3E)	$18.95
_____	1-57248-139-0	Grandparents' Rights (3E)	$24.95	_____	1-57248-216-8	Social Security Q&A	$12.95
_____	1-57248-188-9	Guía de Inmigración a Estados Unidos (3E)	$24.95	_____	1-57248-221-4	Teen Rlghts	$22.95
_____	1-57248-187-0	Guía de Justicia para Víctimas del Crimen	$21.95	_____	1-57248-366-0	Tax Smarts for Small Business	$21.95
_____	1-57248-253-2	Guía Esencial para los Contratos de	$22.95	_____	1-57248-335-0	Traveler's Rights	$21.95
		Arrendamiento de Bienes Raices		_____	1-57248-236-2	Unmarried Parents' Rights (2E)	$19.95
_____	1-57248-103-X	Help Your Lawyer Win Your Case (2E)	$14.95	_____	1-57248-362-8	U.S. Immigration and Citizenship Q&A	$16.95
_____	1-57248-334-2	Homeowner's Rights	$21.95	_____	1-57248-218-4	U.S. Immigration Step by Step	$21.95
_____	1-57248-164-1	How to Buy a Condominium or Townhome (2E)	$19.95	_____	1-57248-161-7	U.S.A. Immigration Guide (4E)	$24.95
_____	1-57248-328-8	How to Buy Your First Home	$18.95	_____	1-57248-192-7	The Visitation Handbook	$18.95
_____	1-57248-191-9	How to File Your Own Bankruptcy (5E)	$21.95	_____	1-57248-225-7	Win Your Unemployment	$21.95
_____	1-57248-343-1	How to File Your Own Divorce (5E)	$26.95			Compensation Claim (2E)	
_____	1-57248-222-2	How to Form a Limited Liability Company (2E)	$24.95	_____	1-57248-330-X	The Wills, Estate Planning and Trusts Legal Kit	&26.95
_____	1-57248-231-1	How to Form a Nonprofit Corporation (2E)	$24.95	_____	1-57248-138-2	Winning Your Personal Injury Claim (2E)	$24.95
_____	1-57248-345-8	How to Form Your Own Corporation (4E)	$26.95	_____	1-57248-333-4	Working with Your Homeowners Association	$19.95
_____	1-57248-224-9	How to Form Your Own Partnership (2E)	$24.95	_____	1-57248-162-5	Your Right to Child Custody,	$24.95
_____	1-57248-232-X	How to Make Your Own Simple Will (3E)	$18.95			Visitation and Support (2E)	
_____	1-57248-200-1	How to Register Your Own Copyright (4E)	$24.95	_____	1-57248-157-9	Your Rights When You Owe Too Much	$16.95
_____	1-57248-104-8	How to Register Your Own Trademark (3E)	$21.95			**CALIFORNIA TITLES**	
_____	1-57248-233-8	How to Write Your Own Living Will (3E)	$18.95	_____	1-57248-150-1	CA Power of Attorney Handbook (2E)	$18.95
_____	1-57248-156-0	How to Write Your Own	$24.95	_____	1-57248-337-7	How to File for Divorce in CA (4E)	$26.95
		Premarital Agreement (3E)				**Form Continued on Following Page** SubTotal_____	

Qty	ISBN	Title	Retail
_____	1-57248-145-5	How to Probate and Settle an Estate in CA	$26.95
_____	1-57248-336-9	How to Start a Business in CA (2E)	$21.95
_____	1-57248-194-3	How to Win in Small Claims Court in CA (2E)	$18.95
_____	1-57248-246-X	Make Your Own CA Will	$18.95
_____	1-57248-196-X	The Landlord's Legal Guide in CA	$24.95
_____	1-57248-241-9	Tenants' Rights in CA	$21.95

FLORIDA TITLES

Qty	ISBN	Title	Retail
_____	1-57071-363-4	Florida Power of Attorney Handbook (2E)	$16.95
_____	1-57248-176-5	How to File for Divorce in FL (7E)	$26.95
_____	1-57248-356-3	How to Form a Corporation in FL (6E)	$24.95
_____	1-57248-203-6	How to Form a Limited Liability Co. in FL (2E)	$24.95
_____	1-57071-401-0	How to Form a Partnership in FL	$22.95
_____	1-57248-113-7	How to Make a FL Will (6E)	$16.95
_____	1-57248-088-2	How to Modify Your FL Divorce Judgment (4E)	$24.95
_____	1-57248-354-7	How to Probate and Settle an Estate in FL (5E)	$26.95
_____	1-57248-339-3	How to Start a Business in FL (7E)	$21.95
_____	1-57248-204-4	How to Win in Small Claims Court in FL (7E)	$18.95
_____	1-57248-202-8	Land Trusts in Florida (6E)	$29.95
_____	1-57248-338-5	Landlords' Rights and Duties in FL (9E)	$22.95

GEORGIA TITLES

Qty	ISBN	Title	Retail
_____	1-57248-340-7	How to File for Divorce in GA (5E)	$21.95
_____	1-57248-180-3	How to Make a GA Will (4E)	$21.95
_____	1-57248-341-5	How to Start a Business in Georgia (3E)	$21.95

ILLINOIS TITLES

Qty	ISBN	Title	Retail
_____	1-57248-244-3	Child Custody, Visitation, and Support in IL	$24.95
_____	1-57248-206-0	How to File for Divorce in IL (3E)	$24.95
_____	1-57248-170-6	How to Make an IL Will (3E)	$16.95
_____	1-57248-247-8	How to Start a Business in IL (3E)	$21.95
_____	1-57248-252-4	The Landlord's Legal Guide in IL	$24.95

MARYLAND, VIRGINIA AND THE DISTRICT OF COLUMBIA

Qty	ISBN	Title	Retail
_____	1-57248-240-0	How to File for Divorce in MD, VA and DC	$28.95
_____	1-57248-359-8	How to Start a Business in MD, VA or DC	$21.95

MASSACHUSETTS TITLES

Qty	ISBN	Title	Retail
_____	1-57248-128-5	How to File for Divorce in MA (3E)	$24.95
_____	1-57248-115-3	How to Form a Corporation in MA	$24.95
_____	1-57248-108-0	How to Make a MA Will (2E)	$16.95
_____	1-57248-248-6	How to Start a Business in MA (3E)	$21.95
_____	1-57248-209-5	The Landlord's Legal Guide in MA	$24.95

MICHIGAN TITLES

Qty	ISBN	Title	Retail
_____	1-57248-215-X	How to File for Divorce in MI (3E)	$24.95
_____	1-57248-182-X	How to Make a MI Will (3E)	$16.95
_____	1-57248-183-8	How to Start a Business in MI (3E)	$18.95

MINNESOTA TITLES

Qty	ISBN	Title	Retail
_____	1-57248-142-0	How to File for Divorce in MN	$21.95
_____	1-57248-179-X	How to Form a Corporation in MN	$24.95
_____	1-57248-178-1	How to Make a MN Will (2E)	$16.95

NEW JERSEY TITLES

Qty	ISBN	Title	Retail
_____	1-57248-239-7	How to File for Divorce in NJ	$24.95

NEW YORK TITLES

Qty	ISBN	Title	Retail
_____	1-57248-193-5	Child Custody, Visitation and Support in NY	$26.95
_____	1-57248-351-2	File for Divorce in NY	$26.95
_____	1-57248-249-4	How to Form a Corporation in NY (2E)	$24.95
_____	1-57248-095-5	How to Make a NY Will (2E)	$16.95
_____	1-57248-199-4	How to Start a Business in NY (2E)	$18.95
_____	1-57248-198-6	How to Win in Small Claims Court in NY (2E)	$18.95
_____	1-57248-197-8	Landlords' Legal Guide in NY	$24.95
_____	1-57071-188-7	New York Power of Attorney Handbook	$19.95
_____	1-57248-122-6	Tenants' Rights in NY	$21.95

NORTH CAROLINA TITLES

Qty	ISBN	Title	Retail
_____	1-57248-185-4	How to File for Divorce in NC (3E)	$22.95
_____	1-57248-129-3	How to Make a NC Will (3E)	$16.95
_____	1-57248-184-6	How to Start a Business in NC (3E)	$18.95
_____	1-57248-091-2	Landlords' Rights & Duties in NC	$21.95

NORTH CAROLINA AND SOUTH CAROLINA TITLES

Qty	ISBN	Title	Retail
_____	1-57248-371-7	How to Start a Business in NC or SC	$24.95

OHIO TITLES

Qty	ISBN	Title	Retail
_____	1-57248-190-0	How to File for Divorce in OH (2E)	$24.95
_____	1-57248-174-9	How to Form a Corporation in OH	$24.95
_____	1-57248-173-0	How to Make an OH Will	$16.95

PENNSYLVANIA TITLES

Qty	ISBN	Title	Retail
_____	1-57248-242-7	Child Custody, Visitation and Support in PA	$26.95
_____	1-57248-211-7	How to File for Divorce in PA (3E)	$26.95
_____	1-57248-358-X	How to Form a Croporation in PA	$24.95
_____	1-57248-094-7	How to Make a PA Will (2E)	$16.95
_____	1-57248-357-1	How to Start a Business in PA (3E)	$21.95
_____	1-57248-245-1	The Landlord's Legal Guide in PA	$24.95

TEXAS TITLES

Qty	ISBN	Title	Retail
_____	1-57248-171-4	Child Custody, Visitation, and Support in TX	$22.95
_____	1-57248-172-2	How to File for Divorce in TX (3E)	$24.95
_____	1-57248-114-5	How to Form a Corporation in TX (2E)	$24.95
_____	1-57248-255-9	How to Make a TX Will (3E)	$16.95
_____	1-57248-214-1	How to Probate and Settle an Estate in TX (3E)	$26.95
_____	1-57248-228-1	How to Start a Business in TX (3E)	$18.95
_____	1-57248-111-0	How to Win in Small Claims Court in TX (2E)	$16.95
_____	1-57248-355-5	The Landlord's Legal Guide in TX	$24.95

SubTotal This page _____

SubTotal previous page _____

Shipping — $5.00 for 1st book, $1.00 each additional _____

Illinois residents add 6.75% sales tax _____

Connecticut residents add 6.00% sales tax _____

Total _____